# Fountain of Youth

# Fountain Of Youth

## Strategies and Tactics for Mobilizing America's Young Voters

Daniel M. Shea and John C. Green

ROWMAN & LITTLEFIELD PUBLISHERS, INC.
*Lanham • Boulder • New York • Toronto • Plymouth, UK*

ROWMAN & LITTLEFIELD PUBLISHERS, INC.

Published in the United States of America
by Rowman & Littlefield Publishers, Inc.
A wholly owned subsidiary of The Rowman & Littlefield Publishing Group, Inc.
4501 Forbes Boulevard, Suite 200, Lanham, Maryland 20706
www.rowmanlittlefield.com

Estover Road
Plymouth PL6 7PY
United Kingdom

British Library Cataloguing in Publication Information Available

**Library of Congress Cataloging-in-Publication Data**

Fountain of youth : strategies and tactics for mobilizing America's young voters / [edited
by] Daniel M. Shea and John C. Green.
    p. cm. — (Campaigning American style)
  Includes bibliographical references and index.
  ISBN-13: 978-0-7425-3965-5 (cloth : alk. paper)
  ISBN-10: 0-7425-3965-2 (cloth : alk. paper)
  ISBN-13: 978-0-7425-3966-2 (pbk. : alk. paper)
  ISBN-10: 0-7425-3966-0 (pbk. : alk. paper)
  1. Young adults—United States—Political activity. 2. Political participation—United
States. I. Shea, Daniel M. II. Green, John Clifford, 1953- III. Series.
  HQ799.9.P6F68 2007
  324.7'2—dc22

                                                                        2006015176

Printed in the United States of America

⊗ ™ The paper used in this publication meets the minimum requirements of American
National Standard for Information Sciences—Permanence of Paper for Printed Library
Materials, ANSI/NISO Z39.48-1992.

*Dedicated to all those who see young voter apathy as a problem, and are determined to do something about it!*

# Contents

## Section III Civic Education and Youth Engagement: Past, Present, and Future

## Section IV Nonpartisan Organizations and Turning out the Youth Vote

## Section V Conclusion

# Tables and Figures

## TABLE

## FIGURES

# Preface

This project began with a set of grants from the Center for Information and Research on Civic Learning and Engagement (CIRCLE). We are quite grateful to Bill Galston, Peter Levine, Mark Lopez, and all the others at CIRCLE for seeing the potential of our ideas, for their willingness to invest in our scholarship. We are thankful that nearly 900 county, state, and national party leaders took time out of their busy schedules to provide us invaluable information about their committees and the future of the party system in America. They do good work, work that is essential for our democratic system but is often under the radar. We appreciate what they do and their willingness to lend a team of scholars a hand.

At the Center for Political Participation at Allegheny College, Deanne Dunbar provided assistance in preparing the manuscript. Ann Areson and Diana Brautigum of Allegheny's Foundations Support Office were very helpful in developing the grant proposals, and the staff at the Office of Public Affairs provided their assistance in releasing elements of the study at various points. At the Ray C. Bliss of Applied Politics at the University of Akron, Janet Bolois prepared the final manuscript and Michelle Henry was instrumental in conducting the survey data.

We would like to thank Niels Aaboe and Karolina Zarychta and all the folks at Rowman and Littlefield for helping us publish this book. We surely owe much gratitude to the scholars and practitioners who provided chapters for this volume. Their understanding of the problem and ways to address declining youth voting fills the pages to follow with novel, keen insights.

Finally, as always, we wish to thank our families—and especially our wives, Christine Gatto Shea and Lynn Rittenhouse Green—for their unwavering support.

# I

## BACKGROUND ON YOUTH PARTICIPATION IN AMERICA

# 1

## The Turned-Off Generation: Fact and Fiction?

### *Daniel M. Shea and John C. Green*

We've all heard that young Americans are apathetic, self-absorbed, lazy, and certainly indifferent to civic matters. It is a turned-off generation, we are told. Youngsters are too interested in having a good time, hanging out at the mall, bopping around with headphones glued to their heads, riding their skateboards, and hooking up to care about civic matters. After all, this generation was reared under the omnipotent buzz of video games, instant messaging, cell phones, and iPods. It is little wonder that kids these days are violent, promiscuous, lazy, angry, whiny, insolent, and self-indulgent. Youngsters are "binge drinkers, test failers, test cheaters, drug users, and just all-round spoiled brats" (Howe and Strauss 2000, 3). It is hard enough to get youngsters off the couch to do some work around the house, much less convince them to do volunteer work for the good of the community. And when they do get involved, it's all about résumé padding!

It has become a near truism that young Americans are indifferent to public affairs. Scholar and commentator James Q. Wilson wrote that America's youth represent nothing more than "30,000 more muggers, killers, and thieves than we have now," all of whom come from "dysfunctional families" and "disorderly neighborhoods" (as cited in Giroux 1998, 68). As noted by one team of scholars, "According to a national survey, barely one adult in three thinks that today's kids, once grown, will make the world a better place" (Howe and Strauss 2000, 3), and "hardly a week passes in which the public does not hear some urgent pronouncement about how the nation must produce a better generation of children" (13).

But of course nothing could be further from the truth. It is one of the great myths of our day that young Americans are amoral, lazy, and self-centered. This generation is caring, involved, and committed to positive change. A host of data suggests they give their energy, time, and money to their schools, community, and nation. A recent report by the Center for Information and Research on Civic Learning and Engagement (CIRCLE) is illustrative. Citing a host of data collected by several reputable organizations, including the University of Michigan's Survey Research Center, the Department of Education, the Bureau of Labor Statistics, and Independent Sector, the report notes, "Volunteering rates among young people are generally higher than they are among adults 26 and older." Whereas about 40 percent of fifteen- to twenty-five-year-olds regularly volunteer in one form or another, the percentage for thirty-eight- to fifty-six-year-olds is only 32 percent. This figure is just 22 percent of those over fifty-seven years of age. Rates of volunteer work for those under twenty-five are now twice as high as for those over fifty-five. The frequency of pitching in has also increased in recent years: in 1990, some 65 percent of college freshmen reported volunteering in high school, and by 2003 that figure had risen to 83 percent.

The Higher Education Research Institute (1999) at UCLA does an annual survey of college freshmen. Their data suggest that by 1999, volunteerism among this group had grown to an all-time high. Roughly 75 percent of incoming freshmen had undertaken a volunteer community project in the past year, a jump of about 10 percent from a decade earlier. "Volunteerism on a regular basis also is up," the study noted, "with 42.1 percent of freshmen donating their time for at least one hour a week, compared with 39.9 percent a year ago and 26.6 percent when this question was asked in 1987. A record high one in five students (20.6 percent) volunteers at least three hours a week." One of the study's authors suggested, "Despite speculation that students' high level of volunteerism may be due to service requirements in the high schools, these findings suggest that the majority of students who engage in volunteer work do so of their own volition." According to Youth Service America, a Washington-based organization designed to foster higher levels of civic involvement among young Americans, the number of high school students involved in service-learning programs grew by some 4,000 percent in the 1990s (as cited in Eisner 2004, 73). Simply put, this is *the* activist generation.

Yet civic and community involvement of this generation is limited to those attending college, right? Again, hard data tell a different story. In 2003, the United States Census Bureau published a report on the shared attitudes among young Americans regarding civic engagement and community involvement (U.S. Census Bureau 2003). But instead of focusing their analysis on all young Americans, they set their sights on hard-to-reach populations — such as ethnic minorities, lower socioeconomic classes, and immigrants. They found that, "contrary to popular belief, most . . . in this study have by no means opted out of civic life—they are civically engaged" (13). They are engaged in a number of civic responsibilities at home, in their church, through neighborhood programs, and in cultural activities. They donate food, give blood and money to local charities, recycle, help out at senior centers, tutor, voice their opinion on talk radio shows, and much, much else. Beyond this *actual* involvement, some 85 percent of the study's respondents suggested they would like to become more involved in their community (13). The authors of the report write, "By and large, our research data reveal that respondents demonstrate their civic seriousness in large numbers" (14).

Nor is this generation especially characterized by anger, pessimism, amorality, or rule breaking. In a comprehensive, eye-opening look at young Americans (what they call the "millennials"), Neil Howe and William Strauss point to reams of data that challenge popular perceptions. Are millennials self-absorbed, for example? "By a huge ten-to-one majority, they believe it's their generation—and not their parents'—that will do the most to help the environment" (2000, 9). Are they a violent generation? "Even including the Columbine massacre, there were only half as many violent deaths at schools nationwide in 1998–9 than there were in the early 1990s" (9). Are they immoral? "Polls [in the late 1990s] showed school kids to be the harshest critics of Bill Clinton's personal behavior" (13). As in past generations, the youth are less involved in organized religion, but nonetheless 38 percent were weekly worship attenders, and 58 percent attended more than once a month, according to the Fourth National Survey of Religion and Politics conducted at the University of Akron in 2004. A number of studies also suggest that the number and percentage of teenage girls becoming pregnant has declined precipitously in recent years, as has the use of drugs by young boys and girls (see, for instance, Martin et al. 2005; National Institute on Drug Abuse 2004). The overall point is clear: young Americans are anything but apathetic and immoral. The above-mentioned census study notes, "Respondents in our study do exhibit a shared consciousness, not in terms of being self-centered slackers, but in concern for others" (U.S. Census Bureau 2003, 12–13).

## ROOTS OF THE MYTH OF A
## SELF-ABSORBED, LAZY GENERATION

Perceptions of young Americans are mistaken. But why have so many gotten things so wrong? Why is the myth of self-centered, apathetic younger Americans so powerful in our culture? One explanation might simply be age-old generational griping. Nothing is more time honored or more common than older generations thinking poorly of younger ones. The grip of nostalgia and a lack of understanding of new trends, fashions, and modes of accept-able behavior can create fodder for the "our generation was better" cannon. In the 1950s, the young were being corrupted by rock and roll music (Elvis and Chubby Checker were the bane of civilization), and by the 1960s, drugs, sexual promiscuity, and lack of respect for authority figures were threatening the nation. "It would be difficult to overstate the cultural importance of that music," noted one observer (Bork 1996, 23). By the 1970s, the rise of cable television and video games were the new blights of society. By the 1980s, greed and laziness had taken hold of youngsters, and the "me" generation was coming of age. By the 1990s, dramatic new technologies (the Internet, instant messaging, cell phones, etc.) had transformed leisure patterns. Good-ness, what a lazy generation! Get outside and get some fresh air! Perhaps the worst change, from the standpoint of older Americans, was the popularity of a radically different form of music: rap. Ice-T's album *Body Count*, with lead song "Cop Killer" and lyrics such as "Die, pigs, die," became an instant hit in 1992, selling over 300,000 in three months (Shea 1999a, 75). How could music like this sell? Surely it was an indicator of a morally corrupt genera-tion. Would kids that listen to such crap also volunteer in their communities? Surely not. Again, older generations looking down upon younger ones are singing an old tune—so to speak.

Another explanation might be the overall decline in civic life among all Americans following World War II. Harvard's Robert Putnam drew our atten-tion to the issue with his oft-cited article and book of the same title, *Bowling Alone* (1995 and 2000a, respectively). "[I]t is important," writes Putnam, "to avoid simple nostalgia" (25). But by looking at trunk loads of data (what he describes as "counting things"), Putnam finds a stunning decline in traditional community involvement—a rapid rejection of social capital. Putnam's research does not focus on young Americans per se, but his conclusions regarding the source of civic decay place the blame squarely on the lap of young Americans. That is, while changes in society such as new patterns of leisure (television use in particular), urban sprawl, and women entering the workforce have had an impact, civic engagement was "killed" primarily by generational turnover (283), to wit: "The slow, steady, and ineluctable replacement of the long civic generation by their less involved children and grandchildren has been a very powerful factor" (283). Others have suggested much the same.

Other researchers, however, have called the overall decline assumption into question, especially as it relates to young Americans. Lance Bennett (1998), for instance, notes that while there may have been a drop in formal group membership, such as in Elks Clubs and PTAs, people continue to be engaged through volunteer networks and loosely organized groups (745). He writes, "Sustained levels of volunteer activity further support a story of continuing, but life-style friendly civic engagement on the part of increasingly individualistic people leading complex lives" (758). The reference, of course, is to the youngest generations. Even Putnam himself, in a later work, seems to appreciate the complexity of accurately assessing a generation's community connectedness (Putnam and Feldstein 2003).

Possibly a stronger reason for the myth of an amoral, apathetic generation has been the emerging cultural war. Regardless of the exact breadth of differences between "red" and "blue" Americans, and the extent to which the "values divide" shapes public policy development and electoral politics, there is little doubt that the debate has become heated in recent years. How young Americans stack up is at the center of the argument. "The bodies of youth are sprawled across the media in a public display of social disorder, laziness, menace, and aberrant promiscuity," noted one commentator. "They are accused of leading the country into moral decline and tearing the fabric of the nation asunder" (Giroux 1998, 1–2).

One of the first to draw a sharp contrast between the values of different generations was William Bennett, former secretary of education in the Reagan administration, in *Book of Virtues* (1993). Things were different with this new generation, and America would turn its back on these sweeping changes at its peril. The book set in motion a vigorous line of attack against youth culture. Robert Bork, Yale scholar and once a nominee to the Supreme Court, followed with *Slouching Towards Gomorrah* (1996), which charts what he believes to be the roots of American decline and perhaps even Western decline (2). "Every generation," Bork writes, "constitutes a wave of savages who must be civilized by their families, schools, and churches" (21). The problem recently, he argues, is that an exceptionally large generation (the baby boomers) came of age during an exceptionally transformative period (demographic shifts, new technologies). "We noticed (who could help but notice?) Elvis Presley, rock music, James Dean, the radical sociologist C. Wright Mills, Jack Kerouac and the Beats . . . [, all] harbingers of a new culture that would shortly burst upon us and sweep us into a different country." By the 1960s, there was a revolt against the entire American culture. Today, campuses are characterized by "violence, destruction of property, and the mindless hatred of law, authority, and tradition" (1). And as for the more general youth culture, there has been nothing less than a collapse—due in large measure to hard rock, unconstrained television programming, an anything-goes movie industry, filth on the Internet, and especially rap music. "Perhaps pop culture is inevitably vulgar but today's is more vulgar than at any time in the past" (127–28).

While not explicitly taking aim at the younger generations, Bork's rant leaves the reader with the clear impression that today's cultural decay has led young Americans down a path of hedonism, violence, vulgarity, and surely an indifference to the greater good.

More recently, James Dobson, the founder and chairman of Focus on the Family, had the following to say about the contemporary culture:

> It is clear that, as standards of decency have continued to erode, it has become increasingly difficult for parents to shield their children from the negative influences of TV, music, video games and other media. It is astonishing to consider just how far we have fallen in recent decades. . . . The offensive content I have just described represents everything that is mainstream and popular in entertainment. These movies, albums, TV shows and games are not simply the choices of the "fringe" kids who dye their hair green and dress in black. (2005)

The implication is that our debased culture has had a profound impact on America's youth. And, by focusing on modes of entertainment that are most attractive to young Americans, the suggestion is that this generation is deficient. All is not lost, work needs to be done, but the bottom line is that young Americans are in grave danger. It is little wonder that the virtues of this generation are not understood.

Leftist scholar and political theorist Henry Giroux has argued that the negative portrayal of young Americans has been a carefully calculated move by conservatives. Appearing to speak directly to Bork and others that rail against youth black culture, Giroux writes, "Scorned as a threat to the existing social order, working-class and inner-city black youth are pushed to the margins of political power within society." The scorn of rap music would seem an apt example. And to young Americans overall, he notes, "Increasingly denied opportunities for self-definition and political interaction, youth are located within a range of images that largely disavow their representational status as active citizens" (66).

## WHAT ABOUT POLITICAL PARTICIPATION?

There is yet another explanation to the myth of apathetic, indifferent youth. Today's youth's civic engagement is perplexing because it does not extend to political involvement. While youngsters seem more than willing to lend a hand cleaning up streams, helping others learn to read, and volunteering at the community soup kitchen, they shun politics—the very process that could produce solutions to polluted streams, poverty, and adult illiteracy. Many have dubbed this the "scissor effect," where "volunteering among young people is increasing rapidly, while political participation is decreasing drastically" (Longo 2004).

To many observers, election turnout is the most overt indicator of civic engagement. In the 1960s, about 60 percent of all Americans turned out to vote in presidential elections, but in recent years, it has been around the 50 percent mark. For the youngest generations, the decline has been staggering. In 1972, when eighteen-year-olds were first granted the right to vote, nearly 50 percent did so. By 2000, this figure had plummeted to about 36 percent. (The 2004 election is discussed below.) During midterm congressional elections, only a scant 20 percent of eighteen- to twenty-four-year-olds went to the polls.

The problem runs much deeper than nonvoting, however. The CIRCLE report cited above finds the rate of participation for younger Americans at similar or higher levels than the overall population for every type of volunteer organization *except* political organizations. Here the rate of participation is just one-third of the overall rate. According to the American National Election Study (NES), published every two years by the University of Michigan, in the 1960s about 35 percent of those less than thirty years old "tried to influence how others voted." NES data also note that the number of young Americans less than thirty who were "very much" interested in campaigns stood at roughly 30 percent from the 1950s to the 1980s. Since then, the decline has been steady, and by 2000, this figure had plunged to just 6 percent. In 2002, 67 percent of all Americans cared "very much" or "pretty much" about the outcome of congressional elections in their area. Just 47 percent of those less than twenty-five years old felt the same way.

The UCLA study "Most of the Nation's College Freshmen Embrace the Internet as an Educational Tool," which draws attention to the high level of community involvement among college freshmen, also underscores the paradox in political participation. In 1966, some 58 percent agreed that "keeping up to date with political affairs" is very important, but by 1999 that figure had dropped to 26 percent. Only 14 percent of freshmen said they frequently discussed politics, compared with the high of 30 percent in 1968. A poll of Americans in their late teens and early twenties conducted by the Pew Research Center found that less than 50 percent were thinking "a great deal about" elections in 2000. This compares to about two-thirds in 1992. Roughly 40 percent suggested that it did not matter who was elected president in 2000, twice as many as in 1992 (as cited in Boyte 2003, 86).

The withdrawal from politics has been rapid, deep, and broad. Political participation is an obvious indicator of civic involvement, and it appears that many have simply jumped to a conclusion: if young folks are not voting, helping out candidates, or talking about elections, then they are probably not volunteering their time to other community projects.

Only recently have we started to understand the relationship between civic and political involvement for young Americans. Why would a generation so eager to be involved in civic life refrain from political involvement? Scholar William Galston suggests that "most young people characterize their volunteering as an alternative to official politics, which they see as corrupt, ineffective, and unrelated to their deeper ideals. They have confidence in personalized acts with consequences they can see for themselves; they have no confidence in collective acts, especially those undertaken through public institutions whose operations they regard as remote, opaque, and virtually impossible to control" (2001, 224). In other words, young Americans are disengaged from the policy process because they feel marginalized within the political process.

In 2001, a group of thirty-three students representing twenty-seven colleges and universities gathered for a conference in Racine, Wisconsin, to discuss the "scissors effect." Again and again, the students did not see their community work as an alternative to civic engagement, but rather as a way to create positive change though community-building efforts. Out of this new concept emerged "service politics" (Longo 2004, 63). That is, younger citizens have become cynical about the political process and believe that the best way for them to make a true difference is to volunteer with a specific project rather than join the political fray. Cleaning up a stream or helping someone to read provides an immediate, concrete payback from involvement. The payoff from political participation, on the other hand, does not seem immediate, nor is there any guarantee that there will be one. Columnist Jane Eisner put it this way:

> The attraction of service for young people is undeniable, and growing. It is propelled by the characteristics of this generation—their tendency toward compassion and their nonjudgmental concern for others, and away from what they see as a political system driven by conflict and ego. (2004, 80)

## FINDING CULPRITS

That service politics has become more important to young Americans than traditional forms of participation has done little to quell fears of a disturbing transformation of American politics. As noted by one scholar, "This trend leads many to conclude that a widespread and pervasive political deficit disorder exists, the consequences of which is nothing less than a crisis of our democracy" (Longo 2004, 61). Much effort has been spent searching for the root of the withdrawal of young Americans and in finding ways to reverse the trend. One route is to explore the roots of cynicism and alienation. Surely the antiestablishment, counterculture revolution of the 1960s and 1970s was part of it. Young people of that time became frustrated at the pace of change and sought alternative avenues of involvement. The rise of interest-group politics and the decline of party organizations, for instance, can be traced to this period (White and Shea 2004, 88–90). We might say, then, that youngsters of the period socialized their children (today's newest generation of voters) to refrain from certain modes of behavior and to engage in other forms of civic action. Be involved, certainly, but worry less about elections and attending city council meetings than about direct volunteer activities. The root of service politics may well extend back to the 1960s.

Similarly, perhaps the larger context in which politics now operates has turned off a generation. Specifically, the rise of scandal-based politics, or what Ginsberg and Shefter (1990) call "RIP" (revelation, investigation, and prosecution), has led young Americans to conclude that the entire process is corrupt. Sabato (1991) and others have documented a dramatic rise in attack journalism. "Post Watergate reporting about government has been unrelentingly negative, scandal giving way to scandal, so that Americans not unreasonably conclude that all politicians must indeed be crooked" (207). We might add to this the growing use and increasingly venomous nature of attack ads during campaigns. Elections have always been dirty, but in recent years, with the advent of slick television production, the cruelty of campaign commercials has taken Americans aback. Most scholars now agree that negative advertising does not depress turnout, as once thought, but that does not mean that it affects all types of voters in the same way. Ansolabehere and Iyengar (1997) present convincing data to suggest that the least partisan voters are the ones most likely to walk away from highly negative elections. Of course, young voters are generally the least likely to be partisan. Between RIP, feeding frenzies, and attack advertising, it seems entirely likely that the context of contemporary politics has turned off a generation. While older generations also vote less than they once did, going to the polls is considered habitual; once someone starts voting, they tend to do so throughout the rest of their life. The youngest generation sees little point in starting.

Another unfortunate cycle may be at work as well. Many young citizens believe that older politicians do not listen and do not care about their concerns. Jennifer Kingsley, a senior at the University of Wisconsin, attended a gathering of politicians, scholars, practitioners, and other students concerned with a "turned-off generation" in January of 2005. Her comments are most illustrative:

> Now more than ever, we are stuck in the same sort of limbo. Young people don't want to make an effort to make politicians hear them, and politicians don't

want to make an effort to cater to young people. So where does this leave us? Growing up without voting, without making our voices heard, and without being involved. . . . Until we hand our youth the right tools to become a powerful voice among Americans, I don't foresee the number of young voters rising. (*Wingspread Journal* 2005, 9)  but what are the right tools?

Many are quick to point to lifestyle changes, such as those factors that Putnam discusses when confronting the overall decline in social capital. Perhaps television, instant messaging, surfing the Web, and online chat rooms distract young Americans. Maybe there is simply less time for involvement in politics. But is this explanation satisfactory, however, given their high level of community involvement? Could it be that young Americans have enough time to volunteer in their community but not enough to vote? Another line of inquiry has focused on changes in civic education. Two studies in the early 1990s painted a "very disturbing picture" of the failure of civics classes in America (Cogan 1997). While civics education may be able to better socialize students into the democratic processes than it once was, it seems to be less effective in creating participatory citizens. These reports suggest that "this generation is ill-prepared to keep democracy alive in the 1990s and beyond" (Cogan 1997). High school programs have "traditionally been seen as mechanisms by which young people can be socialized to more participatory lifestyles" (Eagles and Davidson 2001). Yet only 64 percent of young people ages fifteen to twenty-six report that they have taken a high school course on civics or American government (Kurtz, Rosenthal, and Zukin 2003). One report by a prominent organization found that one-third of high school seniors lacked a basic understanding of how government works (Carnegie Corporation of New York and CIRCLE 2003). The problem, many speculate, may be in the content of traditional courses. *The Civic Mission of Schools* illustrates how the curriculum of civics courses has become diluted. The standard civics class only describes and analyzes government "in a more distant way, often with little explicit discussion of a citizen's role" (14). The authors of the report suggest that "teaching only rote facts about dry procedures is unlikely to benefit students and may actually alienate them from political participation, such as voting" (20).

There is still another possibility—perhaps the strongest. Even a cursory look at levels of participation in American history underscores the importance of *mobilizing institutions*—such as local political parties. Simply put, participation in America has been highest when intermediary groups are vibrant and local. Given the transformation we have seen in party politics during the past three decades, especially the decline of grassroots parties, it is not surprising that involvement among citizens has declined as well. The tight relationship between vibrant intermediary organizations and high levels of participatory politics has been a common theme in political science literature. One often-cited scholar to suggest such a connection was E. E. Schattschneider. In his 1942 book, *Party Government*, he writes, "Parties have extended the area of popular participation in public affairs enormously" (208). He also suggests that parties draw traditionally shunned groups (such as young voters?) into the process: "Once party organizations become active in the electorate, a vast field of extension and intensification of effort is opened, the extension of the franchise to new social classes, for example" (47). Conceivably, then, parties have focused less attention on bringing voters to the polls than they did in the past. Likely they have found that persuading undecided voters is more cost efficient than trying to mobilize groups that traditionally do not vote—such as the youngest cohort.

There are numerous other possibilities. It could be that the spiraling amount of money in politics has turned off younger voters, or maybe the overall pro-fessionalization of politics has played a role. Is it a mere coincidence that at about the same time that young voters dropped out of the system, campaign consultants took the helm of most campaigns? It is quite feasible that politi-cians have responded to the changing demographics of voters—that is, the aging of the electorate—and have neglected the concerns of young Ameri-cans. Politicians, we are often told, don't pay attention to young voters. Politi-cians might respond that *if* this were true, it is likely because young people do not vote, which raises the whole chicken-versus-egg question. The shrinking number of competitive state legislative and congressional races, due largely to computer-enhanced gerrymandering, may contribute to the problem. And it is certainly possible that the media does not take young citizens seriously. Do reporters really care whether or not a presidential candidate wears box-ers or briefs, or if he used a Mac or PC (scripted questions in 2000 and 2004 debates, respectively)? In a piece entitled "Citizens or Cynics," columnist Ellen Goodman (2003) notes, "In some ways this Mac-or-PC moment was just another bad example of what the older generation thinks the younger generation thinks."

Some suggest that young voter withdrawal is an expression of content-ment and thus nothing to worry about. Robert Kaplan, writing in the *Atlantic Monthly*, suggests, "Apathy, after all, often means that the political situation is healthy enough to be ignored. The last thing America needs is more voters—particularly badly educated and alienated ones—with a passion for politics" (1997, cited in Patterson 2002, 11). Columnist George Will, in a piece entitled "In Defense of Nonvoting," went so far as to argue that good government is a fundamental human right, not the right to vote. He suggests that a surge in high voting rates in Germany's Weimar Republic enabled the Nazis to come to power (cited in Patterson 2002, 11).

We disagree. Derek Bok, former president of Harvard University, was correct when he noted, "Democracy is a collective venture that falters or flourishes depending on the efforts citizens invest in its behalf.'[ Given that we have a limited government—a government by and for the people—the withdrawal of a cohort of citizens from politics is problematic] Our democracy is threatened when individuals embrace civic endeavors but shun the policy process. Among many other things, the departure of young Americans from the electoral sphere may have profound policy implications. Galston writes, "The withdrawal of a cohort of citizens from public affairs disturbs the balance of public deliberation—to the detriment of those who withdraw, but of the rest of us as well." At the very least, the departure of a generation of Americans from the electorate may have a profound influence on the outcome of elections. ⊘ Yes, a generation removed from politics *is* something to worry about.

## THE 2004 ELECTION

Much to the surprise of scholars, pundits, and older Americans, the decline in youth voting made a dramatic turnaround in 2004. Turnout increased among all Americans by about 4 percent, but the rise was greatest for eligible eighteen to twenty-four. Whereas just 36 percent of this group voted in 2000, an impressive 46.7 percent did so in 2004. These represented a stunning 11 percent increase—double the rate of increase among any other age group. What is more, several indicators of broad participation jumped up in the 2004 election. The National Election Study found that some 48 percent of all Americans tried to influence how others would vote, an increase of 14 percent from 2000 and a 20 percent jump from 1996. Fifty-six percent of those under thirty tried to influence how others would vote—the highest percentage of any other age group defined by NES summary reports. Some 8 percent of those under thirty attended a political meeting during the 2004 election, roughly double the figure from previous elections, and the percentage of young citizens "very much interested" in the campaign essentially doubled from previous years. Young voters still vote less than older Americans, but the 2004 election suggested that the decline among this group may be slowing, and that the disparity among age groups may be narrowing. Simply stated, the young were engaged in the 2004 election.

As to why the young became so involved in the election, there are a number of possible explanations. For one, the decline in youth participation was so startling that many organizations and programs were initiated to bring them back to the polls, such as Rock the Vote and Choose or Lose, Justvotenow. org, New Voters Project, Smack Down Your Vote!, and Youth Vote Coalition, to name only a few (see chapter 10). Six nonpartisan organizations spent approximately $40 million on youth turnout efforts (Levine 2005, 5). The New Voters Project, for example, was likely the "largest grassroots mobilization of young voters in history" (Frishberg and Delli Carpini 2005, 14). In six states, this nonpartisan organization registered nearly 350,000 young citizens, mobilized tens of thousands of volunteers, partnered with hundreds of college organizations, and conducted more than half a million conversations near the end of the campaign to bring people to the polls. In some areas, their hard work appears to have boosted turnout among the young by as much as 36 percent over 2000 levels (14).

Unlike previous elections, campaign operatives set their sights on voter mobilization in 2004. This was the result of two developments. First, given the tie in the 2000 presidential election, and given how close the 2004 contest appeared throughout the summer and fall, campaign operatives on both sides reasoned that any new handful of voters could swing certain states and put them over the top. Second, and closely related, initial polling suggested an unusually large portion of traditional voters had made up their minds early; there were few existing voters left to persuade by October. Groups of voters traditionally on the sidelines were considered campaign gold. Young voters fell into this category and were courted as in few other elections. In contested states, young voter turnout was about 17 percent higher than in nonbattle-ground states (Levine 2005, 5).

Because of new legal limits on the expenditure of campaign funds on electronic media during the final phase of federal elections, much effort was put into "ground war" activities in 2004. Of course, among the most efficient of such activities are get-out-the-vote programs. Also, due to changes in campaign finance rules, several new election-centered organizations exempt from most regulations were created, including America Coming Together and MoveOn.org. Indeed, the major campaign finance story of 2004 was the involvement of these independent "527" organizations. These organizations spent a great deal on television, especially in battleground states. But they were also frontline battalions in the ground war. The progressive America Coming Together, for example, registered more than 450,000 new voters and had 50,000 employees on the streets in the days leading up to the election (Currinder 2005, 124). Once again, much of this work was targeted at young citizens.

Finally, it seems entirely possible that young Americans were pulled into the electoral process due to the intensity of the campaign and the weight of the issues. The war in Iraq, gay marriage, the future of Social Security, stem cell research, global warming, and much more captivated public attention and drew young voters into the political process.

## WILL THEY STAY POLITICALLY ACTIVE?

Whether or not young voters will remain engaged and, perhaps, increase their share in the electorate is an open question. Some have suggested that this is a shot across the bow for all politicians; ignore young voters at your peril. Republican pollster and strategist Fran Luntz notes, "No longer will the parties or candidates be able to take that segment of the population for granted" (as cited in Frishberg and Delli Carpini 2005, 14). We are a tad less sanguine, however. It seems doubtful, perhaps even wishful thinking, that the myriad forces leading to young voter withdrawal have somehow evaporated. The higher turnout and general involvement of this generation in the 2004 election will in and of itself lead to higher levels of engagement in the coming years, as operatives on both sides appreciate the potential power of this cohort. Put a bit differently, few candidates or consultants will want to gamble on youth indifference, as they did in the past. But a dramatic turnaround is unlikely.

Much more will need to be done to draw young citizens into the rough-and-tumble world of politics. Unlike community involvement, where a benefit can be immediate and quite visible, electoral politics can take time. Will young voters tolerate the frustration of pouring their hearts into a campaign only to lose on election day? What is the payoff? And even if their candidate wins, can they bear the slow pace of policy change? For a generation accustomed to immediate benefits from involvement, political participation may prove maddening and a disappointment. The danger, it seems to us, is to become complacent and to assume that young citizens have finally found the light. While the 2004 election suggests young citizens can be drawn into the process, it does not imply a guarantee of their involvement.

## THE AIM AND PLAN OF THE BOOK

The aim of this book is to generate a discussion on the roots of youth disengagement from politics and, perhaps more importantly, to explore strategies, tactics, and initiatives that show promise in engaging this generation. There is no one solution, to be sure, but there may be approaches that can make a difference—schemes that can slowly turn the tide of indifference to one of effective political engagement. As such, this book is designed for all students and scholars of the American electoral system, but especially for those interested in seeking innovative solutions to a critically important issue.

We begin with a series of chapters on political parties. As noted above, throughout American history, local party committees pulled average citizens into the political process. Based on a survey of 804 local party chairs in the fall of 2003, the first two chapters are by us. The quantitative piece (chapter 2) explores whether these mobilizing institutions are interested and capable of connecting with young citizens. Many readers will see the findings as quite surprising. This is followed by a qualitative look at what several county and state party committees have tried in recent years to better connect with this group. It is a "best practices" report, of sorts. Political communications scholar J. Cherie Strachan penned the concluding chapter in this section. Strachan explores the decline of party identification among young Americans, why this is a disconcerting trend, and what might be done to reverse it.

While political parties draw citizens into the polling booth, schools have traditionally been agents for socializing young citizens on their obligations in a democracy, broadly defined. But here, too, significant changes are underway. Scholar Bill Galston (chapter 5) offers a thought-provoking look at some of these changes, the significance of civic knowledge in a participatory democracy, and what might be done to enhance classroom instruction to help create better citizens. This is followed by Melissa Comber's sharp attack on the limitations of traditional service-learning programs. Comber argues that civic skills are a key component in the development of political participation, but they are what is often missing in the traditional civic curricula and in most service-learning programs. Scholars Maya Rockeymoore and Mark Rockeymoore pen the final chapter in this section. A vital, yet less explored, component of the engagement puzzle is ways to best engage minority youth. This chapter charts this complex topic and offers a number of innovative, insightful solutions.

The next section of chapters explores the role of nonpartisan organizations in mobilizing young Americans. The first chapter sets its sights on the widely known Rock the Vote (RTV) program. First developed in 1992, RTV has become the most obvious, high-profile effort to engage young Americans. While well-meaning, scholars Michael Hoover and Susan Orr take issue with how the program pitches its message. Their recommendations for improvement will surely draw much attention. This is followed by a chapter by two practitioners that were in the front lines of the youth mobilization efforts in the 2004 election. Activists Ivan Frishberg and Heather Smith helped organize the New Voters Project, which focused its work in six states in the 2004 election. As noted above, this was likely the largest youth-centered grassroots mobilization effort in the nation's history. Their account of the program, both good and bad, is most illuminating and will surely help future mobilization activists better understand potential pitfalls. We provide the final chapter in this section—essentially a catalog of most of the other partisan and nonpartisan mobilization efforts in the 2004 election.

The final chapter in this book is penned by John K. White, the author of numerous works on the transformations of the American electorate. Here White provides a powerful and timely example of why youth participation matters: dramatic changes in the ethnic and racial makeup of American society. The young voters of today and tomorrow will embody the increased diversity of American society in the twenty-first century. Although it is too early to tell exactly how these changes will manifest themselves in politics, these trends are certain to transform the system. In young voters, we quite literally see the "faces of the future."

# II

## POLITICAL PARTIES AND MOBILIZATION OF YOUNG VOTERS

# 2

## Throwing a Better Party: Local Political Parties and the Youth Vote

### John C. Green and Daniel M. Shea

One of the persistent problems with American democracy in the last generation has been a decline in participation in politics, a trend exemplified by low voter turnout. Young citizens have been at the center of this trend. Given the importance of youth political engagement for the future health of American democracy, the topic has attracted considerable concern. Some analysts believe that the youth are poorly prepared for their role as citizens, and in addition, that they are apathetic and self-centered. Others argue that the "new style" of politics, with its focus on negative campaigning, sensational news coverage, and big money, has alienated the youth. A third alternative is that the political institutions that historically mobilized voters have decayed, and this decay has had an especially large impact on the youth.

This chapter focuses on the third explanation for youth disengagement, with a survey of local party leaders across the country. We find that a large majority of local party leaders recognize that youth disengagement from the political process is a problem, but only about one-half of these—roughly two-fifths of the total—give priority to mobilizing young voters. Many local parties have adequate resources and skills to mobilize the youth, and in addition, they appear to be successful when they focus on this task. However, only about one-quarter of the local parties are sharply focused on young voters. In sum, this research suggests that innovation among local parties is a fruitful avenue for increasing youth political engagement. Put another way, many local leaders are throwing a "pretty good party" for young voters, and they need to throw a "better party" to attract young voters back into the electoral process.

## THE SHRINKING ELECTORATE AND YOUNG VOTERS

Over the last generation, the United States has experienced a stunning decline in political participation. Shrinking voter turnout is one indicator of the problem, surely the most recognizable, but other modes of political behavior—such as sending letters to elected officials, helping a candidate or a party, wearing a campaign button, talking about politics with family and friends—have declined as well. According to the American National Election Study, the number of Americans "very much interested" in political campaigns has dropped by nearly 40 percent since the 1960s. This pattern of decline has not been constant, with occasion upticks in participation, such as the 1992 presidential election and the excitement associated with Ross Perot's independent candidacy. Another example is the 2004 election, which saw a surge in voter turnout, reaching back to the level of the late 1960s. It could be, of course, that 2004 marks the beginning of a new era, one with an expanded electorate. Even so, there is overwhelming evidence that Americans have withdrawn from public life in the last generation (Levine and Lopez 2002).

The shrinking electorate is especially pronounced among younger Americans (Patterson 2002). In 1972, the first election in which eighteen-year-olds had the right to vote, 50 percent did so. In recent elections, this figure has dropped to 29 percent. In the last two midterm congressional elections, this figure fell below 20 percent. A recent study of younger Americans, also commissioned by the Center for Information and Research on Civic Learning and Engagement (CIRCLE 2005), found that while attitudes toward government may have improved in the wake of September 11, 2001, the number of young Americans willing to take part in our political system is shrinking. Only about two-thirds of the eighteen- to twenty-five-year-olds in the CIRCLE survey had even registered to vote, a decline from two years before, and 49 percent of the overall group (fifteen- to twenty-five-year-olds) said that voting "is a little important or not at all important to them." Many other indicators in this study, and in numerous other studies, suggest the same: younger voters are turned off by electoral politics.

Many observers assume that the lack of political engagement is part of a generational phenomenon. "Generation X" and its successors are simply a "turned-off generation." While plausible, such a generalization is simply not true. Indeed, a host of data reveals that young Americans give generously of their energy, time, and money to their schools, community, and nation. A report by CIRCLE (Lopez 2004), for example, suggests that young Americans volunteer at significantly higher rates than do older Americans. Moreover, the frequency of pitching-in has also increased in recent years: in 1990, some

65 percent of college freshmen reported volunteering in high school, and by 2003, that figure had risen to 83 percent. Rates of volunteer work for those under twenty-five are now twice as high as for those over fifty-five. From this perspective, this generation is the activist generation—except in terms of electoral politics.

Of course some observers argue that the political withdrawal of our youth is an expression of contentment and thus is nothing to worry about. Arguments refuting this contention stretch from the theoretical to the pragmatic. From a theoretical perspective, Thomas Jefferson aptly noted, "Making every citizen an active member of the government, and in the offices nearest and most interesting to him, will attach him by his strongest feelings to the independence of his country." And from a pragmatic perspective, the departure of a generation of Americans from the electoral sphere may have a profound influence on the outcome of elections and even more importantly on subsequently enacted public policies. Many would agree with University of Maryland scholar William Galston (2001) that the "withdrawal of a cohort of citizens from public affairs disturbs the balance of public deliberation—to the detriment of those who withdraw, and to the rest of us as well." A generation removed from politics is something to fret about. And of course higher or lower turnout by young voters may shape the outcome of future elections. The 2000 and 2004 campaigns are good examples of this kind of impact (see chapter 3 in this volume).

## EXPLANATIONS FOR YOUTH POLITICAL DISENGAGEMENT

Why doesn't the extensive civic engagement among young people extend to voting and other forms of political activity? Most common explanations for the low levels of youth voting have focused on the character of young citizens as individuals. The decline of participation is due to changes in attitudes, especially among younger Americans. On the one hand, they are seen as ignorant of their duties as citizens, in part due to poor civic education in high school (Carnegie Corporation of New York and CIRCLE 2003; Comber 2005). On the other hand, they are seen as apathetic and self-centered when it comes to public affairs. If such attitudes are the problem, then the solution is to change them. For instance, many high school and college programs have been developed to promote students' interest and knowledge of politics. Rock the Vote, which emerged in 1992 and was reenergized for the 2004 presidential contest, is a prominent example (see chapters 9 and 10 in this volume).

A less common approach has been to focus on political elites, including candidates, public officials, journalists, party leaders, and campaign professionals.

Here the main culprit is "new-style political campaigns," which focus on negative campaigning, extensive fundraising, and the precise targeting of voters, compounded by sensational media coverage of politics. This style of politics has alienated many voters, but especially the youth. If such elite behavior is the problem, then the solution is to change the style of campaigning and campaign coverage. And there have been many efforts in this regard. There have been extensive efforts at campaign finance reform (Malbin 2003). There have been parallel efforts to develop codes of conduct for campaigns, such as the American Association of Political Consultants' code of ethics.[1] And there have also been initiatives to improve media coverage of politics, including the Center for the Study of Journalism and Democracy at the University of Southern California.[2]

A final approach has received relatively little attention, and that is the role of political organizations dedicated to mobilizing citizens to vote. Simply put, there has been a decline in the scope, size, and effectiveness of such "mobilizing institutions." Campaigns are now run by candidate organizations that use modern technology to reach voters directly. Such campaigns are aided by political parties redesigned to provide services to candidates rather than control nominations, and they were abetted by an expanded set of interest-group organizations. The net result was the relative absence of broad-based institutions concerned with voter mobilization for its own sake. If the decline of mobilizing institutions is the problem, then the solution is to reinvigorate such institutions. In this regard, new kinds of institutions have been developed, including new grassroots organizations, such as America Votes, and the deployment of new technologies, such as the Internet. Attempts to revive local political parties are part of this effort as well. History suggests that the latter might be a particularly fruitful avenue.

## LOCAL POLITICAL PARTIES AND VOTER MOBILIZATION

Reviving local political parties has considerable support in American history. After all, when was political participation highest, and what brought a large number of ordinary citizens, including young people, into the political process? Most scholars would agree that the heyday of electoral participation was from 1840 to the end of the nineteenth century. Although the voting age was twenty-one instead of today's eighteen and women were not allowed to vote, turnout was still remarkably high. In only three elections during this period did the presidential election turnout dip to less than 70 percent, and on three occasions it breached the 80 percent mark. By way of contrast, since 1972, turnout in presidential elections has averaged 55 percent, and it has not been significantly above the 60 percent mark since then.

Politics during this "golden age of parties" was integral to the everyday lives of most Americans. When Charles Dickens traveled around the United States in the early 1840s, he was overwhelmed by American's passion for politics:

> Quiet people avoid the question of the Presidency, for there will be a new election in three years and a half, and party feelings run very high: the great constitutional feature of this institution being, that (as soon as) the acrimony of the last election is over, the acrimony of the next begins; which is an unspeakable comfort to all strong politicians and true lovers of their country; that is to say, to ninety-nine men and boys out of every ninety-nine and a quarter. (Dickens 1842)

It is little wonder that candidate forums, such as the Lincoln-Douglas debate in 1858, would extend for hours and even days. By all accounts, electoral politics reached new levels of intensity.

What would explain such intense participation in electoral politics? Perhaps the pace of change in the nineteenth century is part of the answer. Industrialization and urbanization of the Northeast progressed with "startling rapidity," notes one scholar (Hicks 1949, 62). The rate of technological innovation during this period was equally quick. New uses of materials (chiefly iron and steel) were discovered, as were new energy sources. Innovative machines, methods of organizing work, modes of transportation, and the general application of science to business changed society and the economic base of the nation. And at this time, successive waves of immigrants also washed onto American shores seeking the opportunity for a better life. Between 1846 and 1856, for instance, some 3.1 million immigrants arrived, representing one-eighth of the existing U.S. population.

Another explanation for the high level of nineteenth-century participation was expanding levels of education, a factor strongly associated with voting. Widespread public education took hold during the midpoint of the nineteenth century. Newspapers and magazines sprang up, many shifting their focus from commercial and legal news to broader topics such as political and cultural happenings. Lyceums, or lecture halls, spread throughout the nation, and soon each community boasted a distinguished lecture series. An extraordinary number and variety of institutions of higher learning were formed, including many on the western frontier.

The nineteenth century was also characterized by major policy debates about the nature of the country itself. A growing tension had emerged between the increasingly industrial and urban North and the agrarian, plantation-centered

South. The clash over slavery took on more immediacy by the midpoint of the century as new territories were added to the union. The conflict escalated into the greatest challenge in our nation's history, and Reconstruction was a turbulent period as well. And once this conflict was over, it was quickly replaced by bitter debates over industrialization, trade, and America's place in the world.

Of course, the dawn of the twenty-first century in the United States is also characterized by rapid economic and social change, technological advance, high levels of education, and fierce policy debates. However, the nineteenth century was characterized by something else: strong local political parties. Indeed, one cannot look very deep into the nature of politics in that era without noticing the dominance of party organizations. American parties were born shortly after the ratification of the Constitution and a generation later had grown into a system of mass-based organizations. Although designed primarily to elect presidents and other officeholders, this system of local political parties had the invaluable side effect of dramatically increasing the level of voter participation, pulling citizens out of their private lives and into the public realm. And, in this regard, it gave citizens an opportunity to participate in governmental responses to the dramatic changes of the period.

Writing of the "golden age of parties," historian Joel Silbey draws a clear link between party activities and voter mobilization: "After 1838, parties were, and were accepted as, the key integrating mechanisms of all aspects of American politics. . . . [As a result,] the American electorate now contained few apathetic, poorly informed, or marginally involved voters" (Silbey 1991, 11). In a very real sense, local parties manufactured mass electoral mobilization in America; when turnout has been high, parties have been active. Indeed, as political scientist E. E. Schattschneider (1942) argued, "Parties have extended the area of popular participation in public affairs enormously" (208), and "once party organizations become active in the electorate, a vast field of extension and intensification of effort is opened, the extension of the franchise to new social classes, for example" (47).

However, the twentieth century was unkind to this system of local parties. A series of reforms, beginning in the progressive era, such as the secret ballot, the direct primary, and the replacement of patronage with civil service, eventually undermined the vitality of many local parties. Innovations in communications technology, such as television, gave national organizations and individual candidates a greater role in campaigns, to the detriment of local organizations. Thus, by the second half of the twentieth century, local parties found it increasingly difficult to perform their historic function of mobilizing the vote. It is not entirely coincidence that these difficulties occurred during the period when voter turnout declined, especially among the youth. Indeed, the party system of the late twentieth century could be fairly characterized as "base-less" because of its lack of direct connection to the citizenry (Shea 2003).

The key culprits in this regard were local political parties, once the dominant electoral organizations in the United States. This decline was partly in the _capacity_ to mobilize the vote; local parties became weaker in both absolute and relative terms, losing out to candidates, interest groups, and higher-level party organizations. But there was also a decline in the *interest* in voter mobilization as local parties became adjuncts to the new style of campaigning and the organizations that practice it. Writing in the *Atlantic Monthly*, Don Peck captured this last point well: "In recent decades, parties have moved away from grassroots mobilization efforts, which reach out to nonvoters, to focus on 'switching' independents that have a strong history of voting" (2002, 48).

Ironically, at about the same time that local party organizations reached this nadir, national and state organizations experienced an expansion in organizational strength (Bibby 1998). By the end of the twentieth century, national and state party committees had more resources than at any point in American history. There is some evidence that this revitalization has extended to local parties as well, so that local organizations are developing the capacity to once again make a difference in elections. One of the interesting results of this body of research is that local parties are still widely perceived as the most important source of campaign volunteers and as critical to voter registration and get-out-the-vote (GOTV) efforts — despite the numerous changes of the last fifty years (see, for example, Frendreis, Gibson, and Vertz 1990; Frendreis and Gitelson 1993; Frendreis, Gitelson, Flemming, and Layzell 1996; Shea and Green 2006).

Simply put, our question is this: are today's local party organizations interested and capable of mobilizing youth voters?

## THE STUDY

This study was supported by a grant from the Center for Information and Research on Civic Learning and Engagement (CIRCLE) to research the current and potential connections between local party organizations and the youth vote. The portion of the study central to this chapter is a telephone survey of a random sample of Democratic and Republican local party chairs drawn from the one thousand most populated counties across the country. According to the 2000 census, these counties contain 87 percent of the American population. So this sample covers the local parties most capable of influencing the electorate, and thus the youth vote.

The survey was between October 1 and November 10, 2003, at the University of Akron Survey Research Center, producing a total of 403 Democratic and 402 Republican responses, with a cooperation rate of about 50 percent. The responses were found to deviate only slightly from the geographic and demographic characteristics of the original sample of counties; the data were weighted to correct for these modest differences. These results have a margin of error of plus or minus five percentage points for each party, and plus or minus four percentage points for the sample as a whole.

Each interview lasted roughly thirty minutes and included batteries on organization strength, party activities, and the political environment, as well as extensive questions on youth mobilization. These survey data were then matched with U.S. Census data for all of the counties, and for 455 counties, the 2000 voting records aggregated by age were appended.

## LOCAL PARTY LEADERS AND YOUTH DISENGAGEMENT

How do local party leaders view the political disengagement of the youth? We asked the local party leaders to respond to the statement "The lack of political engagement by young people is a serious problem"; the results are listed in table 2.1. Overall, more than four-fifths of the respondents agreed that youth disengagement was a problem: some 52.4 percent "strongly agreed" with the statement, and 36.6 "agreed." Only about one-tenth disagreed or had no opinion.

There were interesting differences by party. Almost two-thirds of the Democratic leaders "strongly agreed" with the statement, compared to 39 percent of GOP leaders. Conversely, just 3 percent of Democrats disagreed that youth disengagement was a serious problem, compared with 13.4 percent of Republicans. One plausible explanation for this difference is strategic calculation: these leaders may see young voters as a Democratic constituency so that youth disengagement imposes different costs on the Democrats and Repub-

**Table 2.1 Youth Political Disengagement: Is it a Problem?**

The lack of political engagement by young people is a serious problem.

|            | Strongly Agree | Agree | No Opinion | Disagree | Strongly Disagree | Total |
|------------|------|------|------|------|------|------|
| Democrat   | 65.4 | 30.6 | 1.0  | 3.0  | 0.0  | 100  |
| Republican | 39.1 | 42.7 | 4.8  | 12.1 | 1.3  | 100  |
| All        | 52.4 | 36.6 | 2.9  | 7.5  | 0.6  | 100  |

*Source:* Survey by authors

licans (see chapter 2). However, a large majority of both parties agreed that youth disengagement is a problem (96 percent of Democrats and 82 percent of Republicans).

If leaders down in the local political trenches see the lack of youth participation as problematic, then what is its cause? Table 2.2 reports the local leaders' responses to statements that concern the individual characteristics of the youth. Overall, some 70 percent disagree with the statement "High schools do a lot to prepare young people for their role as citizens." Here, Republicans held a bit more intense opinions than Democrats, but there was a consensus that young people are poorly prepared to be good citizens.

Overall, a slight majority of the local party leaders agreed with the statement "People do not become interested in politics until they reach middle age" (the second item in table 2.2). Although this statement does not directly address allegations that the youth are apathetic and self-centered, it is relevant to these claims because it suggests that there is something about the youth that

**Table 2.2 Causes of Youth Disengagement: The Characteristics of Youth**

High schools do a lot to prepare young people for their role as citizens.

|  | Strongly Agree | Agree | No Opinion | Disagree | Strongly Disagree | Total |
|---|---|---|---|---|---|---|
| Democrat | 4.3 | 26.3 | 2.7 | 42.2 | 24.5 | 100 |
| Republican | 2.3 | 19.0 | 3.0 | 39.0 | 36.7 | 100 |
| All | 3.3 | 22.6 | 2.9 | 40.6 | 30.6 | 100 |

People do not become interested in politics until they reach middle age.

|  | Strongly Agree | Agree | No Opinion | Disagree | Strongly Disagree | Total |
|---|---|---|---|---|---|---|
| Democrat | 12.5 | 45.0 | 2.2 | 32.8 | 7.5 | 100 |
| Republican | 13.4 | 45.5 | 4.0 | 30.3 | 6.8 | 100 |
| All | 12.9 | 45.2 | 3.2 | 31.5 | 7.2 | 100 |

How difficult is it to mobilize young voters?

|  | Very Difficult | Somewhat Difficult | Not at All Difficult | Total |
|---|---|---|---|---|
| Democrat | 55.6 | 39.1 | 5.3 | 100.0 |
| Republican | 36.1 | 51.7 | 12.2 | 100.0 |
| All | 46.0 | 45.3 | 8.7 | 100.0 |

*Source:* Survey by authors

renders them uninterested in politics. However, this opinion is not strongly held by the respondents (just one-eighth "strongly agreed"), and some two-fifths disagreed with the statement. There was little difference between Democrats and Republicans on this matter.

The effect of such attitudes by the youth is to render them difficult to mobilize politically. The final item in table 2.2 addresses this difficulty directly. Overall, almost one-half of the local party leaders said the youth were "very difficult" to mobilize, and as many said youth mobilization was "somewhat difficult" to achieve. On this question, there was a significant party difference: more than one-half of the Democratic leaders reported the youth to be "very difficult" to mobilize, compared to a bit more than one-third of their Republican counterparts. This pattern may be surprising given that more Democrats identified youth disengagement as a problem. However, it could be that the Democratic leaders' assessment of the problem reflects in part a stronger desire to mobilize the youth.

Of course, an alienated youth may be difficult to mobilize as well. Table 2.3 reports the respondents' views on allegations that the behavior of contemporary political elites has alienated young voters. Overall, some 70 percent of the party leaders agreed that "young people are turned off by negativity in campaigns." Democrats were a bit more likely to agree than Republicans, but neither set of party leaders held especially strong opinions on this matter (between one-fifth and one-quarter "strongly agreed").

Overall, some two-thirds of the party leaders agreed that "the media has done much to turn young people away from politics." Here, Republicans were more likely to agree than Democrats (73 to 57 percent) and to have a more intense opinion (36 to 24 percent "strongly agree"). And overall, three-fifths of these party leaders agreed that "candidates ignore the youth vote." The Democrats were more in agreement on this matter than the Republicans (65 to 55 percent), but both groups lacked strong opinions.

Thus, local party leaders affirmed some of the complaints about the effect of contemporary campaigns on youth participation. However, a clear majority disagreed with the statement that "young voters are turned off to politics because of the amount of money involved." This overall pattern may reflect the fact that it is expensive to mobilize voters and especially the youth. However, here the Republicans were more likely to disagree than the Democrats (59 to 46 percent), but once again neither group was especially intense in their opinions.

What about the role of mobilizing institutions in youth disengagement? Table 2.4 offers a partial answer to this question. Overall, more than nine of ten local party leaders agreed with the statement "Local parties can make a difference getting young people involved in politics," and nearly two-fifths

**Table 2.3 Causes of Youth Disengagement: The Behavior of Political Elites**

Young people are turned off by the negativity of campaigns.

|  | Strongly Agree | Agree | No Opinion | Disagree | Strongly Disagree | Total |
|---|---|---|---|---|---|---|
| Democrat | 24.1 | 50.6 | 6.5 | 17.0 | 1.8 | 100 |
| Republican | 19.3 | 45.1 | 8.8 | 24.2 | 2.6 | 100 |
| All | 21.7 | 47.9 | 7.6 | 20.6 | 2.2 | 100 |

Candidates ignore the youth vote.

|  | Strongly Agree | Agree | No Opinion | Disagree | Strongly Disagree | Total |
|---|---|---|---|---|---|---|
| Democrat | 13.8 | 51.4 | 8.5 | 24.3 | 2.0 | 100 |
| Republican | 11.5 | 43.4 | 7.6 | 34.2 | 3.3 | 100 |
| All | 12.6 | 47.4 | 8.1 | 29.2 | 2.7 | 100 |

The media has done much to turn young people away from politics.

|  | Strongly Agree | Agree | No Opinion | Disagree | Strongly Disagree | Total |
|---|---|---|---|---|---|---|
| Democrat | 23.9 | 33.2 | 7.4 | 32.5 | 3.0 | 100 |
| Republican | 35.9 | 37.0 | 5.6 | 19.7 | 1.8 | 100 |
| All | 29.9 | 35.1 | 6.5 | 26.1 | 2.4 | 100 |

Young voters are turned off to politics because of the amount of money involved.

|  | Strongly Agree | Agree | No Opinion | Disagree | Strongly Disagree | Total |
|---|---|---|---|---|---|---|
| Democrat | 10.1 | 33.2 | 10.4 | 41.3 | 5.0 | 100 |
| Republican | 6.4 | 27.7 | 6.9 | 51.9 | 7.1 | 100 |
| All | 8.2 | 30.5 | 8.6 | 46.6 | 6.1 | 100 |

*Source:* Survey by authors

"strongly agreed." And almost as many respondents agreed with the statement "Young voters will respond to the right candidates and issues" (87 percent; 32 percent "strongly agree"). Clearly, these local party leaders see their organizations as a possible solution to the lack of youth voting, but they also believe that effective politics can attract young voters, much as it attracts their elders.

If political institutions can mobilize the youth, to what extent are these institutions directed toward this task? Table 2.5 reports the party leaders'

**Table 2.4 Possible Solutions to Youth Disengagement: Candidates and Local Parties**

Local parties can make a big difference getting young people involved in politics.

| | Strongly Agree | Agree | No Opinion | Disagree | Strongly Disagree | Total |
|---|---|---|---|---|---|---|
| Democrat | 35.8 | 54.7 | 1.8 | 7.7 | 0.0 | 100 |
| Republican | 43.1 | 51.6 | 2.7 | 2.3 | 0.3 | 100 |
| All | 39.5 | 53.2 | 2.2 | 5.0 | 0.1 | 100 |

Young voters will respond to the right candidates and issues.

| | Strongly Agree | Agree | No Opinion | Disagree | Strongly Disagree | Total |
|---|---|---|---|---|---|---|
| Democrat | 33.3 | 56.6 | 2.8 | 7.0 | 0.3 | 100 |
| Republican | 30.2 | 54.7 | 4.3 | 10.3 | 0.5 | 100 |
| All | 31.8 | 55.7 | 3.4 | 8.7 | 0.4 | 100 |

*Source:* Survey by authors

perceptions of the commitment of a variety of political actors to mobilizing young voters. The first entry is for the respondent's own local party committee. Here, 39 percent claimed that their committee was "very committed" to youth mobilizations (and another 53 percent "somewhat committed"). On this matter, there was little difference between the Democrats and Republicans. It is worth noting that the first figure is almost exactly the same as the percent of respondents who "strongly agreed" that local parties could make a "big difference" mobilizing young voters.

Overall, the local party leaders had a similar view of their party's major candidates and state committees, with a bit more than one-third reporting that these actors were "very committed" to youth mobilization. However, the respondents gave much lower marks to their national party committees, with a little more than one-fifth rating these national organizations as "very committed" in this regard. Of course, national committees have traditionally worked through state and local parties with regard to voter mobilization. It is interesting to note, however, that the Republicans gave their national committee higher marks than the Democrats (26 to 18 percent). Overall, the respondents reported that interest groups (12.7 percent) and campaign consultants (15.6 percent) were the least committed to mobilizing young voters. Campaign consultants received the lowest score, with 45.7 percent claiming they were "not at all committed" to mobilizing young voters.

**Table 2.5 Perceived Commitment of Political Groups to Mobilizing the Youth**

Given scarce resources, how committed are the following groups to mobilizing young voters?

| Local Party Committee | Very Committed | Somewhat Committed | Not at All Committed | Total |
|---|---|---|---|---|
| Democrat | 38.9 | 53.9 | 7.2 | 100.0 |
| Republican | 39.1 | 52.4 | 8.5 | 100.0 |
| All | 39.0 | 53.1 | 7.9 | 100.0 |

| Candidates for Major Offices | Very Committed | Somewhat Committed | Not at All Committed | Total |
|---|---|---|---|---|
| Democrat | 32.9 | 54.5 | 12.6 | 100.0 |
| Republican | 38.1 | 54.2 | 7.7 | 100.0 |
| All | 35.5 | 54.3 | 10.2 | 100.0 |

| State Party Committee | Very Committed | Somewhat Committed | Not at All Committed | Total |
|---|---|---|---|---|
| Democrat | 36.1 | 52.1 | 11.8 | 100.0 |
| Republican | 33.8 | 56.0 | 10.2 | 100.0 |
| All | 35.0 | 54.0 | 11.0 | 100.0 |

| National Party Committee | Very Committed | Somewhat Committed | Not at All Committed | Total |
|---|---|---|---|---|
| Democrat | 17.7 | 57.6 | 24.7 | 100.0 |
| Republican | 26.4 | 54.1 | 19.5 | 100.0 |
| All | 22.0 | 55.9 | 22.1 | 100.0 |

| Interest Groups | Very Committed | Somewhat Committed | Not at All Committed | Total |
|---|---|---|---|---|
| Democrat | 12.7 | 55.6 | 31.7 | 100.0 |
| Republican | 12.7 | 50.7 | 36.6 | 100.0 |
| All | 12.7 | 53.2 | 34.1 | 100.0 |

| Campaign Consultants | Very Committed | Somewhat Committed | Not at All Committed | Total |
|---|---|---|---|---|
| Democrat | 14.0 | 40.9 | 45.1 | 100.0 |
| Republican | 17.3 | 36.3 | 46.4 | 100.0 |
| All | 15.6 | 38.7 | 45.7 | 100.0 |

*Source:* Survey by authors

Taken together, these responses support the notion that inadequate mobilizing institutions can contribute to youth disengagement in the political process, but that local political parties are less among the culprits.

## MOBILIZING THE YOUTH VOTE:
## PRIORITY AND PROGRAMS

The local party leaders' reports of their organizations' commitment to youth mobilization are plausible, but their accuracy may be suspect. To further investigate the extent to which youth mobilization was a priority to these respondents, we asked a series of questions to ascertain if young voters were on top of the local leaders' minds. Near the beginning of the survey, we asked an open-ended question: "Are there demographic groups of voters that are currently important to the long-term success of your local party?" We recorded the group listed and then asked for a second and third group. Thus, the local leaders were given three opportunities to mention any group of voters. Table 2.6 reports the percentage of respondents who mentioned young voters and, for purposes of comparison, senior citizens as well.

Overall, just 8.4 percent of the respondents mentioned youth in the first question, another 11.6 percent mentioned it in the second questions, and 17.5 percent mentioned it on the third try. Thus, a total of 37.5 percent mentioned young voters—even though the question addressed the "long-term success of the party." By way of comparison, senior citizens were mentioned more often: 20.7 percent on the first mention (more than twice the first mentions of youth), 18.8 percent on the second mention (roughly 50 percent higher than youth second mentions), and 9.4 percent on the third (about one-half of the third youth mentions). In total, 48.9 percent of the local party chairs mentioned seniors.

These figures clearly suggest that the local parties gave lower priority to the youth compared to seniors. This relative priority makes some sense, given that seniors typically have a much higher level of voter turnout than their grandchildren. But note that the 37.5 percent who mentioned young voters is about equal to the percentage who reported that their local party committee was "very committed" to youth mobilizations and who "strongly agreed" that local parties could mobilize the youth. These figures suggest that when it comes to a focus on young voters, the local party's glass is two-fifths full.

Here there were some variations by party. Republican leaders were nearly twice as likely to mention young voters on the first mention, but on the next two opportunities, the Democrats did better. With the three opportunities combined, 40.9 percent of Democratic leaders mentioned the youth, compared to

**Table 2.6   Voter Age Groups and Priority: Youth and Senior Citizens**

Are there demographic groups of voters that are currently important to the long-term success of your local party?

| Youth | Democrat | Republican | All | Seniors | Democrat | Republican | All |
|---|---|---|---|---|---|---|---|
| 1st mention | 7.2 | 9.5 | 8.4 | 1st mention | 22.8 | 18.6 | 20.7 |
| 2nd mention | 12.5 | 10.8 | 11.6 | 2nd mention | 24.2 | 13.3 | 18.8 |
| 3rd mention | 21.2 | 13.8 | 17.5 | 3rd mention | 11.0 | 7.8 | 9.4 |
| No mention | 59.1 | 65.9 | 62.5 | No mention | 42.0 | 60.3 | 51.1 |
| Total | 100.0 | 100.0 | 100.0 | | 100.0 | 100.0 | 100.0 |
| All youth mentions | 40.9 | 34.1 | 37.5 | All seniors mentions | 58.0 | 39.7 | 48.9 |

*Source:* Survey by authors

34.1 percent of the Republicans. Interestingly, there was an even more dramatic difference for the overall mentions of seniors: 58 percent of Democrats mentioned seniors, compared to 39.7 percent of Republicans.

### Youth Registration and GOTV Programs

Are local parties acting on these priorities? As part of the battery on voter groups, we also asked the respondents if the local party had special voter registration and GOTV programs for the groups of voters they mentioned. In a separate question, respondents who had not mentioned youth were nonetheless asked about such programs for youth. Table 2.7 reports the distribution of these programs; for ease of presentation, this information has been combined with the youth priority measure (the sum of all three mentions of young voters).

In terms of voter registration programs, about one-fifth of the overall sample neither reported youth registration programs nor gave priority to young voters. However, nearly twice as many local leaders (almost two-fifths) reported youth registration programs, but without mentioning the youth as a priority. Less than one-tenth of the sample gave youth registration priority but had no special registration programs. Finally, a little less than one-third of the party chairs reported both youth registration programs and priority. Here there was a strong partisan divide: Democrats were more likely to have both youth programs and priorities than Republicans were (36.0 to 26.3 percent). In contrast, Republicans were more likely to report such programs without a youth priority than Democrats were (42.6 to 36.5 percent).

In terms of GOTV programs, almost two-fifths of the local party chairs reported neither special programs nor priority for youth mobilization. And

**Table 2.7 Registration, Youth Programs, and Youth Priority**

| Special voter registration programs for youth: | Democrat | Republican | All |
|---|---|---|---|
| No youth programs, no priority | 22.5 | 23.3 | 22.9 |
| Youth programs, no priority | 36.5 | 42.6 | 39.5 |
| No youth programs, youth priority | 5.0 | 7.8 | 6.4 |
| Youth programs and priority | 36.0 | 26.3 | 31.2 |
| Total | 100.0 | 100.0 | 100.0 |

| Special GOTV programs for youth: | Democrat | Republican | All |
|---|---|---|---|
| No youth programs, nor priority | 35.2 | 38.0 | 36.6 |
| Youth programs, no priority | 23.9 | 28.0 | 26.0 |
| No youth programs, youth priority | 7.2 | 6.5 | 6.8 |
| Youth programs and priority | 33.7 | 27.5 | 30.6 |
| Total | 100.0 | 100.0 | 100.0 |

*Source:* Survey by authors

approximately one-quarter reported youth GOTV programs despite the absence of youth as a priority. Once again, less than one-tenth had no such programs but nonetheless said that youth was a priority. Finally, some three in ten respondents combined special youth GOTV programs and priority. Although not as sharp as for the registration programs, there was a partisan divide for GOTV programs as well, with Democrats besting the Republicans in the combination of youth GOTV programs and priority (33.7 to 27.5 percent), while the Republicans did better with such youth programs without priority (28.0 to 23.9 percent).

A follow-up question asked the respondents to describe their special youth programs. Upon inspection, we found that only a handful of these local party leaders mentioned significant and innovative activities (see chapter 4 for a fuller description of some of these cases). Instead, most of these programs could be dubbed "modest" and "traditional." For example, a common response was "Some people in our party have spoken at area schools" or "Our people set up booths at fairs and malls." Moreover, many respondents were unable to provide any detail about their special youth programs.

## College Party Clubs and Party Youth Groups

Roughly one-half of the local leaders describing youth programs mentioned college party clubs, such as working with the college Republicans or Democrats. In separate questions, all the respondents were asked directly about college party clubs and also about youth groups or divisions, and the results are reported in table 2.8.

Overall, a little more than one-quarter of the local leaders reported neither any involvement with a college club nor a priority for youth. And more than one-third reported working with a college club but had no youth priority. Roughly one-sixth did not work with a college club but nonetheless gave priority to young voters. Finally, a bit more than one-fifth of the sample was both connected to a party club and gave youth priority. Here, too, there were some partisan differences. The Republicans were more likely to report working with such a club than the Democrats, and the difference was especially striking for those who did not give priority to youth (40.4 to 30.9 percent).

Similar patterns held for party youth groups or divisions. Better than one-third of these local leaders reported neither such involvement nor youth priority. Another one-quarter reported a youth group or division but did not give young voters priority. And about one-fifth did not work with such a group but gave priority to youth mobilization. Finally, a little more than one-sixth of the respondents combined a youth group with youth priorities. Some party differences appear in these data as well. As with college clubs, Republican leaders were more likely to report involvement with a youth group, and this was especially true for those who expressed no youth priority (31.3 to 20.6 percent). However, the Democrats offset this figure with a greater presence in the combined category (20.3 to 15.3 percent).

**Table 2.8   College Party Clubs, Youth Groups, and Youth Priority**

| Work with college party clubs: | Democrat | Republican | All |
|---|---|---|---|
| No college club nor priority | 28.2 | 25.6 | 26.9 |
| College club, no priority | 30.9 | 40.4 | 35.6 |
| No college club, youth priority | 16.8 | 12.2 | 14.6 |
| College club and youth priority | 23.9 | 21.8 | 22.9 |
| Total | 100.0 | 100.0 | 100.0 |

| Have active party youth group or division: | Democrat | Republican | All |
|---|---|---|---|
| No youth group nor priority | 38.4 | 34.6 | 36.6 |
| No youth group, no priority | 20.6 | 31.3 | 25.9 |
| No youth group, youth priority | 20.7 | 18.8 | 19.7 |
| Youth group and youth priority | 20.3 | 15.3 | 17.8 |
| Total | 100.0 | 100.0 | 100.0 |

*Source:* Survey by authors

It is worth noting that the vast majority of local party leaders who reported a lack of involvement with college clubs or youth groups also claimed that they would like to have such involvement in the future. This finding reinforces the dominant pattern: most local party leaders see youth disengagement as a problem, but many are unable to solve the problem.

## Youth Focus and Local Parties

How do all these measures fit together? Table 2.9 reports a summary measure of youth programs and priority among local parties, arrayed from the least to the most focused on youth mobilization. Overall, one-tenth of the local parties had "no focus" on youth, reporting no youth programs and giving youth mobilization no priority. More than one-quarter had a "weak focus," with one or two of the four types of programs discussed above, but with no youth priority. Almost one-fifth had a "modest focus" on youth, with few or no programs, but gave priority to young voters. Meanwhile, about one-quarter had a "moderate focus," reporting three or four types of youth programs, but had no youth priority. Finally, almost the same proportion of the sample had a "sharp focus" on youth mobilization, combining three or four types of youth programs with youth priority.

There are two ways of looking at these patterns. On the one hand, almost one-half of local parties were at least moderately focused on youth mobilization. However, only about one-half of these respondents had a sharp focus on youth mobilization. On the other hand, nearly two-fifths of the local leaders gave young voters priority, but only three-fifths of these were sharply focused on youth mobilization. And almost two-fifths of all the local parties had a modest, weak, or nonexistent focus on youth mobilization.

**Table 2.9    Focus on Youth Mobilization, Local Parties**

|  | Democrat | Republican | All |
|---|---|---|---|
| No Focus |  |  |  |
| *(No programs nor priority)* | 11.0 | 9.0 | 10.0 |
| Weak Focus |  |  |  |
| *(One or two programs, no youth priority)* | 27.2 | 28.3 | 27.8 |
| Modest Focus |  |  |  |
| *(None, one or two, youth priority)* | 15.2 | 13.5 | 14.3 |
| Moderate Focus |  |  |  |
| *(Three, four programs, no youth priority)* | 20.9 | 28.6 | 24.8 |
| Sharp Focus |  |  |  |
| *(Three, four programs, youth priority)* | 25.7 | 20.6 | 23.1 |
| Total | 100.0 | 100.0 | 100.0 |

*Source*: Survey by authors

The partisan differences in these summary categories were straightforward. Democrats were more likely than Republicans to be sharply focused on youth mobilization (25.7 to 20.6 percent). However, Republicans were more likely than Democrats to be moderately focused on youth mobilization (28.6 to 20.9 percent). Respondents from both parties were about equally represented in the three less-focused categories of respondents.

Figure 2.1 brings this discussion full circle by showing the relationship between youth focus and the reported commitment of the local party to mobilizing young voters. Note that for both the Democrats and the Republicans, the level of reported local party commitment to youth mobilization rises steadily with the degree of youth focus. For example, among the Democrats, the figure increased from just 6.8 percent among local parties with no focus on youth mobilization to 58.3 percent among local parties with a sharp focus. For the Republicans, the comparable numbers were 11.1 and 60.5 percent.

## YOUTH FOCUS AND THE CHARACTERISTICS OF LOCAL PARTIES

What are the characteristics of the local parties that are focused on youth mobilization? For one thing, they tend to be stronger organizations. Table 2.10 displays the degree of youth focus by the bottom, middle, and top thirds of a scale of party strength. Following the literature, this scale includes standard organizational

**Figure 2.1   Youth Focus and Local Party Commitment to Youth Moblization**

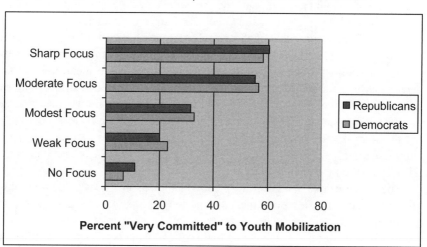

**Table 2.10   Youth Focus and Party Organizational Strength**

|  | Focus on Youth Mobilization | Organizational Strength: | | | |
|---|---|---|---|---|---|
|  |  | Low | Moderate | High | Total |
| *Entire Sample* | No Focus | 46.2 | 25.0 | 28.8 | 100.0 |
|  | Weak Focus | 36.5 | 35.1 | 28.4 | 100.0 |
|  | Modest Focus | 53.0 | 32.2 | 14.8 | 100.0 |
|  | Moderate Focus | 22.7 | 36.9 | 40.4 | 100.0 |
|  | Sharp Focus | 23.2 | 31.4 | 45.4 | 100.0 |
|  | All | 33.3 | 33.3 | 33.4 | 100.0 |
| *Democrat* | No Focus | 40.9 | 31.8 | 27.3 | 100.0 |
|  | Weak Focus | 39.8 | 32.4 | 27.8 | 100.0 |
|  | Modest Focus | 65.5 | 23.0 | 11.5 | 100.0 |
|  | Moderate Focus | 28.6 | 32.1 | 39.3 | 100.0 |
|  | Sharp Focus | 22.3 | 31.1 | 46.6 | 100.0 |
|  | All | 37.0 | 30.5 | 32.5 | 100.0 |
| *Republican* | No Focus | 51.4 | 18.9 | 29.7 | 100.0 |
|  | Weak Focus | 33.9 | 37.5 | 28.6 | 100.0 |
|  | Modest Focus | 40.0 | 41.8 | 18.2 | 100.0 |
|  | Moderate Focus | 18.4 | 40.4 | 41.2 | 100.0 |
|  | Sharp Focus | 23.5 | 32.1 | 44.4 | 100.0 |
|  | All | 29.8 | 36.1 | 34.1 | 100.0 |

*Source: Survey by authors*

measures, such as permanent headquarters and paid staff (Cotter et al. 1984), as well as per capita party budget and the percent of the local committee positions that are filled (see Shea and Green 2006 for more details).

Overall, nearly one-half of the party committees with no focus on youth mobilization were found in the bottom third of the organizational strength scale. In contrast, only a little more than one-fifth of the local parties that were sharply focused on youth were organizationally weak. A similar pattern occurs among the strongest party organizations: a little more than one-quarter of the no-focus respondents were strong organizations, while nearly one-half of the sharp-focus committees were. Thus, the committees that were sharply and moderately focused on youth mobilization tended to be strong organizations with the resources to carry out youth programs.

These figures rise in a generally steady fashion as the focus on youth mobilization sharpens. However, there is one major anomaly: the modest-focus committees are unusually concentrated among the weak party organizations. Recall that the modest focus is made up of respondents who gave priority to the youth but did not have extensive youth programs. This pattern suggests that these party committees may lack the resources to act on the priority they assign to youth.

This pattern by organizational resources held for both Democrats and Republicans. For the Democrats, the proportion of strong parties increased from 27.3 percent in the no-focus category to 45.4 percent of the sharp-focus committees. The comparable figures for the Republicans were 29.7 and 44.4 percent, respectively. Table 2.11 complements this picture by reporting the respondents' response to the question: is there typically heavy party involvement or limited party involvement in campaigns in your area? Overall, more than three-fifths of the local leaders claimed there was "heavy party involvement." But note that the percentage of respondents choosing this answer increases steadily as the focus on youth mobilization sharpens. Overall, this figure rises from 51.9 percent of the no-focus committees to 74.2 percent of the sharply focused committees. The same basic pattern held for Democrats and Republicans.

Thus, party resources and activity seem to be an important part of the story: while only a minority of the local party committees are focused on youth

**Table 2.11   Youth Focus and Local Party Campaign Involvement**

|  | Focus on Youth Mobilization | Degree of Local Party Involvement in Campaigns: | | |
|  |  | Heavy Party Involvement | Limited Party Involvement | Total |
|---|---|---|---|---|
| *Entire Sample* | No Focus | 51.9 | 48.1 | 100.0 |
|  | Weak Focus | 56.0 | 44.0 | 100.0 |
|  | Modest Focus | 53.0 | 47.0 | 100.0 |
|  | Moderate Focus | 72.1 | 27.9 | 100.0 |
|  | Sharp Focus | 74.2 | 25.8 | 100.0 |
|  | All | 63.3 | 36.7 | 100.0 |
| *Democrat* | No Focus | 53.5 | 46.5 | 100.0 |
|  | Weak Focus | 52.8 | 47.2 | 100.0 |
|  | Modest Focus | 48.3 | 51.7 | 100.0 |
|  | Moderate Focus | 67.9 | 32.1 | 100.0 |
|  | Sharp Focus | 72.5 | 27.5 | 100.0 |
|  | All | 60.5 | 39.5 | 100.0 |
| *Republican* | No Focus | 50.0 | 50.0 | 100.0 |
|  | Weak Focus | 59.5 | 40.5 | 100.0 |
|  | Modest Focus | 58.2 | 41.8 | 100.0 |
|  | Moderate Focus | 75.2 | 24.8 | 100.0 |
|  | Sharp Focus | 76.2 | 23.8 | 100.0 |
|  | All | 66.3 | 33.7 | 100.0 |

*Source:* Survey by authors

mobilization, these local parties tend to have the wherewithal to conduct the necessary programs. These data suggest two ways that youth mobilization could be enhanced. First, strengthening the local organizations in the sharp-focus, moderate-focus, and especially the modest-focus categories could greatly expand the level of attention to young voters. Second, persuading the existing strong organizations among the no-focus and weak-focus committees to care about the youth vote could also increase youth mobilization.

Our survey suggests that local party committees are dedicated to voter mobilization in general, regardless of their youth focus. Overall, GOTV programs accounted for an average of 31.7 percent of the local party efforts, followed by campaign services to candidates (mean of 20 percent), campaign events (mean of 19 percent), and voter registration (mean of 17 percent). In addition, more than one-half of the local committees reported receiving aid from the state parties, and about one-eighth from national parties, with the largest portion of these funds going to GOTV activities. Interestingly, these proportions of GOTV effort did not vary much by party, organizational strength, or youth focus. Thus, it appears that local parties specialize in electoral activities across the board (Shea and Green 2006). This finding bodes well for the possibility of improving youth mobilization: all else being equal, local parties are already in the business of mobilizing voters.

Youth focus is associated with a few additional characteristics. First, youth focus is most common in more populous and competitive counties. And youth focus was also modestly associated with a larger number of young people in the county and with female party chairs. But other factors do not distinguish the youth-focused respondents, including the age or ideology of the local party chair, or a more participatory style of politics. For example, when asked to choose "helping candidates win elections" or "helping voters develop attachments to the parties," 63 percent of the local leaders chose winning elections over building loyal supporters. This pattern varied little by youth focus or party.

## SUCCESSFUL YOUTH MOBILIZATION

Does a greater youth focus succeed in mobilizing young voters? A variety of evidence suggests that it may. Table 2.12 displays the local party chairs' assessment of their own success with their reported special youth registration and GOTV programs. Overall, nearly as many local party leaders reported these programs to be "very successful" (14.2 percent) as "not at all successful" (12.9 percent), with the vast majority saying that the programs were "somewhat successful." But note the striking differences by youth focus: more than one-fifth of respondents with a sharp focus on youth mobilization

**Table 2.12     Perceived Success of Youth Programs**

|  | Focus on Youth Mobilization | Youth Programs Have Been: | | | |
|---|---|---|---|---|---|
|  |  | Very Successful | Somewhat Successful | Not at All Successful | Total |
| *Entire Sample* | Weak Focus | 4.1 | 71.2 | 24.7 | 100.0 |
|  | Modest Focus | 1.7 | 76.6 | 21.7 | 100.0 |
|  | Moderate Focus | 19.1 | 74.2 | 6.7 | 100.0 |
|  | Sharp Focus | 21.8 | 71.5 | 6.7 | 100.0 |
|  | All | 14.2 | 72.9 | 12.9 | 100.0 |
| *Democrat* | Weak Focus | 1.3 | 67.9 | 30.8 | 100.0 |
|  | Modest Focus | 0.0 | 71.9 | 28.1 | 100.0 |
|  | Moderate Focus | 11.0 | 85.3 | 3.7 | 100.0 |
|  | Sharp Focus | 17.0 | 73.4 | 9.6 | 100.0 |
|  | All | 9.1 | 75.2 | 15.7 | 100.0 |
| *Republican* | Weak Focus | 7.4 | 75.0 | 17.6 | 100.0 |
|  | Modest Focus | 3.6 | 82.1 | 14.3 | 100.0 |
|  | Moderate Focus | 25.2 | 66.7 | 8.1 | 100.0 |
|  | Sharp Focus | 26.8 | 70.4 | 2.8 | 100.0 |
|  | All | 19.1 | 71.2 | 9.7 | 100.0 |

*Source:* Survey by authors

reported that the special programs were "very successful," compared to just 4 percent of those with a weak focus. (The no-focus respondents were not asked about program success since they did not report any special youth programs.) This pattern holds by party, with the Republicans reporting a somewhat higher level of success than their Democratic counterparts.

Overall, 98 percent of the respondents with special youth programs reported that they planned to continue them, and roughly one-half of the respondents had specific plans to improve their youth programs. Only a small number planned to discontinue their programs or were pessimistic about improvement. These local leaders universally cited the great difficulty in mobilizing young voters as the reason for their view. Interestingly enough, the perceptions of such difficulty were closely related to youth focus, as can be seen in figure 2.2. For the Democratic leaders, four-fifths of those with no youth focus said that mobilizing young voters was "very difficult." In contrast, only two-fifths of those sharply focused on youth mobilization made the same claim. The comparable numbers for Republicans were more than one-half and less than one-quarter of the respondents, respectively.

These patterns strongly suggest that experience with and interest in youth mobilization changes the local party leaders' perceptions of the possibilities of doing so. Other evidence supports this conclusion as well. For example,

**Figure 2.2   Youth Focus and Difficulty of Mobilizing Youth**

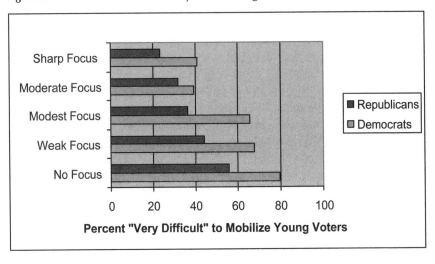

figure 2.3 reports the relationship between youth focus and the view that local parties can make a difference in mobilizing the youth. A positive assessment of the capacity of local parties in this regard rises to a high point among the local leaders with a sharp youth focus (with the exception of the anomalous figure for no-focus Republicans). Here, too, Republicans tend to have higher scores than their Democratic counterparts.

These patterns certainly suggest that local parties can and do have success in mobilizing young voters when they focus on the task. Table 2.13 offers some additional evidence on this point: the mean level of turnout among voters eighteen to twenty-four years old for 455 of the counties (records were not available for the remaining counties). The table shows a statistically significant difference between the counties with a sharp youth focus and those with no focus on youth mobilization. Of course, many factors go into explaining aggregate voter turnout, and a full explication is beyond the scope of this chapter. Nevertheless, simple controls for factors such as socioeconomic status and electoral competition do not eliminate the differences. Although simple, these data support the survey findings.

What about the future of local parties? We asked the local leaders if the role of local parties would increase, stay about the same, or decrease in the next ten years. Table 2.14 reports the results. Overall, some two-fifths of the respondents said that local parties will become more important, slightly more said things will remain the same, and just one-eighth said local party

**Figure 2.3   Youth Focus and Local Parties Can Mobilize Youth**

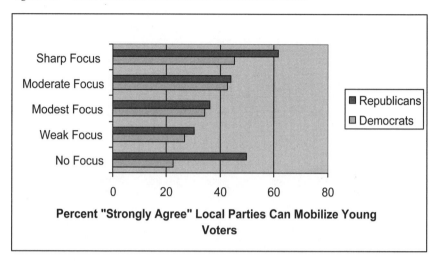

influence will decline. Note, however, that the expectation that local parties will be more important expands as youth focus sharpens. For all the respondents, these figures increased from 28.8 percent in the no-focus category to 48.2 percent for the sharp-focus category. Similar patterns occur for the Democrats and Republicans. An important anomaly occurs for the modest-focus respondents, who are less optimistic about the future of local parties. As before, this may reflect the lack of resources available to these local leaders. In sum, these data suggest considerable potential for local parties to expand their efforts at mobilizing voters, and especially the youth.

**Table 2.13   Youth Focus, Youth Turnout, and Registration, 2000 Presidential Election**

|  | Turnout, Voters, 18-24 Years Old | |
|---|---|---|
|  | *Mean* | *Standard Deviation* |
| No Focus | 24.8 | 9.1 |
| Weak Focus | 26.1 | 11.3 |
| Modest Focus | 26.4 | 13.2 |
| Moderate Focus | 26.0 | 12.7 |
| Sharp Focus | 30.6 | 18.2 |
| All | 27.5 | 13.6 |

*Source:* Survey by authors, county voter records aggregated by age, 455 counties

**Table 2.14   Youth Programs, Priority, and Views on Mobilizing Young Voters**

| | Focus on Youth Mobilization | How Important Will Local Parties Be In the Next Ten Years? | | | |
| | | More Important | About the Same | Less Important | Total |
| --- | --- | --- | --- | --- | --- |
| *Entire Sample* | No Focus | 28.8 | 55.0 | 16.2 | 100.0 |
| | Weak Focus | 40.7 | 43.9 | 15.4 | 100.0 |
| | Modest Focus | 34.2 | 51.8 | 14.0 | 100.0 |
| | Moderate Focus | 46.9 | 42.9 | 10.2 | 100.0 |
| | Sharp Focus | 48.6 | 43.2 | 8.2 | 100.0 |
| | All | 42.0 | 45.7 | 12.3 | 100.0 |
| *Democrats* | No Focus | 31.8 | 54.5 | 13.7 | 100.0 |
| | Weak Focus | 35.8 | 45.9 | 18.3 | 100.0 |
| | Modest Focus | 32.8 | 47.5 | 19.7 | 100.0 |
| | Moderate Focus | 45.2 | 42.9 | 11.9 | 100.0 |
| | Sharp Focus | 47.1 | 45.2 | 7.7 | 100.0 |
| | All | 39.8 | 46.3 | 13.9 | 100.0 |
| *Republicans* | No Focus | 24.3 | 54.1 | 21.6 | 100.0 |
| | Weak Focus | 45.1 | 41.6 | 13.3 | 100.0 |
| | Modest Focus | 36.4 | 56.4 | 7.2 | 100.0 |
| | Moderate Focus | 48.2 | 42.9 | 8.9 | 100.0 |
| | Sharp Focus | 50.6 | 40.7 | 8.7 | 100.0 |
| | All | 44.0 | 45.0 | 11.0 | 100.0 |

*Source:* Survey by authors

## CONCLUSIONS

Let's return to our initial question: are local parties interested in and capable of mobilizing young voters? We find mixed evidence in terms of interest in the youth. Although a large majority of local leaders agreed that youth disengagement was a problem, less than one-half of that number—about two-fifths of the total—gave priority to youth voters. In terms of capacity to mobilize the youth, the situation is more positive. At the present time, local parties specialize in voter mobilization, and many have adequate resources for the task. About one-half of the local parties have extensive programs directed at young voters, and many of the rest say they would like to do better in this regard.

All told, it appears that local parties can successfully mobilize the youth when they focus on the task. However, only about one-quarter of the local committees are sharply focused on youth mobilization. Thus, one reason for youth disengagement in politics may well be inadequate mobilizing institutions, including local parties. And a sharper focus on the youth could well bring more young voters to the polls. Put another way, many local leaders are throwing a "pretty good party" for young voters, and they need to throw a "better party" to attract young voters back into the electoral process.

Some party leaders need to be convinced of the importance of the youth, and others need financial help to develop better programs. Most could benefit from innovation in approaching the youth. Simply put, traditional approaches to registering and GOTV are ineffective with the new generation. It does not appear to be enough simply to "hand out voter registration cards at the high schools" or to "make calls before election day." This generation wants to be engaged in the process, and such superficial approaches have limited success.

The local party leaders interviewed for this research are correct: mobilizing young voters is a difficult chore—and one likely to become even harder in the years ahead. Yet, astute political operatives will look at this group of potential voters with a keen eye—especially if they are interested in the long-term success of their party. Young voters, it would seem, are increasingly up for grabs. Perhaps the necessity of mobilizing young voters in order to win elections will also lead to a more healthy democracy. Local parties can make a difference in youth participation, but they may also be the link to a more vibrant political process overall. We hope they will seize the moment.

## NOTES

1. See www.theaapc.org/content/aboutus/codeofethics.asp.
2. See http://ascweb.usc.edu/asc.php?pageID=351.

# 3

## Tales from the Trenches: Party Organizations that Are Connecting with Young Citizens[1]

*Daniel M. Shea and John C. Green*

As noted in chapter 2, we believe political parties can play a critical role in bringing young Americans into the electoral realm. One of the many functions parties provide our system is voter mobilization. Simply stated, communities with vibrant, active party committees bring more voters, including young voters, to the polls on election day. Yet many state and local party committees are finding mobilization difficult in the twenty-first century, and connecting with young voters has proven an even harder task. Not for want of trying, many party organizations are at a loss as to what activities might make a difference with young voters. Is there anything that might be done?

With financial assistance from the Center for Information and Research on Civic Learning and Engagement (CIRCLE), we have explored how local parties might better connect with young voters. In the fall of 2003, we conducted an unprecedented telephone survey of 803 county party chairs from across the nation. This study produced a wealth of information, which is summarized in chapter 2. The present chapter represents the second step of the project, an effort to detail some of the most successful efforts to mobilize the youth vote. Using the survey data as our starting place, during the summer of 2004, we conducted interviews with a few dozen party leaders who seemed to be doing innovative work to attract young voters. We compiled some of these interviews into "case studies," found in the pages that follow (see Shea and Green 2004). Our goal is to applaud these organizations for their efforts and, more importantly, to make these "best practice" stories available to scholars and other party leaders across the country.

Two important disclaimers are in order: First, the organizations highlighted below are not the only ones doing good work. Nor are they necessarily the finest youth-centered committees. Doubtless there are many other committees rolling up their sleeves and doing innovative work with young voters. Second, our findings lead us to conclude that neither party is "out in front" of the other. Indeed, there are success stories among both Democrats and Republicans.

## NATIONAL PARTY COMMITTEES AND THE YOUTH VOTE

It has often been noted that innovation in party politics heads in both directions, upward and downward. That is, in many instances the national committees seem "first off the mark," and their innovation spreads downward to state and local party operations. A good example is the use of direct mail to raise funds and persuade voters. The Republican National Committee, in particular, began using aggressive direct mail operations in the early 1980s. It proved successful, and the Democratic National Committee headed down this same path, and that particular innovation spread downward through the structure of both parties in the following years. At other times, it seems that innovation has moved upward—from the local party committees to the state and national level. There are many reports, for example, of national committee operatives organizing "meet-and-greets," "coffee socials," and neighborhood gatherings for their presidential candidates in 2004. Of course, local party committees have used these sorts of activities for centuries.

Much the same is happening with youth outreach activities: a number of innovative programs and activities are emerging at different levels of the party structure. The bulk of our analysis explores local party committees, where we believe voter mobilization is most important and where we think young voters will have the greatest opportunity to become involved. This section looks briefly at national party endeavors.

## THE NATIONAL PARTY COMMITTEES

### Democratic National Committee

Our interviews with Democratic National Committee (DNC) staff clearly suggest that youth participation is deemed a key part of the party's long-term strategy. Yet DNC staffers were frank about the difficulties of bringing young voters into the party rubric in recent years. According to Stephanie H. Sanchez, the executive director of the College Democrats of America and adviser to the DNC chairman on youth outreach in 2003:

> Young people are involved in their communities, but not in politics. Yet young folks, especially students, are very important to the DNC because we believe

the Democratic Party is on track with the issues that are important to this age group. We have to worry about Republicans and what they're doing, but we also have to worry about apathy. We're fighting apathy as much as we are fighting Republicans.

Ryan Friedrichs, head of the Young Voter Alliance, a branch organization dedicated to mobilizing Democratic young voters in five target states, echoed these sentiments with a mix of both pragmatic and ideological concerns:

> It's the broken wheel of democracy right now. Young voters can make or break an election. They're the ones who have friends in Iraq and experienced 9/11, and they never had challenges to their generation like that—so they're going to step up now. They are the core of Democratic beliefs, and they are key to the progressive heart of this country.

In terms of youth-centered programs at the DNC, it seems that the College Democrats of America (CDA), the official student outreach arm of the Democratic Party, is front and center. Its goal is to mobilize campuses across the country for Democratic candidates, train new generations of progressive activists, and shape the Democratic Party with voices from America's youth. As for specific voter registration programs, several have been conducted by the CDA, the DNC, and other branch units in the past few years, including Every Vote Counts, Youth to the Booth, New Citizens Voter Registration Project, 2002 Get Out the Vote Initiative, Give a Damn 2002 Pledge Card Drive, and Get on Board, a voter registration program through which thirteen states registered more than seven hundred voters. DNC operatives saw "Campaign Invasion" as a bold, aggressive step. Here, college students go door to door to talk to potential voters in swing states and swing districts. In South Dakota, for example, they knocked on over fourteen thousand doors. By giving students something concrete to do, and by suggesting that their involvement is critical to the prospects of victory, the DNC believes it can pull young people into the party for the long term. The DNC also helped sponsor a College Democrats of America National Convention in Boston during the same week the DNC was nominating John Kerry.

The DNC's "Something New" events are designed to create an exciting atmosphere for eighteen- to thirty-five-year-olds. According to Sanchez, the idea is to "call upon a talented group of forward-thinking young professionals, entertainment industry executives, professional athletes, and urban promoters to create an educated and registered army of young, new voters." Events have been held in cities across the country and include voter registration drives, town hall meetings, and events at local hot spots. In October of 2003, a Something New event held at a nightclub in Washington, D.C., attracted some 4,500 participants and contributors.

Finally, the DNC made a number of moves to use the power of the Web. For example, democrat.meetup.com is a new DNC Web page initiative designed after Howard Dean's success with Meetup.org. Young voters can sign up to be "eCaptains" and build an online team of activists. There are several blogs, including "Kicking Ass" and a College Democrats blog. The idea is to bring young voters into Democratic politics by reaching them through the Internet.

## Republican National Committee

Not surprisingly, the Republican National Committee shares a sense with the Democrats that young voters are critical to their party's long-term efforts. As the 2004 presidential race began to heat up, the chair of the Republican National Committee (RNC), Ed Gillespie, remarked to the media that

> young Americans have an optimistic vision of America's future. They are reject-
> ing the Democrats' political hate speech for President Bush's positive message
> and positive agenda. Their excitement, energy and organization will be a power-
> ful force for President Bush and Republican candidates around the country on
> Election Day.

Voter registration was conducted at college campuses across the country, with special attention paid to battleground states in 2004. The RNC also works with national volunteers to get graduating high school seniors involved in the process. There is an attempt to target students who have just turned eighteen or soon will. The idea is that if people begin to vote at a younger age, voting may become habitual for them, and they will become lifelong voters. The party engages in an absentee ballot program for all voters, which helps to ensure that college students can vote even though they are away at college.

In the summer of 2004, the RNC did not plan to host a lot of events specifically for younger people, but the party is taking advantage of opportunities that arise. Indeed, it regularly sends people to as many events as possible. At concerts, for example, the party will send a group and set up a table. Recently the party sent a group to a Third Day concert. The party chairman went to Rock the Vote to speak to younger voters to help get them involved. The party is also involved in "Stand Up and Holla!," a contest in which eighteen- to twenty-four-year-olds submit an essay to win a trip to the national convention. MTV launched the program to get younger people motivated and participating in the political process.

The RNC also sends "Reggie the Voter Registration Rig" to events around the nation. Reggie is a fifty-six-foot semi truck that serves as a mobile voter registration table. Through Reggie, the party has registered three million new voters. Reggie is outfitted with televisions, Xbox game systems, DirectTV satellite dishes, and other equipment. It appears at sporting events, including NASCAR races and minor-league baseball games, college campuses, state fairs, parades, and other public events. Reggie's stops can be followed online at the GOP website and through the "Track Reggie" link or the "Reggiecam," which broadcasts footage of the truck during voter registration events.

Although not formally affiliated with the national party because of campaign finance restrictions, the College Republicans are helping to activate students as well. They have conducted outreach at universities that do not have a College Republicans chapter, at historically black colleges, and in battleground states. The College Republicans reached out through an active field program. They sent sixty field representatives and four field directors, who serve as managers, to campuses across the country. They started new College Republicans chapters, conducted voter registration drives, and helped with the presidential election and local area elections. They also have a College Republicans Convention that draws many students.

As with the Democrats, the Internet has also been a way for the GOP to reach younger people. On the party website are campaign videos, games, political cartoons, updated news, and so on. The party is trying to get younger people to use the Internet as a means for political participation.

## STATE PARTY ACTIVITIES AND THE YOUTH VOTE

### Delaware Democratic Party

Over the past two and a half years, the Democratic Party in Delaware has been quite successful in increasing the number of youth outreach programs. Such success stems from two principal factors. First, Delaware is a very small state with only three counties, each of which has a liaison that focuses specifically on youth outreach. The state executive committee consists of twenty-three members who are spread throughout the state helping youth groups. Second, the state party is actually run by young voters. Executive Director Nicole Majeski is twenty-five, and her other staff director is twenty-four. Majeski believes that this is beneficial because young people feel that they are on the same level with their state party leaders and are more receptive to their efforts because of this.

Young voters are vital to the Delaware Democratic Party. Majeski noted that they are "of huge importance. . . . They come to our meetings, and we help them in any way that we can. The youth vote can shift an election here, so it's very important to us." Recognition of that importance has led to great changes over the past few years in Delaware. Previously, events were held for young voters, but there was nothing to keep them interested. Erik Schramm, president of the Delaware Young Democrats, noted that people were not attending meetings or events, and it was necessary to find ways to keep people interested and involved. Majeski suggested that having isolated registration drives or events does not result in successful youth outreach. "Everything is tied together. The first step is to register young voters, and then you have to keep them excited through events and organizations, which ideally ends in getting out the vote. It's all a process to keep them engaged," noted Majeski.

Schramm, who became president of the Delaware Young Democrats three years ago, said, "It became obvious that youth outreach had to begin at the county level." The organization is directly connected with the state party committee, and Schramm is an actual voting member of the state executive board. In order to facilitate youth outreach beginning at the county level, liaisons were placed in each of the three counties. The liaisons rotate among counties and are responsible for attending county meetings and finding new and exciting activities within the county. All liaisons then report back to Schramm. Over the past three years, the Delaware Young Democrats have grown from 5 members to 135. Majeski also suggested that the state committee works with local committees on youth outreach projects by providing funding and advertising via word of mouth, and by making sure that events are posted on the state committee's website and in their newsletter.

When it comes to specific outreach programs, the Delaware Democrats have voter registration drives but focus heavily on getting young people involved in the party and the democratic process as a whole. Both Schramm and Majeski note that, over the past few years, the party has added an educational component to its projects. For example, training is held to teach young voters how to affect the way campaigns are run. Schramm also noted that they try to take advantage of other organizations by having joint events. For example, the Delaware state convention is usually held on the same day as the Delaware Stonewall convention.

The Delaware Young Democrats will often participate in service projects not only to get young voters involved but also to give back to the community. Schramm stated, "People are more likely to check out a community service event than go to a meeting when they're just starting out and not sure about everything." One of their recent service projects was with AIDS Delaware. The Delaware Young Democrats assisted with a personal products drive and then on a Saturday morning assisted AIDS Delaware in cleaning and sorting their food pantry, creating over five hundred personal hygiene packs to hand out to their clients. The Delaware Young Democrats also try to hold fun events at which young people can meet their members and elected officials in a more relaxed atmosphere. "You get to sit and mingle rather than drilling them with the ideals of the Democratic Party," said Schramm. Such an event took place over the summer, when the Young Democrats purchased tickets to a Wilmington Blue Rocks game for any young people who might be interested in their organization and a fun afternoon out. Schramm noted that it was "an opportunity to come hang out and see what Delaware Young Democrats is all about in a setting that was extremely informal. We have found that meetings are not always the most conducive environment to check out for your first time."

Plans for future youth outreach projects in Delaware include reaching out to more and more young people. Majeski noted that there are a lot of programs for college-age and young Democrats, but the state party would like to work with colleges more on voter registration. Majeski also hopes to increase outreach in high schools as students are turning eighteen, because there are not as many programs at that level. The state party also hopes to increase the number of liaisons at the county level. Majeski noted that they hope to organize at the county level. That way the party can have people in different areas in the county to assist the state committee and more effectively mobilize voters.

## Indiana Republican Party

The Indiana Republican Party has a strong focus on mobilizing young voters. One party official interviewed suggested, "The party stressed the importance of voting to youth in a nonpartisan way, agreeing that voter participation for youth voters is the most important goal."

Voter registration efforts take place largely on a county-by-county basis, so state assistance to local committees is crucial. The county parties register voters at the county fairs. The party has an absentee ballot program in which they work to "maintain contact with the voter throughout the entire process, from requesting the ballot to submission of the ballot." They also work with College Republican chapters, groups, county parties, and high schools to register new eighteen-year-olds. What is more, they send people into high schools whenever they are invited and otherwise seek opportunities to speak to younger people.

The state party also makes an effort to involve young people in fundraising activities. The party sponsors dinners with special guest speakers, depending on who is available to speak. Attendance is usually between eight hundred and a thousand. Jim Kittle, state party chair, noted, "How many younger people attend the fundraisers generally depends on the cost of the tickets." It is difficult for students to attend more expensive events. The state committee works to include College Republicans by offering them tickets at reduced rates, especially if they assist with setup or teardown at the events. Sponsors (people or groups) also buy tables for the dinner, and younger people are often included in the groups at these tables.

The 2004 gubernatorial candidate increased youth interest by speaking to them about issues that are important to them, especially the economic issues that concern youth. "Speaking to the younger people on issues that are important to them gets them fired up," offered an official of the party. The job losses of the last seven years and the negative export of college graduates (brain drain) have been key issues that have gotten the attention of many younger people.

The state party also has an internship program that helps bring young people into the process. At any given time, four or five college interns are working for the party. Some students are receiving college credit, while others intern for the valuable work experience. Interns have multiple responsibilities. "They do a little bit of everything. They perform administrative and clerical tasks, as well as staffing phone banks. Interns also canvass door-to-door, place signs, and participate in literature drops." The College Republicans and other young volunteers perform valuable work in campaigns throughout the election season. On average, there are 150 to 200 volunteers throughout an election cycle.

## Maryland Republican Party

In 2004, the Republican Party in Maryland set a goal to register twenty-five thousand new voters. The College Republicans are conducting voter registration drives on college campuses. The chair of the party also occasionally goes to colleges to speak. This is the only time party speakers directly target young audiences.

The College Republicans have the opportunity to participate at fundraisers. In exchange for working at the fundraiser, they are allowed to sell T-shirts to make money for their group. The College Republicans and Young Republicans groups also provided volunteers for the Bush-Cheney campaign. State parties were limited in what they could do for the Bush campaign because of campaign finance laws. This made youth participation more valuable, and the party cooperated with the Young Republicans groups to obtain information such as lists of potential volunteers.

The state party does its part to increase the membership of the Young Republicans. When people under thirty-five register to receive e-mails from the state party, their information is forwarded to the Young Republicans, who use these referrals to recruit members through additional mailings or other contacts.

When people call or e-mail the state party to ask about volunteer opportunities, the state committee forwards this information to the Young Republicans as well.

## Michigan Democratic Party

Mark Brewer, executive chair of the Michigan Democratic Party, noted, "We really believe that there is a lot of potential among young people. When you're in the business of politics, you go where the greatest potential for voters is." Furthermore, Chris Cornwell, president of the Michigan Young Democrats, stated, "I believe, number one, that young voters have to be a priority because they feel disenfranchised with the system. They are leaving the state because of this. They aren't participating in anything across the board." In years past, Michigan had programs to reach out to youth, but in 2002, they expanded their outreach, utilizing a program that allowed the Democratic Party to reach out to greater numbers of youth. The program was called the Youth Coordinated Campaign.

Ryan Friedrichs, author of the report "Mobilizing 18–35 Year Old Voters: An Analysis of the Michigan Democratic Party's 2002 Youth Coordinated Campaign," wrote,

A targeted Youth Coordinated Campaign, led by the Party's newly formed Youth Caucus, reached out to 98,000 voters age 18 to 35, through 24,000 phone calls, 14,000 door knocks and 60,000 door hangers. The Youth Coordinated Campaign mobilized young voters in fourteen target sites from October 5 to November 5. The campaign utilized thirteen paid staff, 174 paid volunteers, 266 unpaid volunteers, and had a total cost of $53,317. Target sites were in fourteen of Michigan's fifteen congressional districts as well as fourteen State House and State Senate districts; selected based on an area's number of 18–35 year old voters and its number of competitive 2002 races.

In his study, Friedrichs found that door-to-door conversation was the most effective means of mobilizing youth.

Brewer noted that the 2004 Coordinated Campaign would be similar to the 2002 effort. As of June 2004, the program was still in its planning stages. However, Brewer expected the effort to be on an equal scale, if not larger than in 2002, and for the majority of the footwork to be again carried out by volunteers to keep costs down. The report written by Friedrichs noted not only that personal contact was the most effective method of mobilization, but that it was made even more effective if the contact was started at least four weeks before the election. Brewer commented that the state party was trying to do things earlier and more often in 2004. For example, a statewide canvassing program was started in 2003 so that people would get multiple contacts before election day. When discussing personal contact, Brewer stated, "We do rallies, but door to door is most effective. The study confirms this, so we really stress this. We won't do an event in place of door to door if we can do door to door."

Chris Cornwell noted that the Michigan Young Democrats work very closely with the Michigan Coordinated Campaign. "We have a rep that sits in on the Coordinated Campaign meeting and vice versa. We're kept aware of what both coordinated campaigns are doing." He also said that many of the volunteers working on the coordinated campaign are young, and even high school students are included. What do the volunteers' knocking on doors and personal contact entail? Cornwell stated, "We don't necessarily hand them a bunch of stuff. We do more identifying and letting people know who we are. We try to reach out to 'identified' Democratic voters." Volunteers then asked if people would like any literature from the Kerry campaign and if they would like to get involved. Cornwell also mentioned that volunteers may hand out targeted literature in a targeted race and that all areas are targeted for a different reason. When volunteers come across voters who are registered as Independents, Cornwell said, "We offer our Democratic view. We may ask questions like: Are you satisfied with the way your community and country are going? Did you vote in the last election? Why/Why not? What can we do for you? What do you need? Are you a student? Do you have student loans? and so on." Cornwell noted that personal contact and peer-to-peer outreach are incredibly effective. "We're steaming ahead full speed. Every day that we do youth outreach, we pick up new volunteers. They then reach out to other young people. That's how we build our army of young foot soldiers."

### Mississippi Republican Party

Mississippi has Republican groups at all colleges and junior colleges and at most high schools. These groups pull from a ready-made base in other organizations. Chair Jim Herring said, "Approximately 60 percent of the students are involved in the youth Right to Life groups or the youth National Rifle Association. So they are already active in political causes through these groups." Because these organizations are popular in high schools, it is easy to recruit for the Young Republicans.

Frequent, informal meetings work best for students. The state party makes it a priority to attend football games and other core student activities. The Republicans also hold rallies and pizza parties and often host movie events or television sports events. "These events are a lot of fun for the kids," said party leader Herring. The Republicans also offer classes on effective campaigning. The state party sponsors workshops on conducting phone banks, canvassing door to door, purchasing media advertisements, and writing a campaign plan. These classes are taught by people from the state party, as well as people in the field, such as someone who works in radio sales. These classes not only enable students to be involved in politics now but also teach them valuable skills that they will be able to use into the future.

The Mississippi Republican Party aggressively monitors local party activity. Field representatives in the state are constantly in contact with citizens. The field representatives must hit seven counties per week, so forty-two counties are covered every week in the state. This means that the whole state is covered every two weeks.

The party also participates in an extensive internship program. There are roughly seventeen interns right now. One current intern is only fourteen years old. "She wanted to work on a political cause, and she felt the Republican Party is the place to be. She said it is good to know that you're helping a cause that you support while having fun." Interns and youth volunteers have multiple responsibilities. They update voter files for target mailings. They also enjoy what many characterize as exciting experiences: attending press conferences and meeting party chairs. The party engages youth of all ages. Working parents in the party often leave their children at party headquarters, where the kids participate in data entry or other appropriate projects.

These young workers feel that they are having a good time while working on something meaningful. "It's not just getting it started, but keeping it going that is important," commented Herring. "This can be difficult to do, but it is worth the effort." Working as part of a team on a meaningful project is a motivational draw for many young people. It pays off for the party as well. Young volunteers will work hard long after their initial involvement. Youth involvement is also a strategic part of growing the party organization. Herring sees these activities as critical for the long-term success of the party: "Young people often encourage friends to participate, and their youth means they will be part of the organization for many years. They will be involved and voting for a long time and will be around to keep the party strong." Party leaders feel that young participants are very important. They work hard, and they are significantly involved by the time they go to college. This provides a strong leadership core for vital college organizations that influence campuses and have more organizational responsibilities.

## Wisconsin Democratic Party

Although the Wisconsin Democratic Party works hard to register young voters and stresses the importance of their votes, there seems to be a stronger concentration on getting young people to participate in the activities of the

Democratic Party and to train them for future work in politics. Lynda Honold, chair of the state party, noted, "Young voters are the future of the state. I, as state chair, got involved in the Democratic Party in college. For our party to grow in the future, it's important to engage young people. Many young people want to see a better world, and that's the vision of the Democratic Party, so we want to attract young people so they can help us carry out that vision." Because youth are so important in Wisconsin, the entire staff and board from the state party, a total of about thirty people, are involved with youth outreach projects.

The state party works very closely with the College Democrats organization. The president of the College Democrats, Mike Pfohl, works directly out of the state party office and is very active with all of the chapters throughout the state. Pfohl noted that the College Democrats are very fortunate to receive such extensive support from the state party. He stressed that his organization is "hooked in" with a lot of the state party activities. For example, College Democrats are recruited to go to the state convention, and party officials are invited to do campaign training at the College Democrats convention to get more students to understand the different processes of elections. Using the College Democrats to reach out to other young voters is extremely beneficial because they understand what methods work best. Pfohl stated, "How you package the message is helpful. College students don't just want to come to meetings. Recruit to an event or rally instead of a meeting, and more people are likely to come." Pfohl pointed out that organizations can often have "meetings in disguise" by simply bringing young people together to make signs and talk about new issues on campus.

Honold said that the College Democrats are incredibly useful when it comes to voter registration and voter turnout. She pointed out that because college students change residences quite frequently, the state tries to coordinate a massive get-out-the-vote drive right around election time on college campuses. Also, Wisconsin is a unique state when it comes to registration because people are able to register at the polls. Thus, Honold noted, there is a "Knock and Drag" program through which the College Democrats literally knock on their friends' doors and take them to the polls to register and vote. She also feels that it is important to have young people helping with the party so that they are prepared to be leaders in the future. There are generally about twenty interns per semester that do work for the state party. Many of them subsequently get hired to work on campaigns. "What often happens is an individual mentor will take a young person under their wing, and the young person is the one who gets things up and running. There's not necessarily a program, but it's more centered around individuals," suggested Honold.

One of the most innovative and effective programs in Wisconsin, however, is the Democratic Leadership Institute (DLI), which has become one of the state party's longest-running programs to engage youth. Andy Engel, political director of the state party, noted that DLI "brings in about 150 young people from across the state to learn about Democrats, politics, and campaigns." Lynda Honold said that the program was started ten years ago because there was a vacuum and "there weren't many young people getting involved in the party." DLI started with about seventy-five young people who would meet for a weekend and learn some basics for campaigns and spend one day learning about issues. Over the years, the program has grown; last year, 140 people attended DLI. Many graduates of the program have become county chairs, members of legislatures, and campaign workers. The purpose of the program is to train young people and not only get them engaged but also keep them active. On average, DLI costs about fifteen thousand dollars a year, and the committee that runs the program raises all of the money to pay for the costs. The DLI board is made up of fifteen to twenty people, and there is also a recruitment committee. The state party is also able to reach into the county level through DLI because there is a county party activist program in which members of county organizations are trained in youth outreach and are able to attend workshops such as "How to Attract Young People to Your County Party." Andy Engel stated, "DLI keeps us tapped in all the time. . . . There is a buzz about it that it is a fun event that a lot of major politicians come to. It's the place to start if you ever want to continue in politics."

### Tennessee Republican Party

The Tennessee Republican Party has had success using College Republicans groups to register younger voters. They register voters at the numerous universities and technical colleges in the state. The College Republicans have their own state organization, with elected leadership. The board of the College Republicans initiates chapters at universities lacking a Republican organization, sometimes targeting a specific university or college. Many groups are initiated by internal interest as well. Usually there are a few interested people who approach the state organization to inquire about starting a group. Chair Beth Harwell suggested, "There are self-starters who come to the state party and ask for help and information about how to get started. Once they come to us, we help them." At that point, the organization assists in the establishment of the group, providing information and leadership. College Republicans plan several events at the beginning of each school year for the campus and state levels.

The Republican National Committee has also helped to register young voters in Tennessee using Reggie the Registration Rig, which allows the party to have mobile voter registration setups at concerts and other places. In Tennessee, Reggie was used at "Dancing in the District" and "Memphis in May," among other events. Reggie has enabled the RNC to "register a couple thousand voters through all of the events."

Younger people also participate in the state party through an internship program. Most of them are college students, and approximately half of the interns obtain college credit for their internship. The state party usually has about six to twelve interns throughout the year. They complete a variety of tasks, including research, writing for campaigns and the state party, working with volunteers, and clerical tasks. The interns "do many of the same jobs as the staff members and are given a range of responsibilities. This helps to keep them interested in their internship experience because they are always doing something different."

Occasionally, special opportunities arise for young voters from the state party. In a presidential election year, there are many special ways for younger people to get involved. In 2004, the state sent three interns to the convention—one student from each region of the state. There was an application process to select which students would be sent. It was an open process, and anyone could submit an application. The chair reported, "At the convention, the party has set up special activities for interns and younger people." The Bush-Cheney campaign also had opportunities available. On the website was a special area for students, giving them information and volunteer opportunities. Many students began their volunteer work through the Bush-Cheney campaign.

The party contemplated some other opportunities for younger people, such as a scholarship program to provide money for dedicated young Republican volunteers to assist them with college.

## COUNTY PARTY COMMITTEES AND YOUTH OUTREACH

### Miami-Dade County Democrats, Florida: The Importance of Youth Networks

In Miami-Dade County, Florida, the Democratic Party seems to be completely in sync with the local youth. Ray Zeller, chair of the county party, stated, "They are the future of the party, and they have to step up to the plate now. My focus has been on youth to ensure that the party is there in the future. If you don't prepare for the future, you're dead." Zeller felt that it would be the young voters who would be instrumental in the 2004 presidential election. He has discovered that young voters not only can affect the outcome of an election, but they are also capable of reaching out to other young people to increase participation. Zeller commented that young people are very innovative, and he uses the young people he has working or volunteering for the county Democratic Party to reach out to other young voters.

He noted that political youth organizations in the Miami-Dade area have gone through a metamorphosis, for which Zeller and the local Democratic Party are partly responsible. Zeller mentioned that he started with a group of about twelve students who came together with him and had what he calls a "brain trust." Zeller called the initial group the "Democratic Futures," and they met for several months to talk and put forth both their ideas and their criticisms. Zeller stated, "We didn't focus on money, but on involvement and on them. Many of them were in college, so they knew what they were talking about. I wanted their approach to politics and to the Democratic Party." The Democratic Futures voted on ideas for projects. To increase awareness of current events and politics in general, they decided to send out e-mails about articles they had read online or in the newspaper. Eventually, the Democratic Futures started their own organization and became the Young Democrats. Zeller pointed out that the young voters were very effective when they moved into campaigns and spread the word about political activism because they had grown up working with their local party. Now Zeller works on youth outreach almost exclusively through the Young Democrats and the College Democrats in the county. Zeller stated that even though the initial group of students went their own ways into different organizations, they maintain contact with one another. He continues to work with any youth organization that is interested in getting involved. He noted, "We are 100 percent behind our Young Democrats, and we are targeting youth through them. They are dedicated to promoting the party, and we stay in constant contact with them. They are integral to what I do. It's like one mind, and that's the secret of any county—have a strong YD group. They are college students and young professionals."

The methods of outreach used in Miami-Dade County vary greatly. Registration drives are held weekly at the University of Miami, which is near the Democratic Party's office. Non-college students are targeted through precinct walks and door-to-door work. Zeller also noted that the county party depends heavily on the Internet and e-mail to reach young voters, whether they are students or not. He pointed out that young people are integral in helping with the technological aspects of youth outreach. "They are the ones who are prepared to deal with technology. A lot of people are not able to cope with technological changes. If you have a group of young people and someone is qualified in one area, whether it may be computer technology or graphics, or any other area, you utilize that person. Then they move from there into campaigns and become more of a participant physically in the party."

Some of the recent college graduates who work in the county office help take on various projects. One wrote what Zeller calls "a wonderful youth program that was geared toward high schools," which was implemented that September. The idea is to have youth serving youth. Young voters went into classrooms to speak with about forty students at a time and promote democratic values. This project is based on the hope that high school students will be more interested if they realize that people who are not much older than they actively participate in the political process.

Once young people show an interest in politics, Zeller noted that he tries to encourage participation in an internship or a volunteer position to learn more. This is also accomplished as part of an incentive system developed by the Young Democrats in the county to keep their members involved. Each member has a card with six slots on it, which they have to fill in by participating in projects such as voter registration drives or by knocking on a certain number of doors. Zeller stated that, once they complete the six projects, "they become members of the chairman's circle, which is an organization that has high-end donors, and the students are put in contact with more people and are able to have one-on-one contact with certain candidates."

Zeller also tries to support events that the College Democrats or Young Democrats organize to reach out to other young voters. He stated, "They may want to open a club or plan a fun event, and if they come to us, we'll sponsor them." One recent exciting event was planned for July 29, 2004, at a local club on Miami Beach called "State." The owner of the club is a friend of Zeller's, and they have done various events together. Kerry's acceptance speech was televised at the event, a gathering with music geared toward young people. Zeller noted that, depending on the music and activities, as many as four hundred people can attend events such as these. The local Democratic Party has been quite successful in reaching out to the younger generation, and Zeller plans to continue such outreach by working with and supporting the local youth organizations.

## Cameron County Republicans, Texas: Building an Organization Especially for College Students

Cameron County gets young people involved in politics through meaningful, hands-on experience, according to chair Frank Morris. Recently, the county party worked to establish a new College Republicans chapter, through which students learn how to build a grassroots political organization of their own. The vitality of College Republicans chapters tends to depend on the students who are involved. There have been College Republicans "clubs" at two schools in the past; however, they depended on good local leadership to thrive. Recently, the county party tried to get the College Republicans groups connected with the state organization in order to charter the group and provide it with permanent standing.

Chairman Morris noted that once a chapter has a faculty advisor and a few interested students, "depending on the school's rules, an additional five to fifteen students are generally needed" for official school recognition. At that point, the group is allowed to post literature and signs around campus, as well as advertise for new members in the school newspaper. This process can be difficult, especially if the school is highly Democratic. It is important to find a few people who can and are willing to help the group. Morris has noticed that the key is to get "people in good strategic positions to help get the organization started." Once a core group of dedicated members is established, the chapter can build membership. For example, a dedicated professor and a graduate student were instrumental in establishing a recent chapter on one campus.

Building College Republicans membership was a party priority early in August 2004, before election season began in earnest. "The volunteers already need to be trained before the campaign season really gets going, because it is impossible to build the organization and to train people at the same time. Establishing the group of students as early as possible is important." The party finds many new volunteers by organizing the students. Information is best spread by word of mouth so that interested students know whom they need to contact to become involved. Prior to the election, the party had a ninety-day push to volunteer, especially for younger voters.

Working directly on campaigns and experiencing firsthand the fruits of their contribution to the party and the candidates makes party activity exciting and rewarding. "You have to work with their interests, and that helps to get the students involved," Morris said. The presidential election offers an opportunity to take advantage of already heightened interest and introduce students to other candidates and the party organization. However, it is important to make sure that activities fit the students' schedules.

The county party has an awards banquet every two years with the election cycle. At the banquet, those volunteers who consistently worked hard for the previous twenty-four months are rewarded. Two people are also recognized for their longtime achievement. Sometimes young people may be among those receiving recognition for their hard work. Most recently, a student was recognized for his work with the College Republicans group.

The key to getting younger people motivated and interested is giving them functions and duties from the start. It is important to plan what they will be doing and how they can best be used as volunteers. "You can't organize while they're waiting there to hear what you have to say; you have to lay it out ahead of time," Morris said. "They need to feel their time is being used and that they are working on something worthwhile." It does no good to have student volunteers excited to work but with nothing to do.

## Ventura County Democrats, California: Tapping into the Ideas of Youth

In Ventura County, California, the local Democratic Party places a high value on the opinions and impact of young voters. The party always tries to have younger influences on their committee, and usually one or two members are from one of the local colleges that serve as a bridge to students. The Young Democrats in Ventura County are chartered for the organization, and they participate equally with the other chartered clubs. There are also Young Democrats groups in the county at specific colleges and in major cities. Young people throughout the county have an opportunity to participate in clubs. County Chair Sharon Hillbrant noted, "When school starts again, we are going to have a young man going to different college campuses and starting a drive to recruit young Democrats to see if they want to have a countywide organization if they don't have enough people at their own school."

According to Hillbrant, the county's Democratic Party is constantly doing voter registration drives, and college campuses in the county are heavily targeted for such drives. She stated, "We've already started in voter registration and precinct work. We started right after the primary in March because this year is so important that each of our eight chartered clubs is fully active in registration and precinct work. It's an ongoing effort, and we're out there every weekend." One particularly innovative registration drive was a countywide effort in which registration booths were set up at movie theaters during showings of *Fahrenheit 9/11*. The effort was very successful in that young people had a lot to do with setting it up and running the booths.

The county party also tries to bring in speakers who talk about topics of particular interest to students and younger citizens. Recently, a young man who had returned home from serving in Iraq called the Democratic Party in Ventura County and told them that he wanted to get involved. He started speaking at college campuses once school began that fall and spoke to different clubs about what it was like in Iraq. The chair noted that this speaker piqued the interest of the younger generation because they have concerns about young people going to war, the draft, and other related issues. The county committee announces such events through e-mail and posts on Yahoo! Groups. Hillbrant said that "it serves a major purpose, and all of our young groups at the colleges use that."

Technology is used in a variety of ways in Ventura County. The main purpose, of course, is communication. "E-mail and cell phones are about the only way we handle business now," said Hillbrant. A Kerry fundraiser was held in the county, and one of the younger club members got bands to come together for the event. A lot of young people attended because it appealed to their taste. "We take their names and e-mail addresses so we can follow up with them," Hillbrant said. She also understands the importance of having an interesting website. The county party found a young volunteer who is going to work on "jazzing up" their website. He noted, "The state website is so colorful and alive, I said that we had to get ours to be like that. That's one of the things we have found that you really have to have. You can drum up business with an exciting website, and a lot of young people now are really into that. They are much more computer knowledgeable. We are going to have the website be updated more frequently and more exciting to look at."

Technology is also used in Ventura County to assist with precinct operations or door-to-door work. The precinct county group purchased all of the county data and maps, using them to produce computerized data for each of the areas. The county clubs then use that data to go door to door, and it is generally the younger members who do this work. From Hillbrant's perspective, "This is a very visual age that we live in; it's made communication a whole different topic nowadays. We're trying to rethink having headquarters, because technology is so much better now. You can get statistics while you're out in the field, and you don't have to go back to headquarters." Use of technology in this way seems to open the doors for younger people who want to get involved, and greater opportunities are also created for reaching out to voters who may still need to be brought into the process.

### Cleveland County Republicans, Oklahoma: Targeting Young People Where They Like to Be—Outside the Classroom

Cleveland County has built a large, active membership of young Republicans. Local party chair Kathy McBlair reported, "Cleveland County has had success through fun, exciting activities and by using young people to help recruit others their age." Indeed, their peer-to-peer outreach effort is one of the group's great successes.

The county GOP goes to local high schools and colleges two or three times a year. The College Republicans usually work in conjunction with the county party when they go to high schools. This gives the college students a feeling of doing something important while suggesting to youngsters that it's "cool" to be partisan. They also run the tables and hand out T-shirts at "Howdy Week" when they start back to school, as well as setting up a tent where they offer food and beverages.

The local party also reaches out to younger voters by going to football and basketball games and other youth activities to register students and to bolster their interest in voting and politics. The party targets a number of youth-centered social activities rather than visiting government classes.

The party hosts a "Straw Poll—Pizza and Politics" event with voter registration opportunities and also makes an effort to reach out through a Fourth of July booth, where candidates come to meet and speak with citizens. "We make a special effort to get young people to work at the table and shake hands with people at the fair," said McBlair. The party also enters multiple community parades, including the Red Ribbon Week parade. McBlair noted, "The party likes to get involved in all of the local parades that it can. We like to be as visible as possible." Here, too, the local party makes good use of its youth volunteers, as they are called upon to staff floats and pass out literature.

## Story County Democrats, Iowa: Using Organizational Backing and Special Events to Involve Students

As the home of Iowa State University (ISU), Story County is heavily populated by students. Jan Bauer, chair of the Democratic Party in Story County, stated that young voters are extremely important because "they provide the enthusiasm and the energy, and it is the young people that are carrying out the day-to-day operations." In Iowa, canvass teams from the Iowa Democratic Party go door to door, hitting every door throughout the state. Bauer noted that this is where the young people are needed. "In each county office, there is a paid staffer on the coordinated campaign, and they are typically college students or just out of college," she said.

There is also a great deal of youth outreach that is not directly connected to the canvassing teams of the state party. Similar to other chairs that have universities in their county, Bauer tries to work closely with local college organizations. Once students return to school in the fall, the county party coordinates with the ISU Democrats to do registration. "Students aren't always able to man the booths, so we do our best to coordinate the effort," stated Bauer. Her organization will often send people to help with the effort. The county party also has a presence at university gatherings such as Welcome Fest, an event held primarily for freshmen, and Club Fest, which is geared more toward getting people to join the ISU Democrats. Bauer noted, "The ISU Democrats will have events with bands and such, and, although they drive their own events, we provide support for them." Students are also able to get internships with the local Democratic Party, whether they are in high school or college. The students can get credit at their schools for working in the office, answering phones, doing mailings, helping with canvassing and phone banks, and other such activities.

The county party has also tried to increase students' ability to actually cast their votes in Story County. Since Iowa allows early voting through the use of absentee ballots, Bauer noted that they petitioned for satellite voting on campuses. If enough signatures are received, a location has to be made available. Bauer stated, "We requested satellite voting in all of the dorms, which allows them to vote early." Ideally, Bauer would like to have the system organized so that people can register and vote on the same day; however, no one can vote before the close of registration. "So now we have to first get them registered and then get them to the satellite location." Publicizing exactly when and where the students can vote does this.

The Democratic Party in Story County has also found success in events that they have held such as fundraisers with costume themes. A year ago, at an event with a big-band swing theme, people could come in costume, register, and get involved. Young people especially enjoyed attending and participating in the event.

The Democratic Party had similar results when they invited young people to attend and assist with a Mardi Gras soup supper. Plans were being made for something similar in 2004, said Bauer. "We're planning to hold a large fundraising event with a '40s theme."

Another event that Bauer was hoping to bring to the county was house parties. "The Kerry campaign has been working hard on house parties, and we'd like to do some youth-driven ones," she said. Bauer describes a house party as an event at which "someone would open up their home, invite their friends, watch a video, listen to a staff member talk about the campaign, encourage them to get involved, and talk about different opportunities to participate." It seems that this atmosphere would be especially beneficial for young participants because it would be more relaxed and less intimidating if someone is joining the meeting or the group for the first time. The Democratic Party of Story County, Iowa, seems to have found a way to reach out to young citizens of various backgrounds, to get them involved, keep them interested, and give them various ways to cast their vote.

### Garland County Republicans, Arkansas: Active Youth Membership

In Garland County, young volunteers are central to local party activities. To attract young folks to their booth at the Garland County Fair, "we often have prize drawings and give away some nice prizes—such as a television," reported Chairman Larry Bailey. "The larger-ticket items get a lot of people to stop by the booth." Young Republicans and the women's Republican group staff the booth, providing voter registration, information about candidates, and literature on Republican activities. To meet voters, candidates will often work in the booth as well. Volunteers and candidates also conduct voter registration efforts at local churches.

The committee has been able to create groups in three area high schools. "The goal is to build the Young Republicans and to get them involved in the central committee so that they are part of the organization," suggested Bailey. Building a student organization requires a core group full of people who are dedicated and willing to roll up their sleeves and make a difference. Finding these people and helping them succeed has been at the center of the county committee's outreach efforts. Currently, three of seven of the high schools have a Young Republicans group, with approximately fifty to sixty members in each. The county coordinates directly with the students a couple of times in nonelection years. The students are more active in the campaigns, but efforts are made to keep them involved in off-election periods. Experience shows that if students remain active during off years, they are more likely to get involved when the action heats up.

Students are also visible at party events via a "sponsorship program." The party has a fish fry at which candidates and party members come together. Students are "sponsored" so that they can come and meet the candidates and get involved. The idea is that students, who often do not have a lot of extra money, can still get involved in party activities through the donations of older members. The party has one major fundraiser—the Lincoln Day Dinner, which usually raises between twelve thousand and thirteen thousand dollars. About three hundred people attend. Along with the "sponsored students," others serve as pages for the corporate table or help set up the event. In exchange, they are invited to attend the dinner. The party understands the importance of bringing young people into a range of activities, including black-tie dinners.

### Orange County Democrats, North Carolina: Making Use of Technology and the Internet

Barry Katz, chair of the Democratic Party in Orange County, North Carolina, feels that young voters are immensely important not only because they can affect the outcome of an election, but also because "they participate in precinct leadership and they also do a very good job of organizing young voters." Katz has discovered the benefits of working with youth and tries to meet the needs of different youth organizations as often as possible. He noted, "We completely fund everything the Young Democrats do. They've never made a request for us that we have rejected." There are two Young Democrats organizations in the county. One is associated with the University of North Carolina at Chapel Hill, and the other is a countywide organization. Katz feels that it is important to have both in order to capture young voters that are not associated with the university.

Projects such as voter registration drives are organized almost completely by such organizations. Katz noted that there is a massive registration drive at the university in the fall at which hundreds of voters are registered. He said, "Fifty-two weeks a year, there is someone out doing some sort of registration." North Carolina has a motor voter rule. This rule often leads to a high number of registered voters, but not necessarily a comparatively high number of people who actually vote. A motor voter rule means that people are registered to vote when they go to the DMV to get a driver's license. Their voting address is then the same as that on their driver's license. What is more interesting about the rule is that if people change their address on their driver's license, their voting address changes. However, the person's voting address can be changed without changing their permanent address. For this reason, efforts are made during registration drives to change students' voting addresses so they can vote near the university. This is done because many people feel that students are more likely to vote near their school than they are to send in an absentee ballot.

In Orange County, other unique methods are being used to reach out to young voters. The Democratic Party in the county is trying to get current contact information for all registered voters, and in the process they try to register more young voters. Katz noted,

> We've got teams in each of the precincts that will be phoning all the households, and one of the questions that we have is if any youth in the house will turn eighteen before November 2. We're polling all of the households in the county to find out if we can register them that way. . . . When we identify someone who is young and not registered, we contact the family and give them a voter registration form. We check the rolls at the board of elections regularly to find out if they have registered. If they haven't, we call them back and we are persistent. We make an effort to identify unregistered youth and then to follow it up.

He stated that, in order to run an effective get-out-the-vote drive, someone has to be working on the contact list to improve it well in advance of the actual drive.

Katz has also discovered that such efforts require the knowledge and use of technology. He noted that there is a strong supply of expertise with software development in the county. "We have an incredible database that allows us to do fabulous things with our data." The importance of e-mail and a strong website is also taken into consideration in Orange County. E-mail is used to reach young voters, but not in a way that will turn them off. E-mail addresses are taken on a confidential basis by the party and are not shared with any other party organization or candidate. Katz also noted that the party limits the number of contacts that are made via e-mail. Katz is also hoping to improve the county party organization's website because "young people tend to look at the website more frequently than other groups of voters." Eventually, there will be various essays on the website by different people throughout the county expressing their political ideas.

Katz has also found that many young people do not know what precinct they live in and where they have to vote. He stated, "We have a precinct finder that will eventually be online. You type in the name of your street, and it will tell you what precinct you are in and give you directions on how to get to the polls where you have to vote. People can call for now, but eventually it will be on the website so they can do it themselves." The county party also tries to make it easier for young people to get to the polls on voting day by having vans that go to the polls all day long. Katz noted, "We rent the vans, the largest we can find, and for days we put up signs that tell where the vans will pick people up, either near a gym or the dorms." Furthermore, not all students on campus vote at the same location, so the party makes sure that a laptop with the precinct-finder program is available so that students will be taken to the correct polling stations.

## Hillsborough County Republicans, Florida: County-Level Internships Provide Valuable Election Experience

Voter registration, absentee follow-up, and candidate rallies are all used by the Hillsborough County GOP to reach out to young voters. Chairwoman Margie Kincaid noted that they have had some success with high school registration, but the party also reaches out through government offices, banks, and other high-traffic places. The party also has an aggressive absentee ballot program in which volunteers contact people who have requested absentee ballots to make sure that they followed through by sending them in.

Hillsborough County has College Republicans and Young Republicans clubs that help organize both students and the community at large. This year, the Young Republicans club organized precinct walks once per month, not only to reach out to voters across the county but also to give club members something concrete to do. As noted in other county organizations, strong leadership is crucial to the success of these groups.

Younger citizens are introduced to the party through a number of exciting party-sponsored day trips. An internship program provides a direct opportunity for youth involvement. Indeed, area high schools send ten to fifteen students to intern during each election cycle. According to local party leadership, these interns are some of the best workers in the organization. A good bit of effort is also spent on connecting with local college professors and lining up student volunteers and interns.

These interns and other young volunteers are integrated into the party's activities, undertaking a range of projects, which include fundraisers, rallies, literature drops, telephone banks, and much more. The key to a successful internship program, local leaders note, is that it keeps students busy and calls upon them to undertake significant tasks. Conversely, giving interns grunt work often frustrates them and reduces their usefulness to the organization. Their efforts must be meaningful—at least occasionally.

In 2004, the county committee's activity focused primarily on the Bush-Cheney reelection campaign. Here young activists were involved in the full range of campaign work, including conference calls, e-mail alerts, and phone banks to contact likely voters.

## Otero County Republicans, New Mexico: Active Involvement

Otero County is a good example of motivating young people to become politically involved because every party activity offers an opportunity for youth participation. As Chair Manuel Gonzales reported, "Here young people participate in the usual county party activities as well as the programs and activities that are specifically designed to target youth."

Voter registration efforts occur in locations frequented by young people. The county party maintains a table at the county fair offering candidate and party information as well as registering voters. "Around eighteen thousand people attend the county fair, and we were able to register approximately eight hundred people," said Gonzales. The party is also a visible participant in the Fourth of July parade and the fair parade, and students are encouraged to participate in the literature drops and sign crews for local campaigns. The party also conducts voter registration drives at local high schools, as well as at the branch of New Mexico State in Otero County. Other voter registration efforts occur at local shopping centers and malls.

Otero County Republicans (OCR) provide a unique scholarship opportunity to local high school students. The "Tigers, Knowledge, Activities," or TKA, scholarship program is cosponsored by the Republicans, a local newspaper, and a youth radio station. Students submit an application to be considered for the scholarship. Each week, one student is selected from approximately twenty-five to thirty students. Weekly recognition is given via a classroom presentation, as well as by a congratulatory ad broadcast throughout the day on the radio. The student is awarded a gift certificate for lunch, a T-shirt, and a CD copy of the radio ad. At the end of the year, one student is chosen from among the weekly TKA winners to receive a five-hundred-dollar scholarship. The student is recognized at the school's annual awards banquet.

Every time there is a political event, Otero Republicans try to get students involved. For example, when President Bush came to the area, members of the high school ROTC, football and basketball teams, cheerleaders, and marching band were all part of the welcome program.

Otero County is a conservative area in which Republicans hold nearly every elected partisan office. The OCR website, www.oterorepublicans.com, often gets 2,500 hits a month. The website contains information pertaining to upcoming party events and is updated for each month's events, along with the county party's newsletter, candidate information, and a printable donation form. There is an Air Force base within the county, and many of the young airmen are computer literate and get involved with the party through the website. The website also has links to the New Mexico government and the Republican National Committee. Otero Republicans also use an e-mail alert system, and the party is currently working to build e-mail lists.

For Otero County, the key is to be steady and always involved. "Positive exposure and a commitment to engage young people on their turf encourages participation in local party activities. There is nothing we do in Otero County that doesn't have an element of youth," noted Gonzales. The party features the youth whenever possible and keeps them involved in every event at some level. They believe it is important to include youth in all of the party's events.

### Benton County Democrats, Washington: Reaching Out to Kids with Different Backgrounds

When speaking of the importance of young voters, Mimi Latta, chair of the Democratic Party in Benton County, Washington, noted, "You stagnate without younger voters; you don't understand issues from their perspective if you don't have them in your organization. They are the ones who will take over after us, and they'll have to reinvent the wheels if they aren't brought in now, so that's up to us to do." There has been a great deal of youth outreach in Benton County, whether it be to high school students, college students, or nonstudents.

The Democratic Party in Benton County has been particularly successful at reaching out to young citizens of different backgrounds through voter registration drives and registration booths. On the Fourth of July, the party set up a booth in the park to register people. Latta noted that posters advertised the booth "so young people would realize that we are interested in their issues too. We also try to talk with parents and grandparents so that they make young people realize that voting is a priority. We were able to register people who will be turning eighteen between now and November. A lot of parents were bringing their children over to register." During the summer, registration booths are set up more generally at fairs, and the booths are staffed by voters young and old. During the school year, the party also sets up registration booths at junior and four-year colleges in the area, with booths set up at least once a week throughout the fall.

The Democrats in Benton County also make it a point to reach out to high school students. The organization does not have specific internships with the party, but they do pair students up with candidates. Latta noted that the students usually come to the party and show interest, and they are then introduced to different candidates to find a good fit. Latta stated, "If people want to increase their participation with youth, they need to keep in touch with and be friendly with local and public schools. They appreciate the fact that we're checking in. I try to keep it low key, whether it's going to be Democratic or nonpartisan; I let the principals know that. It's an ongoing relationship." The Democratic Party also has a variety of strategies to make sure that high school students will register to vote. Some of the party members will go to the schools to speak to classes and hand out registration forms. They will also give registration forms to civics teachers to keep in their classrooms. The most interesting way that registration forms are distributed, however, is by handing them out with the students' high school diplomas so that they have them in their graduation packets.

The local party organization also tries to have events such as forums and meet-ups to attract younger voters. In July, at a forum at a local coffeehouse, issues such as separation of church and state were discussed by three Democrats who were running in the fourth congressional district. Events such as the forum are announced in the local papers and in e-mails as well. Latta stated, "We just make sure that we get the word out. The kids at this point look for it because they know that we do it practically on a weekly basis." The party also had Kerry meet-ups, which were basically gatherings of John Kerry supporters that happened on a regular basis. Latta noted, "We kept all of the info from our caucuses, and we worked really hard to get young people out for the caucuses. We retained the names and contact info to make them aware of the events that they should attend."

The party operated their booth at a local fair, and young people helped significantly. The party participates in parades throughout the summer in various towns within the county, and Latta noted, "We make sure that we reach out to the youth, especially for that, because it's fun. They walk the route and help with construction of entries." Latta and the Democratic Party in Benton County try to reach young voters of different ages through various methods because, as Latta stressed, "It's trying to figure out how to reach out, not just pizza at a meeting, but to get them interested in issues."

## LESSONS LEARNED

Our review of the best practices by political parties in mobilizing young voters reveals a wide variety of approaches and techniques. No two areas are exactly the same, and many different programs have been successful. However, we did learn ten lessons from the most successful party organizations we studied.

1. *Leadership is extremely important.* Many of the new branches of College Republicans and College Democrats were started by a few interested people, and then the club grows from there. A few people in the right place at the right time are needed to get an organization off the ground. Strong leadership is needed to keep the group going so that it does not fade.

2. *Target youth on their turf.* Younger people are often involved in a lot of activities. Come to them at these activities with a positive message and show an interest in what they do. This could mean going to sporting events or creating college scholarship opportunities or internship programs.

3. *Get young people involved at every opportunity.* It is important to have events or programs that target younger people, but it is also important to ensure that younger people are included in all party events and functions. Many students do not attend fundraisers because they cannot afford them. Get other party members to buy extra tickets to fundraisers so that students can attend, or allow students to attend free for helping with setup.

4. *Give young volunteers meaningful work.* Once young people are involved, give them work that they will feel is important so they will want to come back. Have their tasks planned out in advance. If they are going to put up signs, for example, have the signs and the address lists ready to go when they arrive so that they can get to the hands-on part immediately. This is often the most fun part for them because they can see the results of their efforts and how they are helping the party. Young people are often busy with other activities, and if they feel they are wasting a lot of time "just sitting around," they are less likely to participate.

5. *Make it fun whenever possible.* Even if the work is hard work, find ways to reward the students if possible. This could mean a pizza party at the end of a project, a free ticket to a party event, or a special meeting with a party representative.

6. *Make use of different outreach technologies.* Young Americans reach out to friends and family in many ways, including e-mail, cell phones, and instant message technology. Conversely, their dependency upon "snail mail" (that is, through the U.S. Postal Service) is dramatically less significant than for other generations. Of course, innovative Web pages and blogs have proven helpful in reaching out to young voters. Party operatives should be aware of this important difference and consider reaching out to youngsters in unique, high-tech ways.

7. *Peer-to-peer programs are effective.* Time and again, party leaders have said that some of their best outreach programs are when young

people look to connect with other young people. Voter registration and mobilization programs conceived and run by younger people for younger people have had much success. Simply put, youngsters listen to each other.

8. *Reward achievement.* Believe it or not, young Americans look up to older folks. And when their elders recognize their accomplishments, they feel better about their efforts and are even more eager to make a difference. Special mention, awards, or certificates at a party banquet, for example, go a long way toward reinforcing young people's political involvement.

9. *Merge with like-minded youth groups.* A number of organizations on both sides of the ideological fence have organized youth operations. Party operatives should look to merge their efforts with the youth groups of these partner organizations.

10. *Look to combine service with partisanship.* One of the surprising findings of this study is how much young people volunteer in their communities. Again, this is the activist generation. Instead of trying to compete with this natural desire to make a difference, astute party leaders might look to combine service activities with partisan events. Indeed, there may be many ways that service work can be merged with political efforts. Why not, for example, plan an event at which youth are called upon to clean up a neighborhood park, followed by a party picnic?

## NOTES

1. We would like to acknowledge the help of Sara Anderson (Allegheny College) and Anne Cizmar (University of Akron) for their hard work and diligence in helping to compile the information to follow.

# 4

# Building Youth Party Identification and Revitalizing Democracy

*J. Cherie Strachan*

As the title of this volume suggests, educators and policy makers alike have become increasingly concerned over our youngest citizens' declining levels of political participation, party identification, and trust in government institutions (Carnegie Corporation of New York and CIRCLE 2003; Galston 2003). Panel studies of college freshmen indicate that young people's participation in a wide array of political indicators, including thinking that keeping up with politics is important, discussing politics with friends, and acquiring political knowledge, have all declined by about half since the 1960s (Sax et al. 2003). Far more young people voted in 2004 than in the past, but younger citizens' appearance at the polls still lagged behind prior generations of young Americans, as well as their current elders (CIRCLE 2005). Moreover, a single presidential election—characterized by unusually high levels of competition and aggressive get-out-the-vote efforts—is not likely to ameliorate this long-term trend in youth political participation.

Political scientists have blamed a number of sources for declines in youth participation, including shifts in the demographic characteristics of the electorate, a less stable political environment, and of course the onslaught of increasingly cynical political media coverage. Yet Shea (1999b) reminds us of one notable change receiving far less attention: the behavior of the party elite. While the party elite, more specifically the chairs of the national, state, and local party committees, used to see their primary function as serving coalitions of voters in the electorate, they now consider their foremost clientele to be the candidates who win party nominations via the primary process. Instead of cultivating voter loyalties and mobilizing these supporters on election day as they once did, the party elite now "strive to please candidates" (Shea 1999b,

45). The results are baseless parties supported by the elite party officials and the candidates who benefit from their campaign services, but not by average citizens. Such claims regarding the effect of party leaders' choices correspond to long-standing arguments that democracy must be maintained via elite norms of appropriate political behavior and the resulting elite decisions (Dye and Zeigler 1996). Elite political actors' behavior is particularly important because their choices establish the "rules of the political game" that affect the rest of us. Arguably, the political elite in both of America's two major parties have been far more concerned with promoting their own ideological agendas over the past several decades than they have been with promoting participatory democracy. Unfortunately, the unhealthy impact of such choices has taken a toll on political participation.

## DISCOURAGING NEW PARTISANS IN THE ELECTORATE

The source of changes in the behavior of the party elite stems from the Progressive movement of the early twentieth century and the internal party reforms that encouraged the use of primary elections and caucuses. The adoption of these reforms, which were intended to enhance rank-and-file voters' ability to influence the selection of party candidates, eventually denied party officials control of the nominating process (Wattenberg 1991). While party leaders were accused of abusing their authority to influence the nomination of candidates in the past, however, they were also concerned with aggregating the concerns of average Americans and nominating a candidate who could appeal to mainstream voters in general elections. Initially, scholars and pundits were concerned that ideologically motivated activists, who participate in nomination politics because of their strong beliefs, would use the open process to support ideologically extreme candidates (Kirkpatrick 1976; Lengle 1981; Soule and Clarke 1970; Wilson 1962).

Further research suggests that this outcome has not occurred. People who vote in party primaries and participate in party caucuses are ideologically extreme in comparison to the general public. Republicans who participate in these types of activities are more conservative than the average American, while Democrats are more liberal. Yet activists from both parties are also aware that mainstream American voters are moderate. Hence, in order to enhance their parties' chances of winning the general election, activists consider candidates' electability in addition to candidates' ideological positions when deciding whom to support (Abramowitz and Stone 1984; Stone, Rapoport, and Atkeson 1995).

Despite activists' willingness to modify their selections, however, opening up the parties' nominating processes has not mobilized most rank-and-file voters to participate in the nominating process. Nor has it encouraged more Americans to participate in shaping the two major parties' primary political agendas. Yet groups of people who have not been mobilized to engage in these types of activities are less apt to develop party identification, or a strong psychological commitment, to either party. Given the two major parties' prominent role in framing electoral politics in the United States, such people also have less incentive than activists to participate in politics. Indeed, survey research demonstrates that nonpartisans, who refuse to identify themselves as either Republicans or Democrats, are the very same people who often choose not to vote at all (Miller 2002).

Removing responsibility for candidate nominations from party organizations has resulted in a candidate-centered process. In order to win, candidates now rely on their own campaign organizations to mobilize the types of voters who should be their strongest supporters. Whereas ideological candidates may have been suppressed by pragmatic party leaders in the past, they can achieve visibility in the current nominating process as long as they can raise enough money and attract enough support to stay in the race. Even though ideological candidates are often passed over, even by their own supporters, for more mainstream politicians, their candidacies have a long-term impact on the parties, for the nomination activists that such candidates mobilize do not simply fade into the background after their preferred candidate loses. They not only become strong supporters of the eventual party nominee in the general election (Stone, Atkeson, and Rapoport 1992), but they also continue to participate in party politics in the future (Pastor, Stone, and Rapoport 1996). For example, the conservative activists that Ronald Reagan brought to the Republican Party, as well as the members of the religious right who were mobilized to support Pat Robertson, have continued to have a long-standing and substantial impact on the agenda of the Republican Party. Hence the nominating process has become "an important arena in which the party defines and redefines itself" (Stone and Rapoport 1998, 101). Groups of voters who are overlooked in the nomination process play little role in defining what the parties eventually come to stand for. Not surprisingly, given their uncertain voting habits, young people are one such demographic group that candidates often overlook and fail to mobilize.

The result of America's candidate-centered nomination process is that, despite nomination activists' willingness to support moderate candidates, the parties have become more ideologically distinct across the past several decades (Abramowitz and Saunders 1998). Moderate elected officials on both sides of the aisle have complained that their parties have been overtaken, a claim made most publicly by the former New Jersey governor Christine Todd Whitman (2005). John McCain has been identified as the most popular Republican with those who plan to vote in the upcoming 2008 presidential election, but conventional wisdom predicts that he has little chance of surviving the primary process—unless a plethora of right-wing candidates split the conservative vote. As the research described above indicates, McCain probably has a stronger chance of winning the nomination than conventional wisdom predicts. Yet he would govern knowing that he is beholden to the social conservatives and the religious right, who now make up a substantial portion of the Republican base. Meanwhile, Democratic hopefuls such as Hillary Clinton, who have well-established liberal credentials, are making a strong effort to be painted as moderates capable of attracting widespread support in the general election (Glover 2005).

Some might praise this shift to ideological coherence within the parties as a sign of a coming realignment where the parties will reorganize themselves around a new issue of importance to the voting public (Burnham 1970). Others might see the shift as an indication that the parties are moving closer to the Responsible Party model advocated by some party scholars since the 1950s (Committee on Political Parties 1950). Such responsible parties, which promote distinct ideologically based choices, are praised because they would provide clearer options for the electorate. Unfortunately, the ideologically coherent platforms offered by Republicans and Democrats do not appear to be the choices that the American people want. Research suggests that average voters are far more moderate, pragmatic, and willing to compromise than the leaders and activists within their parties (Fiorina, Abrams, and Pope 2005), and some argue that the ideological extremism at the elite and activist level has even increased public disdain for politics (Dionne 1991).

## THE NEED FOR CULTIVATING REMARKABLE CITIZENS

In many senses, the primary processes that were intended to enhance democracy also increased the political responsibilities heaped upon the shoulders of average citizens. Citizens can no longer rely on the party organizations to promote their concerns in the nominating process but must assume this burden for themselves. One way the party organizations could have responded to the shift to primary elections would have been to continue to aggregate the interests of average voters. Doing so under the primary nominating system, however, requires coaxing a wide swathe of average citizens—not just those mobilized by a particular candidate—into the process and serving as an educative force for participatory democracy.

Enhancing the parties' educative function to include helping citizens develop their political goals is especially important under the current nominating process, for as Schneck (1995, 85) notes, "Age-old political thinking has it that participatory forms of government required 'remarkable' citizens." As far back as Aristotle, political theorists have argued that such citizens, who are "willing to trade private interests for the common good," must be cultivated in order for political systems based on participatory democracy to succeed (Schenck 1995, 86). As primary elections offered more opportunities for citizen participation, the need to educate these citizens for greater responsibility also increased. In modern America, the party organizations, with a vested interest in enhancing strong partisanship in the electorate, are one of the few—if not the only—organizations in society with a self-interested motive for performing such tasks.

Moreover, the parties' fulfillment of such civic education functions would be especially beneficial for current generations of young citizens, who have come of age politically during an era of declining associational life. In other words, they have come of age at a time when many scholars argue that membership in voluntary community organizations has been dropping. Political observers have also long argued that democratic control of government is only possible when citizens coordinate their political efforts within these intermediary, community organizations that exist outside of government's control (Putnam 2000a; Tocqueville 1835). Cooperating within such organizations not only teaches citizens effective collective-action skills, but it also encourages deliberation that can transform their self-interested agendas. In short, such organizations serve as the training ground for the cultivation of remarkable citizens. Yet evidence suggests that the social structures that used to integrate Americans into communities—organizations such as the PTA, the Elks, the Kiwanis, and a wide array of other institutions—were declining just as today's young people were receiving their political socialization (Putnam 2000a; Skocpol and Fiorina 1999).

Ironically, even as political reforms placed more power in the hands of the people, the community organizations that help people successfully wield political influence were in the process of disintegrating. In the past, people developed their interests within such voluntary organizations before bringing their concerns to the political process. The parties then responded to these agendas, relying on existing group-based preferences in society to build stable coalitions of voters. If young people have in fact had limited exposure to such organizations, the parties have an even more important role to play in promoting political decision making and participatory skills than at any time in our nation's recent past.

Yet instead of altering their means of voter aggregation and enhancing their efforts to cultivate informed and active citizens, the party organizations responded to changes in the nominating process by wholeheartedly supporting the nominees who emerge from the primary elections. They transformed themselves into service parties, with the infrastructure and financial resources necessary to provide increasingly sophisticated campaign services to candidates (Shea 1999b). In short, the parties enhanced their ability to perform marketing techniques in order to "sell" candidates to moderate voters in the general election. In order to persuade people to vote for these candidates, the parties and candidates quickly learned to emphasize less controversial valence issues—or widely acceptable "motherhood and apple pie issues"—rather than specific policy agendas. According to Lakoff (1996, 2004), for example, conservative Republicans began to study how to persuade voters with alternative messages immediately after Barry Goldwater's crushing defeat in the 1964 presidential election. Republicans discovered that associating candidates with the widely held ideal of the traditional family—with an authoritarian father figure focused on discipline and punishment—could garner support from voters even when they disagreed with conservative policy agendas. Note, this claim does not mean that voters prefer ideologically extreme liberal policy agendas, just that the Democratic Party elite have been less successful in marketing their candidates to the public (Lakoff 1996, 2004).

The new communication technologies have made the task of persuading lukewarm voters with these types of valence issues rather than substantive arguments even easier. Product advertising across the past five decades, for example, has increasingly associated products with an emotional tone or mood rather than touting the specific benefits of product features (Clark 1988). Despite offering more substantive information than news stories, candidate advertising has matured in similar ways, with shorter spots that make more emotional pitches to the voters (Kern 1989). Television's appeal to the visual senses enhances the ability to evoke such uncritical reactions from the audience (Jamieson 1988), while advances in audience research enable campaigns to identify voters' personal "hot button" issues and to evoke knee-jerk responses from them during a campaign (Selnow 1993).

These types of persuasive tactics, carefully honed by America's service parties since the 1970s, can be quite effective in the short term. Yet audiences, in this case the American voters, who receive such messages do not internalize the reasons for their short-term decisions. As a result, their choices at one point in time do not reflect the development of long-term attitudes toward the parties, nor do they predict future behavior (Petty and Cacioppo 1986).

Given the historical circumstances framing their socialization and the failure of the parties to play a more substantive role in citizenship education, the alienation of America's youth should come as no surprise. Young people are entering the electorate with lower rates of partisan identification than that of the preceding generations for good reason (Miller 2002). By failing to mobilize young people to participate in the nominating stage where the parties' agendas are developed, and by relying on uncontroversial valence issues or emotional cues to persuade them to participate for short-term ends, the parties have failed to cultivate a broad base of support from new members of the voting public. Moreover, continued reliance on such approaches by the parties is likely to result in the two major parties' competing for votes in an ever-shrinking and increasingly volatile electorate.

## HELPING YOUNG CITIZENS TO DEVELOP PARTY-CENTERED ATTITUDES

Research on decision-making processes not only underscores the impact of the parties' current choices, but it also provides insight into activities that should help our youngest citizens develop stronger partisan commitments. Scholars who study the connection between attitudes and behavior argue that decision making occurs along a continuum that ranges from active to passive cognitive processing (Petty and Cacioppo 1986). This work begins with the assumption that people want to have the "correct" attitudes, and they want their behavior to correspond to those attitudes. But the way people develop and adjust their attitudes, as well as how they decide to take specific actions, will vary according to the individual and to the circumstances framing a particular decision.

When people rely on passive cognitive processing, for example, they elaborate very little on the decision they are about to make. Rather than engaging in a thoughtful process, they rely on cues or heuristics—such as evoked emotions and prior assumptions—to guide their decisions. Passive processing is an efficient way to reach a decision quickly, but the decision does not reflect the development of a deeply held attitude, nor does it necessarily predict future behavior under similar circumstances (Petty and Cacioppo 1986). Clearly, the types of tactics used in political campaigns have encouraged voters to rely on passive processing and heuristics to make voting decisions.

Alternatively, people relying on active cognitive processing engage in a great deal of elaboration. They are willing to scrutinize information, and they expect logically presented, well-developed arguments. While engaging in active processing, people will typically generate their own arguments, seek out additional information, ask themselves probing questions, and carefully critique any information provided to them. Active processing is a less efficient means

of persuading an audience in the short term, but those who use active processing to reach a decision tend to resist counterarguments, remain persuaded for
months afterward, and easily recall the attitudes that they developed throughout the evaluative process. Moreover, these attitudes are predictive of future
behavior (Petty and Cacioppo 1986).

Hence, in order to develop long-term attitudes toward the political parties,
young people must first engage in active processing of political information.
Some factors that influence whether people will choose to engage in active or
passive processing are difficult to alter. For example, research indicates that
personality plays a role in decision-making processes. Some people have a
need for cognition or deep thought, and they enjoy carefully evaluating information before making choices. Meanwhile, others avoid such evaluative processes if at all possible (Cacioppo, Petty, and Morris 1983). Yet scholars have
discovered that many of the factors affecting both the motivation and the ability to engage in active information processing can be influenced by the way
interactions are structured.

Two motivational factors that help to trigger active processing include a
strong sense of personal responsibility or interest in an issue and a strong
sense that the decision will have important consequences (Petty and Cacioppo
1986). It is true that convincing young people that their decisions have self-
relevance or will, in other words, yield important consequences in the future
can be a difficult task. Young people, for example, are more apt to be immune
to fear appeals, as they tend to believe that they are "invulnerable to possibly
serious consequences of their behavior" (Cho and Witte 2004, 227). Moreover, issues that will not affect young people for years to come, such as Social
Security, pension plans, and prescription drug benefits, are too distant and
removed to attract serious attention from young people. Yet contrary to stereotypes about disengaged youth, many young people care about a wide array
of political or potentially political issues (Robbins and Grabow 2004). They
do, however, lack external political efficacy, which means they do not believe
anyone in authority listens or responds to their concerns. Young people also
tend to feel excluded from traditional political processes. Since they lack faith
that their concerns will be addressed by public officials, young people typically prefer to volunteer in apolitical settings where they can see the direct
impact of their efforts (Carnegie Corporation of New York and CIRCLE 2003;
Gibson 2001; Hays 1998; National Commission on Civic Renewal 1998).

Clearly, then, one way the parties could encourage active processing would
be to ask young people to develop their own political agendas and to discuss issues that young people claim to care about. Active processing could
be further triggered by engaging young people in face-to-face, interpersonal
interactions and in small-group settings, or at least by using direct personal pro-

nouns—such as "you" and "we"—rather than third person references—such as "young people" or "students"—to address them (Petty and Cacioppo 1979, 1990). Personal involvement, and the ensuing active processing, could also be enhanced by simply asking young people open-ended, rhetorical questions. People often respond to such questions by beginning to answer the question in their head, and in doing so they begin to actively process information in order to construct an answer. Finally, active processing can also be triggered by creating uncertainty or ambivalence (Maio, Bell, and Esses 1996). Hence, it would help to stop advancing simple solutions for political issues. Instead, young people should be presented with a number of compelling arguments or points of view on the issues they claim to care about. By sorting through the contradictory evidence, they will be compelled to actively process the information in order to evaluate it.

Even when audience members are motivated to actively consider information, they will revert to passive processing if they are not capable of doing so. Factors that affect the ability to actively process information include a sufficient base of knowledge (Wood, Kallgren, and Preisler 1985), which underscores the importance of high school American government courses for political participation, and the comprehensibility of the persuasive messages (Hafer, Reynolds, and Obertynski 1996), which suggests that civic education programs should avoid the use of political jargon and acronyms that a broader audience might not understand.

Yet the factor most relevant to young citizens' capacity to process information is self-efficacy, or their own belief that they are capable of understanding and using political information (Bandura 1977, 1986). This perception that the information will be useful is an essential prerequisite for active processing. People are inundated with a huge array of information on a daily basis, and they cope with this intrusion by becoming cognitive misers who purposefully choose to ignore certain types of information. When people do not think information is apt to be useful to them, they will not expend the effort to actively process it (Graber 1993). Indeed, when asked to explain their lack of interest in politics and their failure to participate, young people provide precisely this explanation. They indicate that they do not believe their involvement will have any effect on the reform of political institutions or the resolution of broad public problems, and, as a result, they choose to tune out (Hays 1998; National Commission on Civic Renewal 1998).

The underpinning reason for young people's lack of internal political efficacy can surely be traced at least in part to the fact that they received their political socialization during a time of declining associational life (Putnam 2000a; Skocpol and Fiorina 1999). If scholars are accurate, young people are less apt than members of prior generations to have learned how to participate effectively within groups, either for the purposes of identifying a common agenda or for pursuing it through collective means. Yet average people, who lack influential connections or access to financial resources, must rely on the power of numbers in a democracy.

The most effective way to make government more responsive to average citizens is to "nourish" grassroots organizations (Putnam 2000b, 50). Yet young people are distrustful of group processes. According to McMillan and Harringer (2002), young people are afraid their own best interests will not be served by the "whims of collective decision-making," and they do not want to be tied to decisions that "might restrict their individual progress and success" (244). These characteristics suggest that young people have not interacted in enough group settings while coming of age to develop the trust in others essential for effective collective political action efforts. Repeated, successful participation in group activities helps foster the belief that other people can be trusted to contribute to the group's overall best interests. These seem to be the types of experiences that young people lack.

Hence, prior to expecting young people to actively process political information, civic education efforts must formally teach the group communication skills—such as deliberation, negotiation, compromise, and persuasion—that were once learned more readily in natural settings. In order to enhance political efficacy, which is the belief that one can achieve political influence, these skills must be tied to the performance of explicitly political collective-action efforts so that young people can learn how their own collaborative efforts can yield results.

The most effective way to improve people's sense of efficacy is to provide them with real-life experiences that create the opportunity for personal accomplishments, because such experiences vividly demonstrate success at performing a given task (Bandura 1977, 1986). Developing civic education programs that provide real-world experiences may be ideal, but they are also apt to be costly and time consuming. In addition, such programs, which would require a high level of commitment from participants, would probably attract atypical young people who are already interested in learning about the political process. Fortunately, however, alternative sources of learning that enhance self-efficacy include both verbal persuasion and vicarious learning (Bandura 1977). Communication research suggests that combinations of vicarious learning opportunities such as modeling, role playing, and rehearsing, often along with verbal persuasion, can improve success in promoting desired behaviors (Anderson 1995, 2000; Maibach and Flora 1993).

Once again, party officials seem particularly well suited to helping young people learn the practical skills needed to develop and pursue a political agenda. They could provide testimonials of their own past experiences to persuade young people that collective organizing can have a dramatic impact on political decisions. Meanwhile, their familiarity with the rules governing participation in both primary and general elections would be useful in developing simulations intended to help young people hone the skills they need to coordinate their voting efforts with groups of their peers. The brevity of this type of intervention could help to overcome one final barrier to active processing, which is the number of distractions a person faces (Petty, Wells, and Brock 1976). Simply put, the more responsibilities a person has, the less time they have to think carefully about decisions, even if they are important. Young people experience a number of distractions, including maintaining an active social life while working and going to school, all of which may limit the amount of time they have to dedicate to actively processing political information. If the parties developed a brief civic education intervention based on the guidelines outlined above, they could work in cooperation with high school government teachers to make their program a mandatory experience. Working in cooperation with teachers would ensure that far more members of our younger generations, even those most disengaged from public life, could be exposed to messages about politics with the potential to make a difference.

## A SUMMARY OF RECOMMENDATIONS

It is clear that if the parties want to restore past levels of party identification in the electorate, they will need to engage in activities that promote active processing of information and the establishment of long-term attitudes toward their organizations. Asking the parties to engage in this type of activity in the midst of a campaign may not be a feasible request, as they are concerned with winning votes under the time constraint imposed by an election day.

### Developing a Long-Term Vision for Party Success

To the detriment of participatory democracy, however, party leaders seem especially focused on electoral activities. As Shea and Green report in this text, the bulk of local party leaders acknowledge that less than 10 percent of their efforts are dedicated to nonelectoral activities, while 63 percent of these same leaders admit that they place a higher priority on helping candidates win elections than they do on building a loyal base of supporters. This emphasis on winning the next election, in combination with young people's low voting rates, is undoubtedly at the root of why local party leaders are not doing enough to educate and mobilize young voters. Indeed, local party officials are focused so intently on upcoming electoral outcomes that they rarely even recognize young voters as a demographic group that is important to the long-term success of their parties (Shea and Green, this volume).

However, the parties should also dedicate themselves to long-term goals that will enhance the health of the party system and American democracy. The two major parties now have substantial financial and organizational resources, which could be used to develop youth and new-voter programs intended to help people develop deeply held political orientations. Declines in American community life make the parties' organizational resources, such as their structure of committees spanning across the entire country, particularly valuable. For while the parties have spent the past several decades reinvigorating their committees at the local, state, and national levels, other community organizations with such federated structures have been replaced by those with only a national headquarters (Bibby 2002; Herrnson 2002; Skocpol 1999). The parties are one of the few remaining organizations with both an interest in civic affairs as well as the national breadth and local depth required to implement civic education programs capable of having a dramatic impact on the political behavior of several generations of young people.

## Identifying Effective Youth Participation Practices

An ideal program to resuscitate party identification in the electorate would encourage young people to develop a political agenda that reflects their own preferences rather than impose the existing agendas of the party elite upon them. Persuading young people that they should invest their time and energy in such a task, however, first requires helping them to overcome the low levels of political efficacy resulting from the historical circumstances framing their political socialization. Current generations of young people must be taught practical political skills such as how to pursue political goals by coordinating their voting efforts—especially during the primaries—before they will be willing to engage in active processing of political issues. Yet if they do learn how to successfully maneuver throughout the nominating process, they are apt to become party loyalists who will contribute to the development of future party agendas and support partisan candidates in elections (Stone and Rapoport 1998).

Despite criticisms that the parties are not doing enough to engage young voters, both Republicans and Democrats at every level have adopted an array of programs intended to increase youth participation and voter turnout (Shea and Green, this volume). Yet most of these programs rely on mobilizing young people who are already interested in the political process and who, most importantly, already agree with existing party platforms. Few of these programs are explicitly intended to reach the most disengaged young people by teaching them how to develop and promote their own political agendas. Hence, the parties may need to supplement existing efforts with programs that would be more likely to have a dramatic effect on large numbers of alienated young voters.

Several promising programs have been developed at the Center for Democracy and Citizenship at the University of Minnesota. One project, titled Public Achievement, for example, attempts to teach the practical organizing skills needed to achieve political influence. The program organizes elementary and high school students into teams in order to work on a public issue of the students' choice over the course of an entire year. Along the way, they are mentored by adults such as teachers, college students, and community members, who help them work toward their goals and learn political skills (Boyte 2003).

This type of program incorporates several of the recommendations made throughout this chapter. Students are directly involved and select the political issue to pursue, which is apt to increase the relevance of political issues in their lives. Moreover, they are exposed to a dramatic, real-life experience, which provides a vivid demonstration of accomplishment capable of enhancing their self-efficacy. Yet the dramatic, real-life nature of such programs may also be a drawback for widespread implementation. Local party officials may be discouraged by the resources it would take to effectively mount such a program, as well as by the sacrifice of control over the choice of political issues to be addressed. Hence they may prefer programs that attempt to accomplish a similar effect by relying on verbal persuasion and hypothetical political situations.

A more attractive model for an effective program may be the one-day conference that was sponsored by the Johnson Foundation and the Center for Information and Research on Civic Learning and Engagement (CIRCLE). The conference brought students and elected officials together in a small group setting for a direct exchange, a personal interaction that should increase students' sense of self-relevance. The agenda for the conference was to help students make connections between their own interests and volunteer work with more traditional political processes, which should increase their sense of political efficacy (Beem 2005). Despite the apparent success of this conference on student attitudes, Beem also noted that "changing the course of youth civic disengagement 20 students at a time is a daunting task" (7). For the parties, with outreach provided by their state and local party committees and their ready access to local elected officials, the task of organizing enough small conferences to accomplish widespread impact becomes far less daunting.

By supporting such programs, the parties would serve an important educative function. They can help young citizens understand how ideology and preferred values can provide a framework for developing a list of political goals. Yet these partisan frameworks, based on either liberal or conservative ideals, should be presented as persuasive arguments for consideration, not as prepackaged, simple solutions that good Republicans and Democrats must either accept or reject without modification. Moreover, the implications of ideological frameworks for specific positions on controversial issues should not be downplayed in favor of vague and widely acceptable "motherhood and apple pie" issues, as the reliance on such passive, short-term cues damages the parties' long-term prospects.

## CONCLUSION

Teaching average citizens how to be involved in the development of party agendas is a risky undertaking for the party elite, especially for those who are invested in the ideological positions that constitute current party platforms. Yet, by returning to the core party function of aggregating voter concerns rather than selling candidates, the parties also have much to gain. Strong party identification in the electorate would once again enhance partisan candidates' chances of winning office. The electorate would be less volatile, and the task of voter mobilization would be a much easier undertaking. In fact, the passive heuristic cue of a candidate's partisanship would once again be an effective means of mobilizing larger portions of the electorate. The cue would be meaningful to voters because they would have helped to construct what the parties stand for. In short, by investing in these types of civic education activities, party leaders would help to fulfill the aspirations for participatory democracy that inspired the reform of our nominating procedures in the first place.

# III

## CIVIC EDUCATION AND YOUTH ENGAGEMENT: PAST, PRESENT, AND FUTURE

# 5

# Civic Knowledge, Civic Education, and Civic Engagement[1]

*William A. Galston*

Although the United States is a stable constitutional democracy, worries about the condition of U.S. civic life are widespread. Scholars, elected officials, and ordinary citizens are concerned about the apparent weakening of civil society as well as documented declines in political activities such as voting. The major political parties are moving toward agreement on responses to this situation, including an increased emphasis on civic education, volunteerism, and national service.

The purpose of this chapter is not to advocate specific public policies, but rather to summarize what is known about the condition of civic and political life in the United States, and to suggest one area in which efforts to make improvement might be focused. I will begin by summarizing current research on civic beliefs and knowledge and then consider current research on civic and political behavior. Throughout the summary, I rely on survey data as the principal support for my conclusions. I analyze both the population as a whole and young adults (ages fifteen to twenty-five), whose attitudes and behaviors help us predict future trends.

After canvassing what is known about the condition of civic life in the United States, I devote specific attention to the importance of civic knowledge. I argue that the decline in civic knowledge is not simply a symptom of the overall decline of American civic life. On the contrary, I contend that civic knowledge directly affects civic competence, character, and conduct. Recent research shows that if we want to revitalize and sustain democratic citizenship, working to raise levels of civic knowledge and information would be one effective strategy, and a sensible place to begin.

The chapter concludes by considering recent research on the pedagogy of civic knowledge. Although there has long been a scholarly consensus that classroom civic education has no effect on civic knowledge, I will demonstrate how recent findings challenge this consensus. Thus, I will suggest that formal education may well hold the key to the erosion of civic life that troubles so many thoughtful people.


## WHAT DO WE KNOW ABOUT BELIEFS AND KNOWLEDGE?

### The "American Creed"

The citizens of the United States remain deeply committed to what many call the "American creed"—an amalgam of constitutional democracy in politics, equal opportunity in the economy, and freedom in society. According to an often-cited survey conducted by the University of Virginia's Post-Modernity Project, support for the basic elements of the creed runs in excess of 90 percent in the population as a whole and in key subgroups (Post-Modernity Project 1996, 5). Decades before the events of September 11, 2001, and continuing into the present, overwhelming majorities have consistently expressed pride in their country (Ladd and Bowman 1998, 15).

There is evidence, however, that young adults are somewhat less committed to the American creed than their parents and grandparents are. Through the last decade, surveys suggested that young people were significantly less likely to say the United States is the greatest country, that its system of government is the best possible, that they are proud to live under that system, or that they would rather live in the United States than in other countries (Rahn 1998). Today's high school seniors are less likely to agree that, "Despite its many faults, our system of doing things is still the best in the world" than was the previous generation. In 1977, two-thirds of high school seniors agreed with this statement; by 2000, agreement had fallen significantly, to only 55 percent (Zill 2002, 28). While numerous surveys have shown a surge in patriotism among young people in the wake of September 11, the most recent evidence suggests that this phenomenon may be short-lived.


### Moral Evaluations of the United States

There is evidence that increasing numbers of Americans perceive their society to be suffering a moral decline. A half century ago, more than 50 percent of Americans responded affirmatively when asked, "Do you think people in general lead as good lives—honest and moral—as they used to?" As recently as the mid-1960s, more than 40 percent agreed. By 1998, that figure had declined to 28 percent (Putnam 2000a). By 2002, it had fallen even further, to only 21 percent (Pew Research Center 2002).

Echoing the argument made in the preceding chapter, this perception of moral decline is especially pronounced in citizens' evaluations of young people. When asked, "Do you think that young people today have as strong a sense of right and wrong as they did, say, 50 years ago?" 57 percent answered affirmatively in 1952, and 41 percent as recently as 1965. Today, that figure has bottomed out at only 19 percent (Pew Research Center 2002).

## Attitudes toward Government

Over the past two generations, Americans' trust in the national government has declined sharply. In the early 1960s, about three-quarters trusted the national government to do what is right all or most of the time. By the mid-1990s, only one quarter did. In the second half of the 1990s, trust in government increased modestly, to nearly 40 percent, before the Clinton scandals knocked it down again (Kohut 1998). September 11 produced a surge in that trust, which has since subsided, although trust remains significantly higher than before the terrorist attacks. Trust in the legislative and executive branches declined about equally, while trust in the judiciary remained stable. Trust in state and local government also declined but is consistently higher than trust in the national government. Through the past decade, scholars in the United States have debated the cause of this historic shift. The most comprehensive exploration reached the following conclusions:

- The early 1960s probably represented a period of abnormally high trust because the World War II generation, with its positive government experiences, was demographically and politically dominant.
- Key events of the mid-1960s through the early 1970s—Vietnam, Watergate, domestic disruption, and the surge in crime—reduced trust but would not have long-lasting effects in the absence of broader structural changes.
- The structural changes that best explain the long-term decline in trust include: (1) value changes in attitudes toward authority and social restraints in general, (2) economic destabilization stemming from technological change and globalization, (3) changes in the political process that weakened political parties and increased the perceived distance between elites and the public, and (4) a more consistent negative stance by the

press toward government as well as other key institutions. (Nye, Zelikow, and King 1997, 268–76)

There is no systematic evidence that younger Americans are more (or less) likely to trust government than are older Americans. In some respects, however, their attitude toward government is more favorable than that of other age cohorts. For example, eighteen- to twenty-five-year-olds are least likely to see government as inefficient and wasteful or to believe that the federal government controls too much of Americans' daily lives (CIRCLE and Pew Center 2002, 18–19). If these youthful attitudes persist over time, they could provide a basis for renewed government activism in areas of national need such as health care (see figure 5.1).

### Trust in Other Key Institutions

Governmental institutions in the United States were hardly alone in experiencing declining public trust during the past generation. Other major institutions that suffered this fate were labor, the legal profession, educational institutions, the media, and even organized religion. Confidence in business and corporations, which increased during the second half of the 1990s, collapsed in the wake of recent highly publicized financial scandals. Only the police and the armed forces have managed to gain increased trust during this period (Ladd and Bowman 1998, chapter 6).

**Figure 5.1   Pro-Government Responses to Questions**

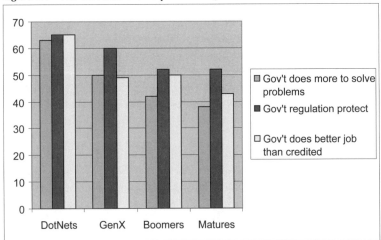

*Source:* The Civic and Political Health of the Nation, A Generational Protrait, 2002.

## Trust in Other People

Americans' trust in one another has declined during the past generation, although less sharply than trust in government. From a high of 54 percent in the early 1960s, trust declined to only 34 percent in the early 1990s, where it remained with minor oscillations for the rest of the decade. Unlike trust in government, there is evidence that young people are significantly less likely to trust others than are older citizens (see figure 5.2) (Rahn 1998). As recently as 1975, high school students trusted other people at the same rate that adults did; by the late 1990s, a gap of nearly fifteen points separated high school students from other adults. Indeed, most, if not all, of the overall decline in social trust since the 1960s can be explained by the changing composition of the population. Older Americans are no less trusting than they were thirty years ago, but younger, less trusting Americans make up a larger share of the population (Putnam 2000a, 140–41).

There is no consensus among scholars about the causes of diminished trust in other people. The most plausible hypotheses include the sharp increase in rates of crime and violence between the mid-1960s and the early 1990s; the disruption of family stability, evident in soaring divorce rates; and immigration, which significantly increased the diversity of the U.S. population. Because these factors tended to affect young people disproportionately, this may explain why they are now less likely to trust others. The events of September 11 appear to have increased trust in government (at all levels), in other institutions, and in other people. Civic behavior has changed much less than

**Figure 5.2   Distrust of People**

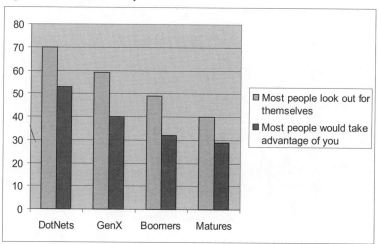

*Source:* The Civic and Political Health of the Nation, A Generational Protrait, 2002.

civic attitudes, however. Robert Putnam asks whether behavior will follow attitudes. If not, "the blossom of civic-mindedness after September 11 may be short-lived" (Putnam 2002, 3).

## Other Key Attitudes

During the past generation, there has been a gradual shift toward materialism. Nowhere has that change been sharper than among young adults. In the mid-1960s, nearly 90 percent of college students believed it was very important to develop a meaningful philosophy of life, while about 40 percent said it was important to become well off financially (see figure 5.3). By the beginning of the twenty-first century, these sentiments reversed: 73 percent of college students said it was important to become well off, versus only 42 percent who felt that way about developing a meaningful philosophy of life (CIRCLE 2002a, 3). Not surprisingly, this trend was different among age cohorts. Toward the end of the 1990s, young adults reported significantly higher interest in money and self-fulfillment than did other Americans, as well as much lower levels of patriotism (Rahn 1999). (Here, as elsewhere, it remains to be seen whether the changes produced by the events of September 11 will be temporary or long lasting.)

Other important attitudinal shifts during the past generation include increased racial, ethnic, religious, and gender tolerance and the increased value placed on unfettered individual choice as the central norm of U.S. social life (Putnam 2000a, 354; Wolfe 1998; Yankelovich 1994).

**Figure 5.3   Changing Priorities among College Freshmen—Money Counts**

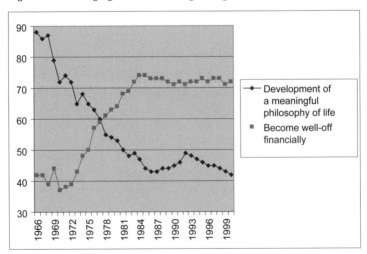

*Source:* HERI Freshman Survey, 1966 to 2000.

## Interest in Public Affairs

In the past generation, Americans' interest in public affairs has steadily declined by roughly one-fifth, with occasional spikes during unusual events (Putnam 2000a, 36). Key measures of declining interest include reading about public affairs in newspapers, watching national television news, discussing politics, and believing that it is important to keep up to date with political developments.

This decline has been especially pronounced among young people. In the mid-1960s, 60 percent said they thought it was important to keep up to date with politics; by 2000, that figure had declined to less than 30 percent. All measures of political interest fell by at least one-half during that period (Bennett 1997, 47–53; CIRCLE 2002b, 5).

## Political Knowledge

Americans today know about as much about political institutions and events as they did fifty years ago. This stability is remarkable, given that education tends to increase political knowledge, and the median amount of formal education has risen by four years during the past half century. It turns out that today's college graduates know no more about politics than high school graduates did fifty years ago, and today's high school graduates are no more knowledgeable than were the high school dropouts of the past (Delli Carpini and Keeter 1996).

Equally disturbing is the developing generation gap in political knowledge. From the 1940s through the mid-1970s, young people were at least as well informed as were older Americans. This pattern has shifted drastically, starting with the baby boomers and has accelerated with their children. As Robert Putnam summarizes the data, "Today's under-30's pay less attention to the news and know less about current events than their elders do today or than people their age did two or three decades ago" (Putnam 2000a, 36). Here, as elsewhere, the events of September 11 evoked an increased interest in political events among all Americans, and especially younger Americans. But current indications are that this surge represents a temporary "spike" rather than a sustained shift toward interest in politics and current events.

## WHAT ABOUT CIVIC BEHAVIOR?

### Voting

A central indicator of civic behavior is citizens' willingness to go to the polls on election day. For much of the twentieth century, voting rates in the United

States were well below those of other democracies. There were substantial variations within that period, however. Overall participation rose to a post–World War II peak in the early 1960s and declined significantly thereafter. Between the mid-1960s and the early 1970s, turnout dropped by about ten percentage points; it has declined much more slowly since then, by about four percentage points.

Recent scholarship has sought to explain this decline. The most persuasive attempt focuses on three factors: resources, interest, and mobilization. According to this thesis, increasing economic inequality has deprived large numbers of poor and undereducated Americans of the resources they need to participate, while the decline of American political parties as grassroots organizations has diminished voter mobilization. Meanwhile, events have tended to depress interest in politics among Americans born after the civic-minded Depression/World War II generation. While it has long been the case that the frequency of voting (and other forms of political activity) tends to increase with age, careful analysis suggests that in recent decades, differences among generations have become more important in explaining voting behavior (Putnam 2000a, 34; Schlozman, Verba, and Brady 1999).

For nearly a century after the Civil War, African Americans were systematically denied the right to vote. The great legal and constitutional amendments of the 1960s began to change that. Today, African American voting rates are close to those of white Americans. (Indeed, once education is taken into account, they are somewhat higher.)

Hispanics make up the most rapidly growing sector of the U.S. electorate. For various reasons, however, their electoral participation has not reflected their increasing weight in the population. On average, Hispanics are younger, poorer, and less educated than other population groups—factors that generally depress turnout among voters. In addition, substantial numbers of Hispanics are not yet citizens and are therefore ineligible to vote in most jurisdictions. Still, turnout among Hispanics who are U.S. citizens remains lower than that of other groups in the electorate. There are signs that this may be changing now, however. Many Hispanics interpreted anti-immigrant legislation enacted in California in the mid-1990s as hostile to their ethnic group. Changes in federal welfare legislation reinforced that view. The result has been highly visible Hispanic voter mobilization, especially in large cities where Hispanics now hold the balance of political power and where promising Hispanics candidates for mayor and city council are coming forward.

An important change occurred in 1972, when, for the first time, Americans as young as eighteen were allowed to vote throughout the nation. At first, they participated in substantial number: in the presidential election of 1972, 52 percent of eligible voters aged eighteen to twenty-five cast ballots. Over the next thirty years, the rate of participation in this age group fell sharply; by the 2000 presidential election, only 37 percent of young Americans bothered to vote, a decline of roughly one-third. Similar trends are apparent for congressional elections held during non–presidential election years, when only 17 percent cast their ballots—again, a decline of roughly one-third. By 2004, there seemed to be a significant turnaround, with some 46 percent of this age group heading to the polls. There were, however, dramatically different circumstances surrounding this election, as outlined in the introduction to this book. We might feel optimistic that young Americans have rediscovered their place in the electoral process, but in all likelihood their inclination to seek other avenues for their engagement will persist.

## Other Forms of Participation in Official Politics

Americans participate in politics in many ways other than voting—for example, writing to their elected representatives, signing petitions, and attending rallies. The conventional wisdom is that while Americans have below-average voter turnout, they are very active by international standards in other aspects of political participation. This belief is less true than it once was. Between 1973 and 1994, the Roper organization conducted an annual survey of political participation that examined trends in twelve different activities. During those two decades, every participation indicator declined significantly. The decline was especially steep (between 34 and 42 percent) for those activities that required working with others in public settings. (By contrast, the more solitary political activities—writing one's congressman or senator, signing a petition, writing a letter to the editor of a newspaper—experienced smaller declines.) Overall, there was a decrease of 25 percent in the share of Americans who participated in at least one of the twelve activities during the prior year (Putnam 2000a, 45).

Like voting, participation in these other political activities is strongly influenced by wealth, education, and social position. Participation increases steadily as income rises, and citizens in the top income quintile are roughly five times as likely as those in the bottom quintile to engage in a political activity (Brady, Schlozman, Verba, and Elms 2002, figure 10-1). (This ratio has fluctuated between four and seven over the past quarter century, with a mean of roughly five [Brady, Schlozman, Verba, and Elms 2002, figure 10-2].)

Age also affects political participation. Young people are least likely to participate, but engagement tends to rise steadily through middle age before falling again among the elderly. In addition, today's Americans at every age level are less likely to participate than were Americans of the same age in previous generations (Putnam 2000a, 253).

Putnam's analysis shows that this process of declining participation has contributed to the polarization of American politics. Individuals who identify themselves as moderate, centrist, or middle of the road have been disproportionately likely to drop out of politics, while those who are more ideologically extreme have tended to remain active. This helps explain an apparent paradox: while an increasing fraction of the U.S. electorate identifies itself as moderate (rather than very liberal or very conservative), fewer and fewer elected representatives are moderates (Putnam 2000a, 342). Political parties have learned that ideologically committed voters are more likely to vote, donate money, and participate in grassroots organizing, so campaigns are increasingly aimed at mobilizing this intense base of support, which further alienates moderates, and so forth, in a vicious circle.

## Voluntary Organizations

Since at least the publication of Tocqueville's *Democracy in America*, Americans have seen themselves (and have been seen by others) as unusually likely to address social and political problems by forming voluntary organizations. While there is much truth to this view, recent scholarship has pointed to some disturbing trends. Since 1995, Robert Putnam has argued that the fabric of American civil society has been fraying over the past generation. With the publication of his comprehensive book in 2000, even the skeptics were forced to concede that there is substantial evidence of decline.

Putnam was able to show, for example, that membership in major national organizations has declined, as has active participation in local clubs and groups. Union membership has fallen from almost 35 percent of the workforce to less than 15 percent. Even church attendance appears to have fallen off, though less steeply than participation in secular groups. In the main, organizations that have grown in the past generation have tended to be "checkbook" organizations that use direct mail to raise funds for the support of national headquarters and professional advocacy rather than face-to-face activities among local citizens (Putnam 2000a, 54, 60–61, 71, 81, 155–61). One might suppose that participation in civil society is less influenced by income and status than is participation in official politics. But in fact, we observe much the same influence of socioeconomic standing in civil society. Once again, there is a linear relation between social position and group membership; those at the top are three times as likely as those at the bottom to participate (Brady, Schlozman, Verba, and Elms 2002, figures 10-3 and 10-4).

The major exception to this generalization is religion. There is no relationship between social position and attending religious services or meetings. Individuals of all income levels are equally likely to participate, and this equality has persisted virtually unchanged over the past thirty years (Brady, Schlozman, Verba, and Elms 2002, figure 10-5). The mobilization of religious Americans over the past generation represents one of the few tendencies toward political and civil equalization during this period. As Brady, Schlozman, Verba, and Elms remark, "It is ironic that, even though many religious institutions are hierarchically governed and democracy is supposed to provide a level playing field on which all citizens are equal, it is religious activity that has consistently been distributed relatively equally across socioeconomic groups" (Brady, Schlozman, Verba, and Elms 2002).

## Giving and Volunteering

Closely related to membership in civil society organizations are the activities of giving (charitable contributions) and volunteering in neighborhoods and communities. Here, trends are mixed. Charitable contributions peaked at about 2.2 percent of national income in the mid-1960s and have fallen fairly steadily ever since, to about 1.6 percent today (Putnam 2000a, 124). (Measured in real dollars per capita, charitable giving rose during this period, reflecting the large increase in per capita income. But most scholars believe that it is more meaningful to measure contributions in relation to individual, family, or national income.)

Volunteering is the principal exception to the general pattern of weakening civic involvement. Over the past quarter century, volunteering by the average American has risen from six times per year to nearly eight times. Much of this increase has occurred among older Americans, who are enjoying longer, healthier, and more prosperous retirements than ever before. (Volunteering is up a remarkable 140 percent among Americans over the age of seventy-five.) We also observe significant increases among college students and young adults (see figure 5.4). Only among Americans aged thirty to fifty has volunteering stagnated or declined since 1975 (CIRCLE and Pew Research Center 2002, 18–19; Putnam 2000a, 128–30).

The explanation for the increase in volunteering among young people is contested. Anecdotal evidence suggests that more and more young people are required to volunteer by their schools as a condition for high school graduation, or by colleges and universities as a condition for admission. When questioned, however, young people deny that these requirements are a major factor. Rather, they claim that they volunteer because someone asked, because it makes them feel good, or because they want to make a difference. Nearly a quarter of all young Americans see volunteering as an alternative to participation in a political system they regard as remote, unresponsive, and beholden to special interests (CIRCLE 2002a).

**Figure 5.4   Volunteering among College Freshmen Is Up Since 1989**

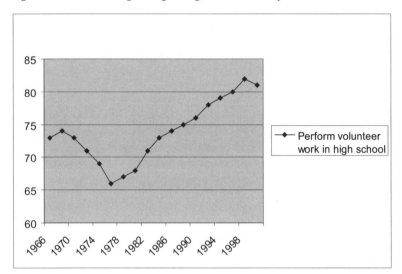

*Source:* HERI Freshman Survey, 1966 to 2000.

## Social Movements

Social movements would seem to be a conspicuous exception to the broad pattern of declining civic engagement summarized in this chapter. After all, since the early 1960s, American society has been transformed by movements for civil rights, feminism, environmentalism, gay and lesbian rights, and many others. Many activists believe that the past forty years have been a golden age for social movements.

The evidence suggests, however, that few of these movements have achieved sustained mass mobilization. Today, most consist of small cadres of professional advocates sustained by large numbers of citizens whose main mode of participation is writing checks. It is doubtful whether this mode of civic engagement builds social capital, especially at the local and community levels (Putnam 2000a, 154–66).

## WHY WORRY ABOUT CIVIC DISENGAGEMENT?

I do want to suggest that the increasing civic detachment of the young cannot be regarded with equanimity. Let me begin with a truism about representative democracy: political engagement is not sufficient for political effectiveness, but it is necessary. If today's young people have legitimate generational interests that do not wholly coincide with the interests of their elders, those interests cannot shape public decisions unless they are forcefully articulated. For example, Congress is moving with unaccustomed speed to repeal the earnings penalty long imposed on the benefits of Social Security recipients between sixty-five and sixty-nine. In the abstract, there is much to be said for this change. But the members of generations X and Y will have to pay for it. I doubt that enough of them will raise their voices to affect the legislative outcome, or even the debate. The withdrawal of a cohort of citizens from public affairs disturbs the balance of public deliberation, to the detriment of those who withdraw (and many others besides).

Second, we might offer an old-fashioned argument from obligation. Most young Americans derive great benefits from their membership in a stable, prosperous, and free society. These goods do not fall like manna from heaven; they must be produced, and renewed, by each generation. When all the subtleties and quibbles are stripped away, the arguments of the Laws to Socrates retain their force; so, too, does John Rawls's injunction to do one's fair share to uphold reasonably just institutions, and the communitarian conjoining of responsibilities to rights.

We come, third, to the perplexed relation between citizenship and self-development. Even if we agree (and we may not) on the activities that constitute good citizenship, one may still wonder why it is good to be a good citizen. I find it impossible to endorse a strong version of civic republicanism; it is possible, I believe, for many individuals to realize their good in ways that do not involve the active exercise of citizenship. Even if we accept Aristotle's characterization of politics as the architectonic activity, it does not follow that the development of civic capacities is architectonic for every soul.

Still, there is something to the proposition that under appropriate circumstances, political engagement helps develop capacities that are intrinsically (not just instrumentally) important. I have in mind the sorts of intellectual and moral capacities that Tocqueville and Mill discuss, or gesture toward: among them being enlarged interests, a wider human sympathy, a sense of active responsibility for oneself, the skills needed to work with others toward goods that can only be obtained or created through collective action, and the powers of sympathetic understanding needed to build bridges of persuasive words to those with whom one must act.

These links between participation and character development are empirical—not theoretical—propositions, and as Jane Mansbridge has rightly insisted, we do not (yet) have the kind of evidence we need to sustain them against doubt.

On the other hand, we do not have compelling reasons to doubt them, and they can at least be advanced as a not-implausible profession of public faith—as long we are not too categorical about it.

Political engagement tends to develop desirable human capacities "under appropriate circumstances." Yet when a political system is distorted by concentrated oppressive power, one engages with it at considerable peril to one's soul. In such circumstances, only those with unusual moral insight and strength can figure out how to engage in ways that enhance their human powers, while the rest of us tend to be brutalized, or at least co-opted and corrupted. (Look at the millions of ordinary East Germans who ended up enmeshed in the operations of the Stasi, the secret police.) Of course, the distinction between those political regimes that are conducive to the good of the soul and those that aren't presupposes some non-context-dependent account of intrinsic human goods and virtues, a premise that may trouble philosophical liberals who think of themselves as principled antiperfectionists. But that is a long story best left to another occasion.

It may well be that even as civic engagement has declined, it has become not less, but more necessary for the development of the human capacities just sketched. Underlying this conjecture is the suspicion that as the market has become more pervasive during the past generation as organizing metaphor and as daily experience, the range of opportunities to develop nonmarket skills and dispositions has narrowed. For various reasons, the solidarity-generating organizations that dominated the U.S. landscape from the 1930s through the early 1960s have weakened, and the principle of individual choice has emerged as our central value. Indeed, citizenship itself has become optional, as the sense of civic obligation (to vote, or for that matter to do anything else of civic consequence) has faded and as the military draft has been replaced by all-volunteer armed forces. When the chips are down, we prefer exit to voice, and any sense of loyalty to something larger than ourselves has all but disappeared. In this context, the experience of collective action directed toward common purposes is one of the few conceivable counterweights to today's hyperextended principle of individual choice.

## THE SIGNIFICANCE OF CIVIC KNOWLEDGE

The portrait of civic life that I have painted provides good reason to worry. It also suggests a question: if we are interested in reversing the decline in civic life, are there particular factors on which we should focus our attention? A part of the answer, I believe, is to emphasize the acquisition of civic knowledge.

Admittedly, it may seem implausible to argue that basic civic knowledge is central to democratic citizenship. Why should it matter whether young people can identify their senators or name the branches of government? Yet, surprisingly, recent research suggests important links between basic civic information and civic attributes that we have good reason to care about (Delli Carpini and Keeter 1996; Leming 1996; Nie et al. 1996; Nie and Hillygus 2001; Torney-Purta 2002; Zaller 1992). The major findings may be summarized as follows:

1. Civic knowledge helps citizens understand their interests as individuals and as members of groups. The more knowledge they have, the better we can understand the impact of public policies on their interests, and the more effectively they can promote their interests in the political process. Political knowledge fosters "enlightened self-interest"—the ability to connect personal/group interests with specific public issues and to connect those issues with candidates who are more likely to share their views and promote their interests.

2. Civic knowledge increases the consistency of views across issues and across time. There is a strong linear relationship between political knowledge and the stability of political attitudes, and more knowledgeable voters display much higher levels of ideological consistency among issues (as measured along a one-dimensional liberal-conservative axis) than do the less well informed.

3. Unless citizens possess a basic level of civic knowledge—especially concerning political institutions and processes—it is difficult for them to understand political events or to integrate new information into an existing framework. (By analogy, imagine trying to make sense of the flow of events in a sports competition for someone who does not know the rules of the game.) Popkin and Dimock (1999) distinguish between "personal character" and "political character" (conduct judged in the specific context of political roles, institutions, issues, and responsibilities). Low-information citizens are much more likely to judge officials according to their perception of officials' personal character rather than their stance on key issues.

4. General civic knowledge can alter our views on specific public issues. For example, the more knowledge citizens have, the less likely they are to fear new immigrants and their impact on the U.S. economy and security.

5. The more knowledge citizens have of civic affairs, the less likely they are to experience a generalized mistrust of, or alienation from, public life. Ignorance is the father of fear, and knowledge is the mother of trust. More knowledgeable citizens tend to judge the behavior of public officials as they judge their own—in the context of circumstances and

incentives, with due regard for innocent oversights and errors as well as sheer chance. By contrast, less knowledgeable citizens are more likely to view public officials' blunders as signs of bad character. Moreover, low-information citizens encountering vigorous political debate, with its inevitable charges and countercharges, are more likely to conclude that there are no white knights and adopt a "plague on both your houses" stance. For those who understand politics, debate can be as clear as a tennis match; for those who do not, it more closely resembles a food fight.

6. Civic knowledge promotes support for democratic values. For example, the more knowledge citizens have of political principles and institutions, the more likely they are to support core democratic principles, starting with tolerance. Knowledge of specific constitutional rights and civil liberties increases tolerance for unpopular minorities.

7. Civic knowledge promotes political participation. All other things being equal, the more knowledge citizens have, the more likely they are to participate in public matters. Political knowledge affects participation, not only quantitatively, but also qualitatively. For example, more knowledgeable voters are more likely to vote on the basis of national economic conditions as well as personal economic circumstances. Political knowledge makes it more likely that citizens will ask not only, "How am I doing?" but also, "How are we doing?"

## THE FAILURE OF CIVIC EDUCATION

The evidence that we have failed to transmit basic civic knowledge to young adults is now incontrovertible. In our decentralized system of public education, the closest thing we have to a national examination is the National Assessment of Educational Progress (NAEP), devised by teams of subject-matter experts and then carefully field tested and revised, a process directed by the National Assessment Governing Board. The NAEP is administered biennially in what are deemed "core academic subjects." Unfortunately, civic education has not yet achieved that exalted status, and we are fortunate if civic knowledge is assessed once a decade. For each subject, four different achievement levels are defined: "below basic," which means little if any demonstrated knowledge of the subject; "basic," which indicates partial mastery; "proficient," which is the level representing a standard of adequate knowledge; and "advanced." These achievement levels represent absolute thresholds, not percentiles. In principle, every student could reach the level of proficient.

The 1998 NAEP Civics Assessment is the fruit of nearly a decade of intellectual spadework, starting with the nationwide consensus-building process that led to the promulgation in 1995 of national standards for civics and government. These standards served as the basis, first, for the official "framework" within which the NAEP Civics Assessment was developed, and then for the specific questions within each category. The result may not be perfect, but it is better than its predecessors, and close to the best possible.

When the results of the 1998 NAEP Civics Assessment were released, they were not encouraging. For fourth, eighth, and (most relevant for our purposes) twelfth graders, about three-quarters were below the level of proficient. Thirty-five percent of high school seniors tested below basic, indicating near-total civic ignorance. Another 39 percent were at the basic level, less than the working knowledge that citizens need.

When we combine these NAEP results with other data from the past decade of survey research, we are driven to a gloomy conclusion: whether we are concerned with the rules of the political game, political players, domestic policy, foreign policy, or political geography, student performance is quite low. This raises a puzzle. The level of formal schooling in the United States is much higher than it was fifty years ago. But the civic knowledge of today's students is at best no higher than that of their parents and grandparents. We have made a major investment in formal education without any discernible payoff in increased civic knowledge.

A recently issued fifty-state analysis of civic education helps explain these unimpressive results. While most states endorse civic education in their constitutions and declaratory policies, fewer have made a serious effort to align their civics-related courses with challenging content standards, and only three administer exams focused exclusively on civic topics. In many states, certification requirements do not ensure that teachers called upon to teach civics will have the education and training needed to do the job. Other studies indicate that a significant percentage of history and social studies teachers, who typically end up leading civics classes, have little formal preparation for that task (or indeed for teaching history and social studies).

## BUT CAN CIVIC KNOWLEDGE BE TAUGHT?

So in the end, there is no compelling reason to doubt that civic knowledge affects civic competence, character, and conduct. But what affects knowledge?

For three decades the scholarly consensus has been that formal classroom-based civic education has no significant effect on civic knowledge. Recent findings challenge this consensus and begin to provide insight into both the overall effects of civic education on political knowledge and specific pedagogical strategies that effectively foster political understanding.

Some of these findings reflect evaluations of individual civic education programs. For example, several research studies conclude that "We the People: The Citizen and the Constitution," a nationwide program of civic education administered by the Center for Civic Education, is especially effective at improving the civic knowledge of elementary, middle, and high school students relative to students in comparison groups. In addition, participants develop a stronger attachment to democratic attitudes and principles and an enhanced sense of political interest and effectiveness.

Other research is broader based. In a study of political socialization of young people in four communities, Pamela Johnson Conover and Donald Searing explored the role of high schools in fostering civic understanding and practice (Conover and Searing 2000). They focus on four elements of the school experience: the sense of the school as a community, the students' level of civic engagement in school and extracurricular activities, the level of political discussion in school, and the formal academic curriculum. They find that all four elements significantly affect young people's civic consciousness and practice, albeit in different ways. Remarkably, the informal civic education that occurs in noncivics courses such as English literature may be more effective than civic education as currently taught.

In a major study based on data from the 1988 NAEP civics assessment, Richard Niemi and Jane Junn (1998) found significant effects from the amount and timing of civic course work, the variety of topics studied, and the frequency with which current events are discussed in class. These course effects are independent of background variables such as gender, ethnicity, and home environment, as well as interest in government and academic aspirations. Classroom effects are smaller for Hispanics than for white students, and smaller for African Americans than for Hispanics (class discussion is the only classroom variable that yields significant results for African Americans). Differences between girls and boys are small, although boys are more strongly affected by their classroom experiences and home background. While formal classes are significant for all dimensions of civic knowledge, not surprisingly they have somewhat smaller effects in areas such as citizens' rights, in which nonschool sources are likely to provide relevant information. (Young people's familiarity with the details of suspects' Miranda rights is stunningly high.)

Niemi and Junn offer an explanation for the divergence of their findings from those of scholars a generation ago, best exemplified by the work of Langton and Jennings (1968, 862–67). In the first place, Langton and Jennings did find some effects of civic education on knowledge, which they downplayed in an analysis heavily weighted toward attitudinal items. Second, they did not take into account the grade in which students took civic education classes; Niemi and Junn show that twelfth-grade classes have more impact than classes taken earlier. Third, they did not include discussion of current events in their analysis, and there are good reasons to believe that these discussions are more likely to provide civic knowledge than are other classroom activities.

Finally, a comprehensive study of 90,000 fourteen-year-olds in twenty-eight countries found that school-based civic education does make a significant difference in developing civic knowledge, skills, and attitudes. Among the most notable findings from this study are the following:

- A classroom climate that encourages respectful discussions of civic and political issues fosters both civic knowledge and engagement.
- An explicit focus on learning about voting and elections increases the likelihood that young people will participate in elections when they reach voting age.
- Participation in student organizations (including student councils) promotes a sense of civic efficacy.

## CONCLUSION

There is a solid empirical basis behind the growing concern about American civic life. Whether one looks at civic beliefs or civic behavior, there have been marked declines in the qualities and characteristics that we associate with successful democratic government—declines that are especially prominent and troubling among young adults.

Yet, if recent research demonstrates the depth of the problem, it also points toward possible solutions. Among other promising findings, current studies demonstrate that civic knowledge is an important determinant of civic capability and character. Moreover, recent findings suggest that formal, classroom-based civic education provides an effective means of teaching civic knowledge. Contrary to a long-standing scholarly consensus concerning the dim prospects for civic education, the recent wave of research furnishes a basis for hope and a guide for action. A key to halting and even reversing the negative trends that have weakened our public life may well be found in the schoolhouse, a central dimension of the complex process through which young people develop civic awareness and motivation.

## NOTES

1. Significant portions of this chapter were drawn from William A. Galston, "Civic Knowledge, Civic Education, and Civic Engagement: A Summary of Recent Research," in *Constructing Civic Virtue*, Campbell Public Affairs Institute, Maxwell School of Public Affairs, Syracuse University, 2003.

# 6

## Political Participation and Service Learning: Civic Education as Problem and Solution[1]

*Melissa K. Comber*

Young Americans have been flooded with the message that volunteerism and community service are essential and honorable avocations. After September 11, President Bush urged young people to care for their neighbors by volunteering, and he created the USA Freedom Corps. Over the last few years, programs such as AmeriCorps and City Year have grown in popularity among young peers. College admissions officers expect applicants to have volunteer and community service experience. Some states and cities are requiring that a certain number of volunteer hours be met before a high school diploma can be awarded. For example, Maryland requires seventy-five hours of student service of its graduating seniors, while numerous other states statutorily encourage service-learning curricula.

Young Americans are volunteering and participating in community service activities in record numbers. These activities, and new service-learning requirements, intend to encourage community service, increase civic engagement, and teach students the value of improving the world around them. Presumably such activities encourage activism and social change. Yet these programs do not teach political participation and the skills needed to attain political change. Can social change occur without political activism? Can community improvement occur without political participation? Community service absent political participation is ultimately ineffective at social change.

Proponents of service-learning programs argue that community service and civic participation result in eventual political activism, as students engaged in their communities become adults engaged in politics (see, for example, Campbell 2000; Flanagan 2003). However, not only is this link fragile within individuals, but it must be nurtured over the passage of time as well. Yet why should we accept any delay in the development of this link within our youngest adult citizens? Shouldn't we be teaching skills necessary for political activity at the youngest feasible age? Political participation skills should be taught concurrently with community service values.

The political preferences and policy interests of twenty-year-olds differ from those of thirty-year-olds. If the political participation skills of twenty-year-olds remain undeveloped, their ability to influence politics will remain disadvantaged. A representative democracy demands that we teach political abilities within the spectrum of skills, abilities, and knowledge required to participate in politics. In accordance with Dewey (1916), democracy is more than just a system of government. In fact, it is "primarily a mode of associated living, of conjoint communicated experience" (87). In this sense, when political participation abilities are absent, the youngest adults have little input in the policy process and miss our shared communicated experience.

Yet political activism beyond voting is difficult. Dahl (1961) reminds us that politics are a foreign activity for most people, and not an innately primary concern in our everyday lives. We must work to cultivate an interest in politics, and to view it as a rewarding activity. Moreover, we are often originally attracted to politics for reasons of private interest, and later our interests turn to public concerns (McWilliams 1995). Despite these difficulties, and because of these difficulties, we must actively nurture the means for political activism within young citizens. A democracy absent an entire age cohort—our youngest adult citizens—is not truly representative.

In order to participate in politics, citizens must have political knowledge, civic skills, and a willingness to be engaged. Youth often learn political knowledge and participation abilities from part-time jobs, extracurricular activities, religious group participation, parents, and civic education. While some civic skills are learned through community service and volunteerism, such as communication skills and group decision-making skills, other civic skills such as participatory skills and news-monitoring skills are not a focus of traditional service-learning requirements. This chapter will explore high school civics courses as sources of political knowledge and civic skills. Potentially, civics courses can provide the abilities to participate politically.

As a source of civic skill development, high school civic education may be more equally available than alternative sources of skill development and political knowledge. For example, some young Americans may not have engaged or knowledgeable family members, a part-time job, or be involved in extracurricular activities. For these citizens, civic education may be their primary exposure to the skills and knowledge needed for political participation. While numerous organizations and segments of society are trying new ways to engage youth and provide exposure to politics and civic skills, the high school civics course remains a steadfast potential source of political knowledge and civic skill development. This chapter will review relevant civic education and political participation literature, consider changes in civics courses over time, examine civics course changes as a problem for political participation, and reflect on the potential of civics courses to engage youth in the political process. It will be argued that newfound levels of civic activity among today's youth, while necessary for a healthy civil society, do not foster the means to politically participate. In turn, while popular service-learning requirements work to teach community participation, how should we teach political participation?

## HOW ARE AMERICA'S YOUTH ENGAGED?

While numerous pundits and researchers decry the lack of participation in community life on behalf of today's youth, the fact is that America's youth are more civically engaged than their counterparts were a few decades ago. Youth participation in community life has increased over the last ten years, with a rise in voluntarism and participation in community service activities (Longo 2004; Lopez 2004). Newer programs that encourage and popularize volunteerism, such as AmeriCorps and City Year, have also contributed to this increase.

Service-learning requirements are becoming more common in high school curricula. Service learning is generally defined as including a "curriculum-based form of community service" (Stagg 2004, 1). In 1999, 30 percent of high school students participated in a service-learning project (Stagg 2004). In 2004, 44 percent of high schools participated in service-learning projects (Stagg 2004). Although data on service learning is difficult to compare over time due to different definitions of service learning, general trends indicate an increase in service-learning participation (Stagg 2004).

However, while service-learning requirements instill civic participation, they are not fostering political participation. Eisner (2004) goes so far as to argue that for many youth, service can be a form of compassionate individualism, or merely consumer behavior through the acts of boycotting or buycotting. For some, these service behaviors may replace political behaviors, such as voting, writing letters to elected officials, or expressing opinions at community meetings. Ironically, AmeriCorps itself, a primary community-service institution, experienced its own funding crisis in 2003, potentially due to its lack of political lobbying. While AmeriCorps alumni certainly learn community service, the organization's own self-preservation was jeopardized due to a lack of political participation among alumni (Eisner 2004).

Declining political participation among young people is a concern. Voter turnout rates, one indicator of political participation, have declined since 1972 for Americans under the age of twenty-five. The exception to this is the most recent presidential election. In November of 2004, 46.7 percent of eligible eighteen- to twenty-five-year-olds voted, compared with 36.5 percent in November of 2000 (CIRCLE 2004a). In all, the rate of decline in voter turnout for young Americans is greater than the rate of decline among Americans aged twenty-five and over (Levine and Lopez 2002).

Other measures of political activism have also declined over time among the youngest American age group. According to the American National Election Studies (ANES), young people are the least likely age group to state that they have attended a political meeting, and the least likely age group to say that they read about a political campaign in a newspaper or magazine. However, after the 2004 presidential election, young people were the most likely age group to state that they had tried to influence the vote of others (ANES 2004). In other words, voting and political activism were higher than usual among the young during the 2004 presidential campaign. The reasons and inspirations behind this should be further explored.

Friedland and Morimoto (2005) provide evidence that a recent increase in community service activities among high school students may parallel increasing pressure on young people to achieve and succeed. For some students, "résumé padding" motivates them to volunteer, in response to the extraordinary pressure put on high school students to attend a good college or university. Friedland and Morimoto suggest that résumé padding is just one factor among many that influence volunteerism. Other motivating factors include altruism, religious beliefs, and love of volunteering. They do not, however, have evidence that a résumé-padding motive for volunteering negates the beneficial effects of volunteering and civic participation.

While participation among youth in civic and volunteer endeavors has risen, participation in politics has declined. Explanations for the decline in political participation among young Americans include poor civic skills, a lack of civic engagement, and little political knowledge. Understanding all these components is crucial to explaining declining political participation among young people. Once understood, remedial measures can be taken to increase youth political participation in American democracy.

## RECENT EFFORTS TO REINVIGORATE THE PUBLIC SPIRIT

On December 21, 2004, President Bush signed into law the American History and Civics Education Act of 2004. The purpose of the bill is to "establish academies for teachers and students of American history and civics and a national alliance of teachers of American history and civics, and for other purposes." The legislation institutionalizes the National Endowment for the Humanities' program "We the People," for elementary and secondary school students. We the People teaches American history and civics through grants to teachers and scholars and provides summer institutes and seminars for American history teachers. The program provides curriculum suggestions for teachers and recommends readings for students. The new legislation allocates funds to establish presidential learning academies for teachers of American history and civics, congressional summer academies for students, and a national alliance of American history and civics teachers.

The legislation is laudable for its focus on teaching American history and civics, and it has inspired national debate on the proper content of history and civics curricula. The legislation also provides much-needed funding for the continuing education of history and civics teachers. In all, this federal legislation legitimizes the importance of teaching history and civics. This is crucial, as No Child Left Behind programs have not prioritized American history and civics.

The We the People curriculum does not, however, focus on civic skills. While a solid history and civics curriculum such as We the People can teach students about the role of political participation in American democracy and even political knowledge, its primary aim is not to teach participatory skills and abilities.

Currently, American civic education appears to embrace either individuality or civicism, without meeting a common center. In practice, civic education is focused on either civics courses or service learning (Boyte 2003). While civics courses emphasize liberal political theory and are rights centered, service learning emphasizes volunteerism and communitarianism (Boyte 2003). Boyte maintains that teaching students about public work and organizing skills is absent from these two common approaches. In particular, Patrick and Hoge (1991) show that high school civics textbooks are focused on teaching American political institutions and do not teach participatory skills.

Westheimer and Kahne (2004) document the accelerated increase in service-learning programs available to high school students. While these programs are important to teach a commitment to serve others, they teach a nonparticipatory form of political citizenship. In particular, the authors find "the emphasis placed on personal responsibility and character an inadequate response to the challenges of educating a democratic citizenry" (243). Conrad (1991) asserts that experiential learning can teach skills directly related to the learning environment, such as child-care skills learned through interaction with a day-care center. However, these skills can be particular to the task at hand and not easily transferable to political participation.

Overall, neither traditional civic education course work nor service-learning approaches always teach participatory skills. With a historical shift in civics course content from a "problems in government" approach to a service-learning emphasis, the teaching of civic skills has been lost. While the "problems" courses taught not just political knowledge but also participatory and communication skills (and hopefully inspired political engagement), service-learning requirements often sacrifice political participation and political skills for a focus on community volunteerism.

We have yet to formulate the perfect civics course content that teaches political knowledge and civic skills and inspires political engagement. What is known, however, is that political participation among Americans under the age of thirty is lacking. If levels of youth participation in politics continue to decline, this subpopulation is in danger of losing any influence on the political conversation.

## The Real Problem

The American founders felt that public education should provide a moral education and form character in future citizens. In particular, President George Washington urged Congress to support a civic education that would consist of "teaching the people themselves to know and value their own rights; [and] to distinguish between oppression and the necessary exercise of lawful authority" (Fitzpatrick 1939 [1790], 493). John Dewey and Charles Merriam also espoused the necessity of education for developing characteristics of citizenship in a democracy, and the responsibility of American schools to teach youth how to participate in a democracy (Niemi and Junn 1998). Benjamin Franklin maintained that good schools should include the value of promoting democracy in their curricula (Hochschild and Scovronick 2000).

Today, the purpose and content of civic education remains a subject of deliberation. Communities often debate which normative purposes and values to teach. Civic education teaches values that can conflict, such as patriotism versus membership in a global society, or socially acceptable attitudes of character versus independent thinking (Nelson 1991). Civic education requirements and curricula differ among states, and again among school districts within states. However, even when civic education policies mandate civic requirements, they often do not mandate the values and norms to be taught.

State policies requiring civics course work or examinations vary widely. In general, over 70 percent of American ninth grade students have studied a civics topic, according to the International Association for the Evaluation of Educational Achievement Civic Education survey (IEA/CivEd) (Torney-Purta et al. 2001). The majority of states require a government or civics course for high school graduation, while fewer have a state statute requiring schools to offer government or civics courses (CIRCLE 2004b). As of 2003, only five states required students to pass a social studies examination as a high school graduation requirement (National Center for Learning and Citizenship 2003). While state assessment systems are often a focus of education reform, only twenty-two states' assessment systems include knowledge of government or civics (Education Commission of the States 2004). State civic education policies are summarized in table 6.1.

The nature of civic education course work has changed over the last fifty years. Course work comprising problems in government has decreased, while coursework about American government institutions has predominated (Niemi and Smith 2001; Weiss et al. 2001). Generally, "problems" courses invite more classroom discussion about public life, while American government courses teach basic facts about government institutions and processes (Carnegie Corporation of New York and CIRCLE 2003). The difference between these two curricula is teaching group discussion skills. In turn, students today may be taking American government and civics courses without learning communication and group discussion skills.

The content of civic education curricula is often discussed. The 1983 Educational Reform Reports promoted literacy as the primary curricular focus for schools. Literacy took precedence over teaching social and civic skills as the primary goal for education (Ascher 1983). Today, current No Child Left Behind legislation prioritizes reading and mathematics skills over civics or arts instruction.

**Table 6.1.   State Civic Education Policies**

| | |
|---|---|
| Course Requirement in Civics for At Least 3 Credits of Social Studies / History | AL, AK, CA, DE, GA, HI, ID, IN, KS, KY, LA, MD, MN, MS, NC, ND, NM, OR, SD, TN, UT, VT, VA, WI, WV, WY |
| Course Requirement Specifically Mentions Constitution | AZ, GA, MA, ME, NM, ND, SC, WY |
| Course Requirement for Social Studies Includes Civics or American Government | AL, AR, CA, CO, CT, DC, FL, GA, HI, ID, IN, IA, KS, KY, LA, ME, MD, MA, MS, MN, MI, MO, NV, NH, NM, NY, NC, ND, OH, OK, OR, PA, SC, SD, TN, TX, UT, VA, WI, WA, WV, WY |
| State Assessment Includes Civics | CA, DE, GA, IL, IN, KS, KY, LA, MD, MI, MO, MT, MA, NC, NM, OH, OK, SC, TX, UT, VA, WI |
| State Evaluations of Schools Measure Civic Outcomes | CA, HI, GA, IL, IN, KY, LA, MD, MI, MS, NH, OH, SC, TX, VA |

*Source:* Education Commission of the States, July, 2005, and the Center for Information and Research on Civic Learning and Engagement (CIRCLE).

Some scholars advocate a focus on civics instruction. Patrick (2000) priori-tizes civic education for schools. Within civic education curricula, he empha-sizes equal teaching of both civic knowledge and skills. Patrick claims that teaching civic knowledge coupled with cognitive and intellectual civic skills is necessary for civic education to be "an effective agent of civic development among American youth" (2).

Gutmann (2000) also calls on public schools to cultivate skills essential for democratic virtues. Gutmann (1987) declares that teaching civic education, including knowledge, virtues, and skills necessary for political participation, "has moral primacy over other purposes of public education in a democratic society" (287). Gutmann further contends that democratic virtue should be taught in history and civics courses. Teaching democratic virtue should care-fully include the "willingness and ability of citizens to reason collectively and critically about politics" (107). She also emphasizes the importance of educa-tion as a means of conscious social reproduction for a society, or a means of transmitting political values to other generations. Patrick (2002) points out the paradox inherent in her emphasis, in that the promotion of specific political ideals is coupled with teaching the importance of free and independent think-ing as a cornerstone to democracy. In this sense, it is essential to teach com-peting ideas of an individual's right to liberties and the importance of civic republicanism (Patrick 2002). Goodlad (1996) also maintains that successful democratic education finds a common center between teaching individuality and civic responsibility.

## Potential Solutions

Numerous researchers have examined whether civics courses contribute to civic engagement and political knowledge. However, little research addresses the rela-tionship between civics courses and civic skill development in young people.

Niemi and Junn (1998), using the National Assessment of Educational Progress survey, find a positive relationship between civics coursework and civic and political knowledge. Torney-Purta (2002), using the IEA/CivEd sur-vey, finds increased civic knowledge and engagement among students who take civics courses. The IEA/CivEd survey examined numerous types of civic education requirements. A recent study by the National Conference of State Legislatures and partners suggests that civic education results in an increased likelihood of voting and increased civic knowledge and engagement (Kurtz et al. 2003). Finally, McDevitt et al. (2003) and the Carnegie Corporation of New York and the Center for Information and Research on Civic Learning and Engagement (2003) recognize program evaluations detailing the positive effects of specific civics curricula on political engagement and knowledge.

A few studies have examined the contribution of civic education to building civic knowledge and engagement. Niemi and Junn (1998), using data from the 1988 National Assessment of Educational Progress Civics Assessment, show that those students exposed to civics instruction display greater levels of political knowledge. Torney-Purta (2002) reports that open classroom climates are linked with greater levels of civic knowledge and that civics coursework can prepare students for engagement in civil society.

Furthermore, while theories of political participation are numerous, theories of the origins of political abilities are scarce. Most theories of political participation explain why people want to participate, not whether they are able to participate. With the exception of resource-based theories, theories of participation do not consider the contribution of skills and abilities to political participation. Resource-based theories document the importance of resources such as money, time, knowledge, skills, self-confidence, and political efficacy in promoting political participation. Yet even resource-based theories do not explain the derivation of civic skills and abilities in individuals. Although incomplete, resource-based theories provide the best available framework for understanding a relationship between civic skills and political participation. However, a clear theory of the origins of civic skills remains absent.[2]

Patrick (2002) maintains that a combination of political knowledge and civic skills is necessary for thriving democratic citizens. In particular, "knowledgeable citizens are better citizens of a democracy in regard to their possession and use of civic skills" (11). He links political knowledge with greater levels of political engagement. He describes knowledge of concepts such as republicanism, constitutionalism, human rights and liberalism, and citizenship as essential civic knowledge components (12). Although Patrick's description of the relationship between civic skills and political knowledge is brief, it is clear that they are distinct components of a democratic citizen.

Delli Carpini and Keeter (1996) define political knowledge as the "range of factual information about politics stored in long-term memory . . . the most important component of a broader notion of political sophistication" (294). The authors strongly link political knowledge with political action. Political knowledge, they assert, contributes to political participation, the construction of citizens' opinions, and political action in relation to citizens' interests (219). Their study also asserts that significant differences exist among Americans' individual levels of political knowledge. Importantly, greater knowledge leads to greater political participation, thus increasing the legitimacy of a democracy. They also contend that political efficacy and trust influence levels of political learning (219).

Popkin and Dimock (1999) study political knowledge, specifically examining citizens' knowledge of how government works. While they agree with

Patrick (2002) and Delli Carpini and Keeter (1996) that higher levels of political knowledge lead to higher political participation in the form of voter turnout, they contend that high levels of political knowledge are not necessary for voters to make informed political decisions. They maintain that voters can be sufficiently competent through the use of information shortcuts to make political judgments (120). These shortcuts are used to help citizens make political decisions by incorporating experiences of daily life, the media, and campaigns to process political information (120).

The study of political knowledge speaks to the question of whether citizens who make public decisions are capable of the task. Lupia and McCubbins (1998) label this problem the democratic dilemma. They conclude that a lack of political knowledge can be acceptable, however, as decision makers will substitute advice from other people and institutions for their own lack of political knowledge. They assert that "reasoned choice does not require full information" (2). Other political scientists agree that judgmental shortcuts, or heuristics, can be substituted for significant political knowledge to make political decisions (Hacker and Pierson 2005; Iyengar 1990; Sniderman et al. 1991).

When civic skills are defined as abilities necessary for political participation, the shortcut process itself is a civic skill. For some citizens, sufficient political decision making may bypass the need for political knowledge when heuristics lead to informed political judgments. Although extensive political knowledge may be unnecessary, the skill of using heuristics is necessary for making political decisions.

Hacker and Pierson (2005) describe "New Pluralism" as the belief that "a rough version of citizen control over politicians exists, even though political resources, including political knowledge, are distributed unequally" (5). In this sense, individuals are capable of protecting their own interests. This differs from "Old Pluralism," or the concept that citizen power to shape politics was held in group memberships. Groups could effectively fight for citizens' interests (5). Page and Shapiro (1992) provide evidence of Old Pluralism. They contend that the aggregate value of voter decisions is more powerful and more rational than individual voter decisions alone. These authors are confident that successful political decision making occurs, despite a lack of political knowledge among individuals.

Though existing literature does not provide a particularly nuanced view of the relationship between civic skills and political knowledge, a clear difference between skills and knowledge exists. Civic skills are abilities necessary for political actions, while political knowledge is familiarity with political information, regardless of the intention of political action. Furthermore, extensive levels of political knowledge can be unnecessary when citizens use judgmental shortcuts to make political decisions. The process of using heuristics to make political decisions is a civic skill. Overall, civic skills are necessary for individuals to make political decisions. Political knowledge is helpful, but potentially not required, for individuals to make political decisions.

Finally, some researchers hypothesize that education can be a source of civic skill development. Verba et al. (1995) correlate education with increased civic skills. They assert that primary skills such as reading and writing are necessary for political participation, and that increased education leads to greater political participation. More common, however, are studies such as Patrick's (2002) that catalog the civic skills that should be taught in schools. Yet his work and others lack a rigorous study of whether schools are actually teaching these skills.

Elsewhere, I describe civic skills as scarce resources that are unequally distributed (Comber 2005). My examination of various data sets shows that minority race/ethnicity students hold lower levels of civic skills than more privileged students, but that all students learn some types of civic skills in civics classroom settings. I provide evidence that for some civic skills, such as political interpretation skills, racial/ethnic minorities and low-income students may only have opportunities to learn civic skills in school. Overall, civic skills are not equally distributed among different race, ethnicity, household income, gender, and noncollege populations.

According to the Civic Mission of Schools report, a promising approach to teaching civic skills includes class discussion, student voice in school government, and simulations (Carnegie Corporation of New York and CIRCLE 2003). All of these methods should be used to teach civic skills. The *New York Times*'s Learning Network Daily Lesson Plan[3] offers numerous lesson plans for civics teachers. Many of these implicitly teach civic skills. For example, in one lesson plan called "Stunning Recommendation," students study current research on stun guns and safety and write letters to their elected officials about whether stun guns should be further regulated. In another lesson, students assess the charitable needs of their community and create a mock charitable organization to address these needs. Still other lessons urge students to form their own opinions on current topics and to express themselves through writing or art. These lessons can teach participatory, organizational, and communication skills to students.

Overall, further research is needed to understand what is happening inside civic education classrooms. While evidence exists that civics courses can teach political knowledge, further research is needed to determine whether civics courses are teaching civic skills and political engagement. Also, a large gap in current research comprises the effects, influence, and interaction of alternative sources of civic skill development with civic education. Alternative sources include parents, families, and students' home environments;

part-time job requirements and activities; after-school group activities; group memberships; and participation in religious organizations.

## CONCLUSION

In the United States, the concept of equal political participation as a human right is relatively new. Women have been voting for eighty-five years, African Americans have had their vote legally protected for only forty years, and eighteen-year-olds have been voting for thirty-four years. While political influence and political participation have historically been reserved for the privileged, equalizing the ability for all to participate is a newer concept. How citizens learn the abilities to participate, and how these abilities can be equalized among all citizens is of grave concern to a fair and representative democracy. Schools, and civics courses, are one reliable source of civic skill and political knowledge development.

However, what is it about civics courses that can inspire political participation, convey political knowledge, and increase civic skill levels? We do know that recent service-learning requirements are associated with an increase in volunteerism and community service activities. While these activities inspire civic engagement, they are not focused on political engagement. We also know that the taking of civics courses is associated with increased political knowledge, and sometimes with increased civic skill levels. But what is it about these classrooms that provides such results? How can success stories be replicated in other classrooms and schools? As researchers and teachers, we have yet to formulate this model.

While young people can learn political knowledge and civic skills from many sources, such as their home environment, extracurricular activities, and part-time jobs, schools remain the obvious choice to take the lead in nurturing political engagement among young people. Schools have unparalleled access to young people and a historical mandate to transfer political values and knowledge to younger generations. Civic education experts recently convened by the Center for Information and Research on Civic Learning and Engagement (CIRCLE) agree that "high schools matter in particular, as they are the last place where messages about democracy can reach all young people regardless of their socio-economic status or future educational goals" (Donovan 2005, 1).

Can civics courses be a solution to the youth participation deficit? The evidence shows that they can, if they engage in open classroom climates, teach political knowledge, and inspire engaged discussion that fosters civic skills. Yet civics is not available to all American students, and, in particular, the teaching of civic skills and civic engagement is not a priority for education reform policies.

Civics courses that take new approaches to teaching, such as open classroom climates, or old approaches, such as discussing problems in government, may have the recipe for success. As the Civic Mission of Schools report recommends, schools should establish civic education curricula at every grade level to incorporate discussion, provide political knowledge, require community service, and encourage student participation (Carnegie Corporation of New York and CIRCLE 2003). Policy makers should consider emphasizing strong civics coursework as a means of equalizing political participation among generations, thereby strengthening our democracy.

Finally, what was it about the 2004 presidential campaign and election that inspired record voter turnout among young people and increased political activism? Along with promising school approaches, the origins of this recent increase in political participation should be explored and examined, and its lessons should be applied toward future politics.

Overall, a new rise in volunteer activity and community service is not to be disregarded. With recent cuts in social welfare spending and social program spending, more and more Americans rely on the hard work and kindness of volunteers and community organizations. Surely the impoverished, the homeless, the hungry, and the environment benefit from volunteer hours and the generous efforts of strangers.

However, voluntarism in isolation will not change cycles of poverty or counter the origins of poverty. Volunteering at a food bank can change the plight of a few families that day, but volunteering coupled with political activism can change the root problems of hunger in America, making the food bank unnecessary. Community service cannot replace old-fashioned lobbying and activism.

Yet political participation does not receive the same attention as service learning currently enjoys. If political participation were similar in focus to community service, President Bush would be urging us to vote and contact our elected officials, college admissions officers and human resources recruiters would ask whether you voted, and holding a voter registration drive and political activism would count toward service-learning requirements. As these are not the case, much work needs to be done to highlight the importance of political engagement. Schools should originate this. As schools have been the primary impetus for an increase in service learning, they can also be instrumental in encouraging political participation and teaching civic skills and political knowledge. Schools and school-related programs need to do the difficult work of teaching both community involvement and volunteerism, along with political engagement and political activism. Only then will a generation of citizens armed to effectuate social change exist.

## NOTES

1. I thank Mark Hugo Lopez, Peter Levine, and Dan Shea for helpful comments on previous drafts of this chapter. Grant support from the Center for Information and Research on Civic Learning and Engagement (CIRCLE) at the University of Maryland School of Public Policy is gratefully acknowledged.

2. Resource-based theorists include Rosenstone and Hansen (1993) and Verba et al. (1995). Other theories of political participation are described in Downs (1957), Green and Shapiro (1994), Barzel and Silberberg (1973), Abramson and Aldrich (1982), and Miller and Krosnick (2004).

3. See www.nytimes.com/learning/teachers/lessons/civics.html.

# 7

## Promoting Diversity in Democracy: Mobilizing the Hip-Hop Generation

*Maya Rockeymoore and Mark Rockeymoore*

As the gains of the civil rights movement have been rolled back, many children of those who fought the desegregation and equality battles of the 1950s and 1960s have passively observed as national leaders have effected or perpetuated laws that leave their communities disadvantaged compared to other communities. Ironically, their passivity in the face of this onslaught has left them voiceless in the world of politics at just the time they have gained a deafening voice in the cultural sphere through hip-hop music and culture.

This sociopolitical imbalance has relegated an entire generation of black and brown young adults to stereotypical images in the mass media, as well as in the greater public imagination. This has resulted in an overarching attitude of dismissive contempt concerning the relevance of young minorities in politics. At the same time, their incentives to vote and participate in the political process have been overshadowed by commonly held opinions that politics and politicians are corrupt, and that political participation—especially voting—is a waste of time and effort. Many minority young men and women simply do not believe that they have the power to make a difference.

The Hip-Hop Generation is now facing a full-blown crisis, as apathy and diminishing educational and economic opportunities have become widespread. More than fifty years after the landmark Supreme Court decision desegregating America's schools, African American and Hispanic youth continue to be marginalized and segregated in the U.S. education system (Orfield and Lee 2005). Many of these students are subjected to high-poverty, low-performing schools with poorly qualified teachers (Rothstein 2004). The lack of quality educational preparation undermines the likelihood of economic self-sufficiency for the individual, and it suggests dire consequences down the road.

Indeed, the consequences are already apparent. "McJobs," low-paying employment at fast-food restaurants and within other sectors of the service economy (Coupland 1991) abound, while real economic opportunities have been reduced to few or none as jobs with decent wages and benefits, traditionally available to low-skilled workers, have been exported abroad. With high minority unemployment and high school dropout rates feeding the cancerous growth of a growing underclass, the lure of the underground economy has become stronger. This has, in part, contributed to the unprecedented number of black and Latino men populating the U.S. prison system (Herivel and Wright 2003; Orfield and Lee 2005).

With so many negative indicators converging to narrow the potential of black and Hispanic youth, the remedy must be rooted in dramatic and comprehensive public policy shifts at the federal, state, and local levels. To date, however, there has been no significant movement to enact policy reforms that would address the issues undermining the progress of the Hip-Hop Generation. On the contrary, all evidence indicates that today's political climate contains perverse incentives that reward politicians for proclaiming that they are tough on crime, even as they overlook the injustices of the system, or for boasting that they are dedicated to strengthening education, even as they fail to take on the gross inequities that make some schools nothing more than low-quality day-care centers. This situation is able to continue because those who stand the most to gain from policy changes—low income, minority, urban, rural, youth—are the most disorganized, disengaged, and politically disempowered of all groups.

To counteract the looming crisis of U.S. democracy, a powerful new constituency must rise up to challenge the policies that are leaving so many behind and subverting the economic productivity of our country. As a growing percentage of the nation's youth and general population, African Americans, Latinos, and other racial and ethnic minorities must become the new constituency that will confront and engage the political system and the public policies that currently keep them marginalized. Indeed, the voice and power of the Hip-Hop Generation must be awakened from its slumber to focus its members on making a purposeful and sustained difference nationally and in their own communities and lives.

## THE PROBLEM

Perhaps one of the most powerful cohorts of all time, the Hip-Hop Generation is loosely defined as those born between the years of 1964 to 1984—although younger generations also embrace the term—who grew to maturity surrounded by the style, vision, and sound of hip-hop music and culture (Kitwana 2003). This generation is powerful because it has used unprecedented creativity, resourcefulness, and brainpower to become a cultural and marketing phenomenon recognized around the globe. From London to Tokyo, Nairobi to Rio, hip-hop music is embraced by those attracted to its irresistible beats, edgy lyrics, and irreverent style. While the culture of hip-hop bonds young people together across race, ethnicity, gender, class, religion, and nationality, the face of hip-hop primarily reflects the lifestyles, preferences, and habits of African American and Latino youth.

And yet, even as the power of the Hip-Hop Generation reigns supreme in popular culture, its influence is negligible in the political sphere. As research and news accounts indicate, this may be due to the feelings of alienation that young people in general—but African American and Latino youth in particular—have expressed toward the U.S. political process. Indeed, black and Latino youth are the most likely to report that voting is not important and that they can make little difference in solving the problems of their communities (Lopez and Kirby 2005). Even with the results of the 2004 presidential elections, when youth turnout spiked 12 percent for whites, 11 percent for African Americans, and 5 to 10 percent for Asian, Native, and Hispanic Americans, voter turnout still hovered around 50 percent or less for all groups (Lopez and Kirby 2005). Lackluster participation and negative perceptions among racial and ethnic minority youth—the fastest-growing population in the United States—present clear evidence that significant efforts to increase their involvement must be undertaken if our nation is to achieve a strong and robust democracy.

Achieving this goal will be difficult, however, given the significant structural and psychosocial challenges facing disaffected groups. Weak political participation among minority youth can be viewed as symptomatic of larger structural problems inhibiting the political socialization process. The education system presents one such problem. The loss of civic education courses in schools with high populations of racial and ethnic minorities has resulted in a "civic achievement gap" (Levinson 2004). This has distinctly negative consequences, as civic education has been proven to produce stronger civic skills—such as interpreting political literature, writing effective letters, and making statements—among African American and Latino youth (Comber 2005). These skills are necessary for building an informed citizenry—the foundation of democratic society.

For those schools that do offer government courses, underfunding has led to a dangerously weakened curriculum that fails to teach students how the political system works and their role in it. Indeed, strapped budgets have produced high school government teachers who lack expertise in the area, outdated text books that keep young people ignorant of contemporary political history and misinformed about not-so-ancient U.S. history, and schools that lack the means to organize field trips to places such as state capitols and local council chambers, where students can see government at work. To illustrate this point, there are young people graduating from Washington, D.C. high schools today who have never entered the nation's Capitol, only two miles from where they have grown up.

A dearth of political learning in the home environment presents another problem contributing to the gap in civics education. Many in the Hip-Hop Generation have never seen their parents vote, have not heard people close to them discussing current political events, and have not been the beneficiaries of stories and discussions that place U.S. history in its proper context. Indeed, a majority of Latino youth (52 percent) report that they have not talked about politics with their parents, followed by African American (47 percent) and white (37 percent) youth (Lopez and Kirby 2005).

A final structural problem lies in the decline in traditional membership in civic organizations that historically served as a bridge to political involvement for some Americans. Robert Putnam (2000a) attributes this dramatic reversal in part to the spread of technologies that promote individual pursuits over group involvement. Ironically, this decline has not made much of a difference for racial and ethnic minorities, since these groups were not actively recruited for membership in mainstream civic organizations during the height of their popularity. However, the decline in these vaunted institutions has exacerbated the challenges of mobilizing minority youth, as previously effective approaches for engaging groups at the grassroots level have disappeared.

Much has been written about the decline of U.S. political parties (Aldrich 1995; Crotty and Jacobson 1980; Wattenburg 1996). Some of this literature has discussed the waning influence that parties have in organizing people at the grassroots level (Shea 2003). Structural deficits such as a lack of strong grassroots infrastructure in the current two-party political system perpetuate the alienation of minority youth. For example, African American (70 percent) and Latino (43 percent) youth are more likely than young whites (28 percent) to identify with the Democratic Party (Lopez and Kirby 2005). Despite their strong party identification, the Democratic Party as a whole lacks a comprehensive strategy for sustaining and growing its base of support within these communities. The existing minority outreach divisions of the Democratic National Committee have no ongoing acculturation programs targeting a younger generation of black and Latino Americans, and the organization's website contains no way of recruiting new supporters. Party get-out-the-vote efforts, which could serve as a recruitment tool, targeting resources toward African Americans and Latinos, are usually conducted in an ad hoc fashion immediately prior to elections. Once the election is over, however, there is no follow-up, and the party position returns to its pattern of benign neglect.

On the contrary, the Republican National Committee has launched an effort to recruit "new faces and new voices" within these communities, and they have the tools, electronic and otherwise, to recruit. Yet the policy message of the Republican Party does not seem to resonate with many black and Latino youth, if party identification is taken as a measure. Although the Republican Party is seeking to increase support in these communities, the proof will be in whether their outreach efforts have long-term impact by creating and communicating policy positions that will appeal to these populations.

A final structural problem is that nonprofit organizations within communities of color that are attuned to this issue are severely underfunded, resulting in piecemeal and insufficient efforts to engage the target audience.

Structural challenges to minority youth participation are exacerbated by a host of psychosocial issues rooted in stark realities. Young minority Americans perceive that there are a number of social ills impacting their communities that appear to be unaddressed or ineffectively addressed by current policies. The grossly disproportionate presence of African American and Latino men in the criminal (in)justice system, the random and not-so-random violence perpetrated in urban communities, the skyrocketing and disproportionate rates of HIV/AIDS infection and other preventable chronic health conditions, the dysfunctional nature of urban education, and dramatic inequities in unemployment rates—especially among teens and young adults—are a few of the stark realities that young black and brown youth face on a daily basis. Exacerbating these problems is the perception that there is a lack of political will from policy makers on "both sides of the aisle" to promote policy alternatives that would alleviate these conditions. In the face of persistent inequities, young minority Americans logically conclude that "the system" does not care about them or the challenges they face.

Their cynicism is fueled by a deep and abiding distrust in the U.S. government. It is no secret that some in the Hip-Hop Generation, like generations before them, express hostility toward government because they understand how it has been used to oppress various groups throughout history. Instead of engaging the system, therefore, they say that it makes no sense to participate in America's institutions of government when America has worked to actively undermine their group's well-being and continues to make no effort to do right by them.

In addition to neglected social ills, young people of color are alienated further due to a paucity of established channels through which they can develop and engage new policy ideas or express their sociopolitical aspirations. While some have used the tools of popular culture (e.g., hip-hop/rap, poetry) to express discontent with, or hope for, their plight, and a few have actually found ways to directly engage the political system (e.g., congressional staff, interns, advocacy groups), countless others have been left without viable outlets through which they can articulate concerns, propose solutions, and work constructively toward implementing their preferred vision for a better society.

Complicating matters is the reality that young people of color see few people that look like them or speak from their perspective in the mass media or in positions of party leadership. With very few exceptions, there seem to be few media opportunities for young black policy analysts, politicos, party officials, and other policy/political professionals (or aspiring professionals) who seek to enter the public debate on contemporary policy issues. A good example of this glaring disparity is that, on both race-specific and general issues that have implications for racial and ethnic populations, white media pundits are most often called upon for their "expert" opinion. The absence of black political and policy professionals in the media is carried over to the influential Sunday-morning talk shows, where one study found that fewer than 8 percent of the guest appearances featured African Americans (Jones 2005). This lack of media representation serves to increase the perception among young blacks that policy and political issues are not for or about them and their lives.

The Census Bureau projects that by 2050, half of the U.S. population will comprise black and brown Americans. This steep growth in minority representation will have dangerous implications for the future viability of U.S. democracy if effective vehicles are not put in place to educate, mobilize, and inspire new generations about the value of civic participation.

## SOLUTIONS

Even though many young people have bought into the hype that they are not politically involved or interested, this conclusion ignores a stark reality: young people have been at the forefront of almost every contemporary social movement that has influenced the political process and made a difference in the quality of life for people in the United States and around the world. From the civil rights movement, the women's rights movement, and Vietnam to the antiapartheid movement in South Africa, the struggle for democracy in China, and the new antiwar and antiglobalization efforts, students and other young people have dedicated their time, energy, and passion to achieving political change. Clearly, then, stimulating young people to involve themselves in politics is not a lost cause; but the systems that should be in place to teach youth civic responsibility may be a lost cause if significant institutional and policy reforms are not adopted.

Despite growing civic-learning deficiencies in traditional institutions such as schools, families, and political parties, there have been independent organizational efforts to mobilize young people of color to become more engaged in politics. The most innovative and recent of these are represented by the National Hip-Hop Political Convention, Black Youth Vote!, the Hip-Hop Summit Action Network, the Hip-Hop Caucus, and the Vote or Die campaign. These culturally specific, community initiated and directed initiatives have used the appeal and marketing tactics of hip-hop music and culture as a platform to reach out to minority youth on political issues. Although no study has directly attributed the increased participation of minority youth in the 2004 election cycle to these initiatives, a solid argument can be made that they heightened awareness about the need for more youth involvement in the political process and provided insight into new ways to engage minority youth.

Even though these nonprofit organizations are helping to address current deficits in civic education, the fact remains that they do not have the capacity to meet the educational needs of all current and future minority youth. Entities that have traditionally been in the best position to mandate and provide widespread support for civic education are federal, state, and local governments through curricula and programs offered through the public school system and strategic grants provided to external organizations. The scope of the need is so great, however, that organizations, institutions, and agencies must develop strategic ways to work together in creating relevant and robust civic education opportunities for youth. The overarching goal of increasing minority-youth political engagement must focus on providing age and culturally appropriate interventions that include leadership development, civic education on contemporary and historical issues, and learning materials and tools that will facilitate the political and policy learning process.

Recommendations to facilitate these strategic objectives are as follows:

- Increase support for civic education programs, initiatives, and organizations. Philanthropists, foundations, and governments should prioritize civic education as a giving or grants strategy to promote democracy in the United States. Significant attention and funds should be directed toward community-based organizations (existing or proposed) that seek to engage young people from racial and ethnic minority populations. City and statewide civic initiatives should also be encouraged as long as they have a well-documented strategy for engaging minority youth.
- Set quality standards for civic education curricula at the secondary school level. All youth should have access to a quality civic education curriculum regardless of their location or background. School systems should expand and strengthen their curricula to meet accepted standards that promote civic knowledge, skills, and community participation.
- Institutionalize civic-focused "field trips" for minority middle and high school students. In an effort to promote real-world exposure and learning,

a broad initiative should be established that links middle and high school classes in urban and rural schools with civic institutions and governmental entities at the local, state, and federal levels. Since these students attend schools that are least likely to dedicate the resources to promote community-based civic learning opportunities, a concerted effort must be made to expose the students to institutions that illustrate how government works.

- Create channels to expose youth to careers in public policy and politics. While they may be unaware of the terminology used by professionals, many young Americans of color have perspectives about the current policy and political environment and ideas about how to achieve a better future. Yet these individuals rarely get an opportunity to share their valuable insight with the nation because there is a paucity of outlets through which they can examine, shape, and engage in communications about politics and public policy. Exposing more young people from diverse backgrounds to professional careers in the policy and political arenas should bridge this gap. Paid internship and fellowship opportunities, such as those offered by the Public Policy and International Affairs Fellowship Program, at institutions such as think tanks, lobbying shops, advocacy organizations, and governmental offices should be expanded to target more individuals from disadvantaged backgrounds. These on-the-job training experiences will help develop a cadre of minority young adults with the skills to produce culturally relevant policy briefs, fact sheets, research reports, and other policy products that help to set the parameters for contemporary political debates. In an effort to diversify the opinions communicated through the mass media, these young adults should also be trained to produce opinion editorials for placement in minority-specific and mainstream news sources, and to participate in television, radio, and other media opportunities.
- Engage students in policy and political issues at minority-serving institutions of higher learning. There are 116 historically black colleges and universities, 32 tribal colleges and universities, and about 164 Hispanic-serving institutions in the United States. These institutions enroll thousands of voting-age students from diverse racial and ethnic backgrounds, yet there have been no sustained, targeted efforts to enlist their support in initiatives to promote civic engagement. College leadership tours, training institutes, and other programs such as an annual retreat or conference for "emerging leaders" should be developed to engage minority students, encourage them to become politically active, build their leadership skills, and help them to learn about contemporary policy issues.

- Develop empowerment products that help reinforce civic education goals. Books, newspapers, audiovisual products, and websites are important sources of information dissemination and political learning in U.S. society. There are many political news sources targeting adults, but few that offer age-appropriate, culture-specific products to reach young people of all ages and backgrounds. There should be a concerted effort to fill this gap by developing products that engage minority youth and empower them to know that they are vital and equal members of society. Examples of learning tools may include coloring books chronicling important minority political figures, teen-zines that highlight how young people can make a difference in their communities, and television shows that cover policy and political issues from a fresh, youthful perspective. These strategies and products can be easily converted to an online format and customized to reach diverse populations.
- Create or expand membership in advocacy organizations that involve minority youth in civic activities. Young people need organized ways through which they can learn civic leadership skills and how to define their role as citizens in a democratic society. Traditionally, programs such as the American Legion's Boys State and Girls State have served as excellent training grounds for high school students to learn about all aspects of government. The intent and the parameters of these programs should be expanded and updated to target young people living in underserved and underresourced areas. These initiatives can be offered through existing organizations such as the NAACP or the League of United Latin American Citizens and can be customized to meet the twelve-to-eighteen age demographic. Political parties that are interested in growing their organizational base could also launch similar programs that engage young people while teaching them about policy issues.
- Use contemporary marketing tactics to engage young people of color. Recent efforts to reach out to members of the Hip-Hop Generation have used innovative record-label advertising tactics to reach out to and encourage young people to vote. The use of high-profile minority celebrities, street teams of young people to engage their peers, radio public-service announcements and interviews, outreach on youth and culture-specific websites, and glossy posters placed in neighborhoods or other locations where young people congregate present several promising outreach tactics that can been studied and expanded upon.
- Involve churches and other nontraditional community-based entities in civic education activities. While churches cannot be involved in partisan political activities, many are centers of learning that can be used

to provide civic education and leadership-development programs. Programs like after-school or Saturday leadership training courses should be offered to young people in church and other community-based settings as a means of supplementing the curriculum offered in schools.

## CONCLUSION

U.S. civic education has traditionally included the "marketplace of ideas" theory to help explain how freedom of expression within democracies is supposed to work. According to this theory, a wide range of ideas and opinions are presented in the public sphere, and the best of those ideas rise to the top to become accepted policies or laws. In the textbook version of this theory, it is implied that any individual from any background or circumstance is eligible to offer ideas that can help to shape the direction and future of this country. In practice, however, the areas of the marketplace with the most influence on public opinion—television, radio, and newspaper opinion pages—have been the most tightly controlled, open almost exclusively to white educated men.

To support broad civic participation in the United States, the marketplace of ideas must be expanded by the deliberate cultivation of people representing a diversity of backgrounds, experiences, and views. This cannot be achieved if the full participation of certain populations in society is stunted by inadequate investments in civic education. The growing racial and ethnic diversity of the country demands that U.S. politics move beyond the archaic formula of government for the few by the few. If our country is to increase the number of minority youth exposed to and involved in the political process, there must be comprehensive and ongoing efforts to develop and engage a new generation of citizens from populations that have been historically marginalized in U.S. society.

# IV

## NONPARTISAN ORGANIZATIONS
## AND TURNING OUT THE YOUTH VOTE

# 8

# Youth Political Engagement: Why Rock the Vote Hits the Wrong Note

*Michael Hoover and Susan Orr*

**W**estern liberal democracies have witnessed declining voter participation in recent decades. Figures indicate that most were experiencing lower turnout at the end of the twentieth century than they had been forty years earlier (Institute for Democracy and Electoral Assistance 2004).[1] According to some, low turnout puts the very legitimacy of the democratic system at risk (Lijphart 1997; Patterson 2003; Putnam 2000a). Observers express particular concern that young nonvoters will exclude themselves from the electoral process throughout their lifetimes; thus, low youth turnout raises particular concerns. With this in mind, let us look at some U.S. figures indicating a general downturn in youth voting, offset by the occasional upward spike (see figure 8.1). Voting among eighteen- to twenty-four-year-olds fell from almost 50 percent of the voting age population in the 1972 presidential election to 40 percent in 1984, hitting a low of 32 percent in 1996 (U.S. Census Bureau 2005). While this decline was offset in 1992 when 43 percent of this group went to the polls, the percentage of eighteen- to twenty-four-year-olds voting in 2000 matched the historic low of 1996. Youth turnout then rose again in 2004 when 42 percent of eligible eighteen- to twenty-four-year-olds went to the polls (turnout among eighteen to twenty four-year-olds who were eligible was 46.7 percent).

While it is indisputable that young people vote less than the general population (Conway 2000; Wolfinger and Rosenstone 1980), the implications of this circumstance are unclear. Is low youth turnout a perpetual consequence of a "life stage," or has there recently developed an "age group" crisis? How someone answers this question is significant in that it will largely determine whether or not they think the situation warrants attention and action. In this chapter, we consider theories that have been posited about the link between

**Figure 8.1**

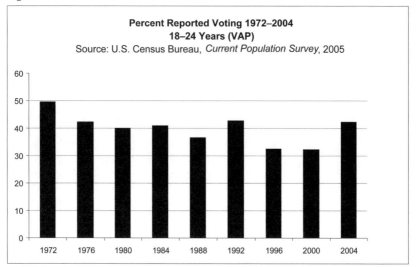

age and voting. We then present survey data conveying young Americans' opinions on politics and political participation. The majority of the chapter is an examination of one well-known response to concerns about low youth voting, Rock the Vote. We sketch the organization's genesis, describe what it does, and discuss the effectiveness of its approach. Finally, we proffer a conclusion about the success of Rock the Vote's efforts.

## ARE THE KIDS ALRIGHT?

Scholars generally dichotomize low youth political engagement in terms of either a *life cycle* or a *generational theory* of participation. Proponents of the former maintain that young people are less likely to perceive the benefits of voting until getting older.

Agnello (1973) suggests that a small number of youthful voters should not be surprising because the young perceive that they are politically powerless. Some opinion even posits that the political process is better served without the participation of reluctant and less-informed youth. Adherents to this view hold that there is little to fear about current low participation rates; young people will become more active as they get married, have children, and settle down. Turnout increases steadily with age and acquisition of a sense of power; it peaks when people are in their fifties and then gradually tapers off for seniors (Campbell et al. 1960; Milbrath 1965; Miller and Shanks 1996; Rosenstone and Hansen 1993; Verba and Nie 1972).

Those employing a generational theory of participation stress the importance of attachments to the political process that citizens develop early in life (Braungart and Braungart 1989; Craig and Bennett 1997; Sigel and Hoskin 1981). In other words, political generations are not born; they are made — oft-cited U.S. instances include those coming of age in both the 1930s and the 1960s. For example, the FDR New Deal generation as senior citizens was the heaviest-voting and by far most Democratic Party–leaning of all age groups, with polls showing them largely supportive of "big" government (K. Anderson 1979; Miller and Shanks 1996). Regarding the "protest" generation of the 1960s, evidence suggests that the most politically engaged young people in that era remained adult participants in political movements that had roots in their earlier youthful activism (Braungart and Braungart 1991; Whalen and Flacks 1989).

Concerning the effects of life-cycle and generational phenomena, Klecka's (1971) examination of Survey Research Center polls from 1952 to 1968 found support for both; moreover, he determined that such effects are only two of a number of variables influencing political behavior. Jennings and Niemi (1974; Jennings 1981) also found evidence of both effects in their analysis of survey data collected in 1965 and 1973. The pair struggle, however, to delineate clear contributions of either effect. More recently, Henn, Weinstein, and Wring (2002) concluded that support for both theories is inconclusive. Even a committed "generationalist" such as Inglehart (1990) acknowledges that there is no precise way of ruling out life-cycle factors. Apparently the only aspect of this research about which there exists consensus is recognition of the difficulty involved in trying to unravel the compound effects.[2]

As previously noted, some evidence suggests a secular decline in voter turnout in established political democracies over recent decades. This pattern might reflect *period-effect* events — such as political assassinations, the Vietnam War, the Watergate scandal, and stagflation in the United States during the 1960s and 1970s — resulting in declining trust in government and lower turnout.[3] Still, electoral data from several decades indicate a growing differential in voter turnout between the younger and older age groups (see figure 8.2).[4] In the United States, for example, the number of ballots cast by the youngest voters has ranged from 13 percent to 22 percent below the number cast by all voters since 1968 (U.S. Census Bureau 2005). In that highly charged and turbulent year, about 50 percent of twenty-one- to twenty-four-year-olds voted in the presidential election compared with 68 percent of all who were eligible, a

**Figure 8.2**

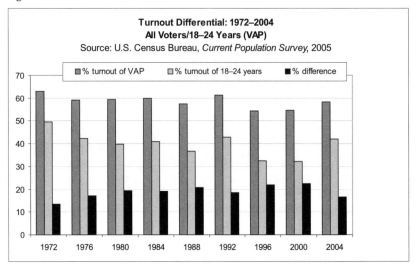

**Turnout Differential: 1972–2004**
**All Voters/18–24 Years (VAP)**
Source: U.S. Census Bureau, *Current Population Survey*, 2005

difference of 18 percent. We could reasonably assume that many young people at the time were turning their backs on what they believed was an unresponsive—even corrupt—system, and therefore they chose not to vote (to which the youth of today might counter "what's new?"). The 18 percent differential for 1968, however, mirrored that of 1964, when 51 percent of twenty-one-to twenty-four-year-olds and 69 percent of the eligible voting-age population reported voting. Then, in 1972, the first election in which those aged eighteen to twenty-one could cast ballots, the gap between the youngest-age cohort and all voters fell significantly to 13 percent, as 50 percent of the youngest and 63 percent of all who were eligible turned out. The differential rose to 17 percent in 1976 and remained above that percentage (with the youngest voters turning out at rates 20 percent below those of voters at large in 1988, 1996, and 2000) in every subsequent presidential election until 2004, when it fell slightly below it.

## TALKING 'BOUT THEIR GENERATION

What do young people themselves say about political participation? Survey research in the United States indicates that the young have low estimations of voting's importance, as well as low expectations that it can make a difference. Studies find that "post-boomer" youth do not discuss politics very much with either family or friends (National Youth Development Center 2000; Panetta Institute 2000). Opinion data reports that young people, when compared to older age groups, possess less political knowledge, express less interest in politics, have a reduced sense of civic responsibility, and perceive a weaker connection between political activity and public policy (Doppelt and Shearer 2001; Keeter et al. 2002; National Association of Secretaries of State [NASS] 1999). Generations X and Y (to use the pop-cult parlance) have grown up in a time of lower generalized trust and confidence in political institutions, and their lives span a period of weakening political party identity.[5] Many contemporary young people think traditional political organizations are out of touch (Brehm and Rahn 1997; Shanks et al. 2002; Soule 2001). Putnam (2000a) relates that the proportion of Americans engaged in civic activities fell by one-third between 1973–1974 and 1993–1994; tellingly, the younger the age group, the greater was the decline in writing letters to Congress, signing petitions, attending rallies and political meetings, working for a political party, serving as an officer in an organization, or running for office. A solely generational focus, however, misses the unevenness of declining youth participation; it is steepest for those with less income, education, and social connections. "Overrepresented" among nonparticipants are African Americans, Hispanics, those who do not attend college, and non-Internet users (Verba et al. 1995; NASS 1999).

Youthful distrust of the electoral system is manifest in the 26 percent of New Millennium Survey (NASS 1999) respondents choosing "don't think their vote makes a difference" as the prime reason for not voting, and in the 30 percent of eighteen- to twenty-four-year-old nonvoters in a Kaiser Family Foundation/MTV (2000) survey agreeing both that "politics is all about money and lying and I don't want to involve myself in it" and that "all candidates are basically the same so it doesn't matter much to me who gets elected." Lacking political efficacy, the young criticize politicians for failing to address their concerns (which appears to be true given that the young don't vote!). Perceiving politics to be corrupt, young people voluntarily remove themselves. As Democratic Party media consultant Dane Strother said in a 1999 National Public Radio *All Things Considered* interview, "I help sell politicians and young adults don't participate in the political process. Whenever we buy television and target our advertising spots we just completely discount anyone under thirty." Unsurprisingly, candidates and parties contact eighteen- to twenty-four-year-olds during election campaigns less often than other segments of the electorate as well.

Some literature on the political behavior of young people questions the notion that they are apolitical. Agnello (1973), writing near the end of the anti–Vietnam War era, concluded that withdrawal from voting could reflect an unwillingness to accept "the ballot box" as an effective expression of political participation in favor of a preference for "unconventional" means of political action. Three decades later, Shanks and his coauthors (2002) found that while youth engage in more protest activities than do their elders, the young are far less likely to be involved in "conventional" political activities such as contacting government officials and making campaign contributions. Young people perceive themselves to be both ignored and misunderstood by the political mainstream. Additionally, their political agenda is somewhat different from that of older adults. Younger Americans seem to be more concerned about protecting the environment, providing health care to the uninsured, and strengthening gun control laws. They also appear more socially egalitarian with respect to minorities, women, and gays, and they support appreciably higher levels of financial aid to higher education (Campaign Study Group 2000; Shanks et al. 2002).

Ostensibly disillusioned with the established electoral structure, some young people may be choosing "service volunteerism" rather than participation in a system they feel does not address their issues and that they feel powerless to change. Studies show that present-day youth are involved in community-based activities to a greater extent than were their politically active "1960s" parents at a similar age. Research also indicates that youth contribute as much as older citizens to service work and that the number of them engaged in volunteerism has been on the rise (Keeter et al. 2002; NASS 1999; Shanks et al 2002). Numerical claims aside, however, it does not necessarily follow that increased volunteerism is a product of the "civic spirit" of today's youth. Many colleges now include community service as a factor in admissions, and scholarship programs are emphasizing it as well; therefore, secondary schools are requiring students to volunteer. Some states have even mandated such work as a requirement for high school graduation. The National Youth Development Center (2000) found that students are much more likely to volunteer when their schools require and arrange the service. When schools did so, 59 percent of sixth through twelfth graders participated, compared with 29 percent when schools did neither.

Young people sincerely choosing to volunteer may be rewarded by what they see to be the instant results of their efforts; something that is not the case with casting a ballot. Volunteering and voting appear to be unrelated to one another, as volunteers are no more likely to vote than nonvolunteers (Keeter et al. 2002; NASS 1999). Strama (1998) reports that focus groups of "active volunteers" expressed drawing inspiration from the immediate impact of their work. Potentially significant was the apparent disconnect between the focus group participants' positive attitudes about their community service efforts and their lack of interest in broader movements for social change. Work at a health clinic for the poor may not be associated with the health care reform movement; literacy mentors are not necessarily active in efforts to reform the educational system. Volunteers tend to focus on direct one-to-one help, often viewing the "political side" of these issues as immovable and unreachable.

Feelings of "incompetence" and lack of information about politics top the reasons young people give for not registering and voting. According to a 2003 Declare Yourself survey of eighteen- to twenty-nine-year-olds, 61 percent of those not registered cited "not knowing enough" about the candidates or the issues for their failure to do so. Similarly, 59 percent of those registered indicated that they might not vote in 2004 because they did not think they knew enough about the candidates to make an informed choice. This data is somewhat surprising given that more people have more schooling and the fact that they have a plethora of media sources available to them. As for formal education, political scientists long held that rising general education levels would lead to higher voter turnout. However, in an early study looking specifically at civic education, Langton and Jennings (1968) determined that citizenship and government classes had little impact on the political attitudes, behavior, and knowledge of students. More recently, Niemi and Junn (1998) concluded that government classes facilitate citizen development, while Torney-Purta (2002) reports that students who had teachers engaging them in political discussion were more politically active than those who did not.

Thus, some analysts suggest that schooling has failed young people in the area of "civic education" (Galston 2000; Murphy 2004); if true, this dereliction has reinforced existing inequalities—relatively affluent, higher-educated youth participate on a par with earlier cohorts (Soule 2001; Verba et al. 1995). The gap in political engagement between "have" and "have-not" young people is further exacerbated by the emergence of a "digital divide." As the Internet becomes an increasingly important tool of political communication and social inclusion, upper-middle-class Gen Xers and Nexters are more likely to be "wired" than their working-class and lower-income counterparts. One consequence is that among all youth who are registered to vote, those who are well off receive more communications at election time.

## IS IT ONLY ROCK AND ROLL?

Having discussed theories and empirical data related to youth political participation, we now turn to an exploration of one response to this issue. Concerns that Generation X was politically "unplugged" (the name of a former MTV program) and on the verge of becoming an "apolitical" age group were ostensibly behind the 1990 creation of Rock the Vote (RTV). Founded by members of the recording industry in response to a series of attacks on artistic

expression and freedom of speech, RTV sought to "make real" the connections between young people's lives and public policy.[6] Always keen to point
out that it is officially nonprofit and nonpartisan, the organization's mission
statement claims that it aims to "politically empower youth." Rock the Vote's
message is that entertainment is the way to get youth interested; to this end,
major record firms generously kicked in seed money at the group's inception,
and media consultants and public relations firms were brought on board. RTV
has championed its voter registration efforts, reporting over three million new
enrollees in the United States between 1992 and 2004 (see figure 8.3). The
organization engages in a multitude of activities, including music concerts
frequently cosponsored with local radio stations, celebrity events on college
campuses and at record stores, "easy" voter registration via a 1-800 number
and the Internet, and "community street teams" of volunteers who attempt to
engage young people and persuade them to register. With links to MTV, and
often working in partnership with corporations, Rock the Vote gained national
and even international prominence, becoming a preferred "establishment"
vehicle for addressing the issue of youth political participation.

RTV began registering new voters in 1992; allied with a number of organizations, including the League of Women Voters and the National Association
of Secretaries of State, the organization announced that it had added 350,000
names to the nation's registration rolls. Rock the Vote claimed—and others
granted it—much of the credit for a near 20 percent rise in the eighteen- to

**Figure 8.3**

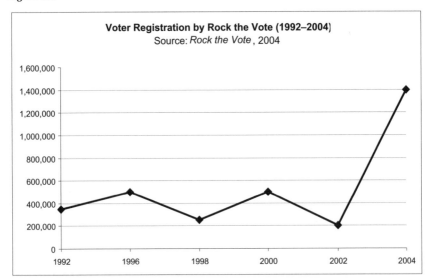

twenty-nine-year-old turnout that year over the percentage that cast ballots in the previous election. Moreover, the largest increase in turnout of any age group occurred among eighteen- to twenty-four-year-olds, with 52.5 percent of them reporting being registered to vote and 42.8 percent reporting voting compared to 48.2 percent and 36.2 percent, respectively, in 1988 (U.S. Census Bureau 2005). Tindell and Medhurst (1998) maintain that MTV's median twenty-one-year-old audience responded enthusiastically to both the organization's "Get Loud" message and its music-video-like public service announcements (PSAs). Featuring the likes of Aerosmith, Pearl Jam singer Eddie Vedder, Queen Latifah, R.E.M., and most memorably, Madonna (partially nude, draped in an American flag, and declaring, "If you don't vote, you're going to get a spankie"), the PSAs suggested to the young that politics could be "cool." Never mind that some of the stars, including Madonna herself, failed to cast ballots after urging young people to do so.[7]

The 1992 presidential campaign was a signature moment in the search by politicians for ways to circumvent the conventional media.[8] In that context, the distinction between Rock the Vote and MTV's "Choose or Lose" election coverage aimed at youth was vague; each was a star-studded affair.[9] Moreover, MTV gave RTV about $20 million of airtime. Democratic nominee Bill Clinton appeared to feed off the energy of this environment, appearing on MTV (recall the infamous "boxers or briefs" moment during one of his appearances) and turning up on Arsenio Hall's late-night television talk show wearing dark sunglasses and playing the saxophone. In contrast, those watching "pop-culture challenged" incumbent George Bush fielding questions from MTV's twenty-something reporter Tabitha Soren while standing on the caboose platform of a train knew that he was not going to "rock" anything. As a candidate, Clinton hyped both the organization and the network; as president, he lauded RTV's lobbying efforts on behalf of a "motor voter" act (National Voter Registration Reform Act) that Bush had vetoed two years earlier.[10] Among other things, the law paved the way for Rock the Vote's first-of-their-kind mail-in, telephone, and online voter registration projects. The organization also touted its role in the passage of legislation (National and Community Service Trust Act) encouraging volunteerism. Within several years, RTV had established an annual award for "significant contributions" to empowering youth, had produced an award-winning dramatic short film on health issues affecting young people, and had received a Ford Foundation grant for a program to bring nonvoters into the electoral process.[11]

Rock the Vote lost some of its luster in 1996 when a not-so-funny thing happened on the way to the polls: a smaller percentage of young people (32.3 percent) managed to get there. Skeptics, maintaining that the organization had ridden a "statistical blip" in 1992, claimed that a youthful Clinton and the candidacy of Ross Perot as a significant alternative drove turnout up among all age groups in that year. Of course, RTV advocates might have cited weeks of public opinion data indicating that President Clinton's reelection "was a given" to explain the all-ages decline in turnout for the 1996 race between himself and Bob Dole. Moreover, a parody button reading "Dole is 96" may have, rather callously, expressed the attitude of certain youth with respect to the seventy-three-year-old Republican candidate. While Rock the Vote announced that it enrolled an additional 500,000 young persons, the percentage of eighteen- to twenty-four-year-olds registered to vote that year fell to 48.8 percent (U.S. Census Bureau 2005). Criticism grew louder when youth turnout was flat (as it was for all age groups) in 2000, despite the tightly contested election between George W. Bush and Al Gore. The percentage of eighteen- to twenty-four-year-old registrants slipped again, this time to 45.4 percent (U.S. Census Bureau 2005), even as RTV advertised signing up another 500,000 youth. Eight years after Rock the Vote burst onto the scene, a smaller percentage of the youngest cohort was registered to vote than at any time since eighteen-year-olds were granted the franchise (see figure 8.4). Stated bluntly, fewer eighteen- to twenty-four-year-olds voted in 2000 than had done so in 1988 before RTV's existence.

In 2004, Rock the Vote joined with other groups under an umbrella campaign called "20 Million Loud" for the goal of turning out twenty million voters between eighteen and twenty-nine years of age. Much like the voter

**Figure 8.4**

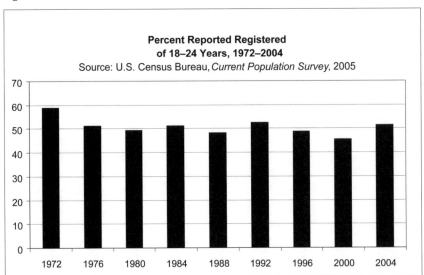

registration numbers about which the organization waxes enthusiastic, the objective seemed impressive. Yet twenty million voters under the age of thirty would have approximated the number that went to the polls in 1992. In fact, the youth vote exceeded Rock the Vote's goal, as almost twenty-one million eighteen- to twenty-nine-year-olds turned out (CIRCLE 2004b). This meant that 51.6 percent—or 9 percent more than in 2000—of this age cohort voted. But turnout rose among every demographic group, and consequently those under the age of thirty casting ballots constituted the same 18 percent of voters that they had in the previous election. The youngest cohort also kept pace; 10 percent of the electorate in both 2000 and 2004 consisted of eighteen- to twenty-four-year-olds. While debate ensued over whether or not the youth vote had been rocked, Rock the Vote wasted little time in changing the "20 Million Loud" message on its website to "20 Million Proud."

## YOU PLAY THE GUITAR ON THE MTV

Having presented data regarding Rock the Vote's voter registration efforts, let's now explore the organization's efficacy and efficiency in this regard. It seems that RTV is similar to the National Voter Registration Act in that it may produce registered nonvoters; call it the "motor-voter" effect (Martinez and Hill 1999; Wolfinger and Hoffman 2001). Granting RTV the registrants it claims, the numbers look more impressive than they really are; a glance at the organization's own statistics indicates that some people who register through Rock the Vote would do so anyway. According to a 2000 Kaiser Family Foundation/MTV survey, only 12 percent of young people agree with the statement "It's complicated to register to vote where I live" (see figure 8.5). Additionally, only 11 percent of first-time voter respondents to a 2004 Pace University/Rock the Vote poll listed "organized drive" as a major reason for registering (see figure 8.6). The eighteen- to twenty-four-year-old voting-age population grew by three million persons—from 24.3 to 27.8—between 1992, when RTV began registering voters, and 2004 (U.S. Census Bureau 2005). Keeping pace with the 52.5 percent registration rate in the earlier year would have resulted in about 14.6 million eighteen- to twenty-four-year-old registrants in the latter; instead, there were about 14.3 million persons (51.5 percent) of that age registered to vote in 2004.[12]

Rock the Vote is only one piece of a larger "turnout puzzle," as the 55 percent of Vanishing Voter Project (2000) respondents who called the 2000 Bush-Gore race "boring" testifies. It is, however, a high-powered, high-profile piece; with that in mind, information about how many of the organization's registrants actually turn up at the polls is sparse. Burgess and her colleagues

*Michael Hoover and Susan Orr*

**Figure 8.5**

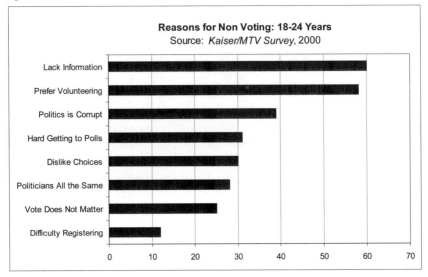

**Figure 8.6**

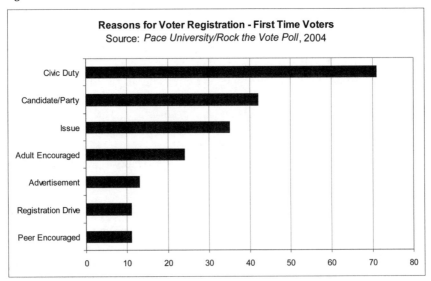

(2000) did examine the impact of RTV by asking individuals to fill out a self-addressed postcard that would be mailed to them shortly before polling day. Some pledge cards asked that persons provide themselves with a "prompt" by completing the sentence "I will vote because _____." Other cards asked someone to sign a card containing the preprinted message "I will rock the system by exercising my right to vote on November 5, 1996." The researchers determined that receiving a pledge card with the personal comment had a 13 percent positive influence on the likelihood of voting (83 percent to 70 percent for those who received a card absent the self-expressed exhortation), irrespective of demographic and psychological predictors.[13] They also speculate that all participants in the pledge-card campaign voted at higher rates than nonparticipants, even as they acknowledge that their study considers only the former and therefore cannot serve as a test of the cards' general impact.[14]

Several studies offer insights as to why Rock the Vote's approach to turning out voters may be ineffective; the Pew Center discovered, for example, that 64 percent of eighteen- to twenty-nine-year-olds "never/hardly ever" watch MTV (Bennett 1998). Moreover, Green and Gerber's (2004) study of "get out the vote" (GOTV) efforts found that face-to-face contact could increase turnout by a statistically significant 8.5 percent. Moreover, such interaction appears to have "spillover" effects as well; the authors indicate that other adults living at the residence visited vote at appreciably higher rates than adults living with voters that received no solicitation. Comparatively speaking, personal telephone calls produced a smaller, but still notable, 5 percent rise in the number of voters. Meanwhile, e-mail, a principal RTV mobilization method of choice, had no discernible effect on turnout. According to Vrome (2004), Internet usage reinforces existing political behavior rather than mobilizing new political actors.

Rock the Vote's celebrity-driven, mass media style is also economically inefficient. According to one estimate, RTV spent ten times more per registration in 1996 than did the League of Women Voters. In terms of money— RTV's 2004 budget was $8 million—the organization's focus on mass media, the Internet, and cross-country "road trips" of pop stars telling youth to vote is much more expensive than concentrated local GOTV drives. RTV and its "partners" spent about $40 million registering 1.4 million youth in 2004 (Schiller 2004). At $37.50 per registration, however, the operation far exceeds the $12 to $20 per vote that Green and Gerber (2001) say person-to-person GOTV campaigns targeting young people cost. On this matter, the authors (2004) conclude that old-fashioned door-to-door canvassing is the most cost-effective method; the pair estimate an additional voter for each $8 spent. They also point out that relatively inexpensive "robo-calls" by celebrities, another Rock the Vote favorite, have not proved cost effective because they do not produce positive turnout results. No matter, RTV communications director Jay Strell states, "We've been in this longer than anyone else, and we know what works. We have the cutting-edge technology and the stars that the kids know" (Kamenetz 2004). In line with such thinking, the organization has added mobile phones and text messaging to its panoply of marketing techniques that include banner ads, chat rooms, and blogs.

## NO VOTE LEFT BEHIND?

Is Rock the Vote's strategy of voter registration an adequate response to youth nonparticipation? We think not; again, a brief perusal of the organization's own survey data suggests as much. Only 4 percent of eighteen- to twenty-nine-year-old nonregistered respondents to an MTV poll gave "too difficult to register" as the reason for not voting (Choose or Lose 2004). Rock the Vote's lack of attention to substantive political education is surprising given that 60 percent of eighteen- to twenty-four-year-olds in a 2000 Kaiser Foundation/ MTV survey cited "lack of information" (meaning information about candidates and issues) as the principal reason for not casting ballots (see figure 8.5). MTV's Choose or Lose news coverage does little to counter the knowledge deficit, consisting as it does of "reports that vary in length from thirty seconds to four minutes, and are integrated into daily news updates, which focus predominantly on music and other cultural news" (Solomon 1996). Highlighting RTV's lack of concern with informing its constituency, Glass (1997) cites a brief survey asking people to, among other things, name one of their state's U.S. senators and to identify how many times the U.S. Constitution has been amended. While the average for presidential inaugural attendees was four correct answers out of six questions, and tourists at the Lincoln Memorial scored a 3.5 average, Rock the Vote partygoers managed, on average, only one correct answer. But then RTV's "organizing" manual advises volunteers to target "the kid who wants to be on MTV" (in contrast, the booklet suggests avoiding those it calls "partisans").

Rock the Vote's website features short snappy synopses of several issues, including censorship, health care, selective service, and, most recently, Social Security. While the information provided is generally informative, those looking for policy guidance on these matters will likely be disappointed.[15] Why might RTV present material that lacks depth and substance? One reason could be that the organization questions the attention span of young people given our contemporary proclivity for "sound bite" culture (which, ironically, the organization's approach perpetuates). Perhaps Rock the Vote thinks it will restrict its audience (bipartisanship offers maximum potential) if it is perceived as too "partisan" or is seen as taking specific stands on issues. Or maybe RTV wishes to protect its tax-exempt status. While the last matter sounds plausible, we perceive it to be factually inaccurate. Given its status as a 501c3 organization, RTV cannot endorse specific candidates or engage in partisan politics. However, the Internal Revenue Service (IRS) neither limits nor prohibits politics-related activities such as analysis of social problems and policies or dissemination of education materials, so long as no references are made to specific legislation and no specific positions are taken. 501c3s can also lobby and support organizing efforts as long as they do not earmark general operating funds for these activities.[16] Therefore, on the issue of health care, a preferred Rock the Vote topic, the organization could provide in-depth information about universal coverage, single-payer plans, HMOs, and health maintenance accounts and tie this information to political party positions. However, RTV chooses to offer a prepared-text e-mail that people can send to Congress asking that family coverage for dependents be extended to age twenty-six and that higher-education institutions be required to offer insurance to students.[17]

An additional explanation for why Rock the Vote skims the surface of politics is that to do otherwise might be bad for business. Early on, RTV abandoned the potentially confrontational politics of censorship (and the music business's particular agenda) in the midst of a flap over "gangsta rap."[18] In contrast, the "positive politics" of voter registration was appealing to companies looking to score brand-name recognition with the MTV demographic (ages twelve to thirty-four). Non–music industry corporate sponsors have included AOL, Doritos (owned by Pepsi), K-Mart, MCI, Winter Fresh gum (owned by Wrigley), and World Wrestling Entertainment. In 2004, 7-UP and Sunkist Orange Soda (both owned by Dr. Pepper/7-UP Inc.) helped Rock the Vote give the "convenience store" concept new meaning by offering voter registration in 7-11 stores and plugging up-and-coming bands signed to labels with RTV connections. Dr. Pepper/7-UP, Ben & Jerry's Ice Cream (owned by Unilever), Motorola, and Cingular Wireless ponied up $1 million apiece for a seat on RTV's voter registration and concert tour bus (Spethman 2004). Recording artists playing free events included A-listers Alanis Morissette, Dave Mathews Band, Dixie Chicks, and Snoop Dogg. Participating companies not only received advertising tie-ins with headlining-status acts for a fraction of what it would otherwise cost them, but they also had an opportunity to add a little "hip" to their image. Meanwhile, lesser-known bands featured on 7-11 "Super Big Gulp" cups played "gigs" to audiences larger than those to which they were accustomed in hopes of quickly building a fan base.[19] As the manager of the eclectic band Squirrel Nut Zippers had said about his group's appearances at several 1996 Rock the Vote events, "Earlier this week we were in Charlottesville, today it's here [Washington, D.C.]. Next it's Georgia. What did you say this Rock the Vote does?" (Glass 1997, 17).

## MUSIC AND POLITICS

Rock the Vote's generic appeals to ubiquitous politicians to "do the right thing" on a few select issues have not protected the organization from criticism that it is, in fact, partisan (Goldberg 2003; Redbord 1996). Dowd (2000) points out that a number of RTV staffers have been employed by Democratic officials and politicians, including former Texas governor Ann Richards, Massachusetts senator Ted Kennedy, and even ex-president Bill Clinton. Additionally, Rock the Vote's nonprofit "partners" are generally "left-leaning" organizations such as the Association of Community Organizations for Reform Now, National Association for the Advancement of Colored People, People for the American Way, and the Service Employees International Union. Examination of the group's website reveals several liberal-like positions—"government program" recommendations (albeit rather lamely) to expand health care coverage, strengthen unemployment insurance, and increase public grants for higher education on the one hand, and "civil libertarian" warnings about protecting free expression on the other. Rock the Vote, so the generally conservative and Republican line goes, is really only interested in recruiting a certain type of young voter. As Buckley (1996, 94) wrote when RTV joined with rapper L. L. Cool J to extend its message beyond relatively affluent white suburbia to urban youth of color, "It isn't likely that adding black votes will do other than enhance Democratic chances."

Attacks on Rock the Vote as a liberal, and therefore Democratic, "front group" became particularly pronounced in 2004; first, country-pop group The Dixie Chicks signed on to RTV after arousing controversy for remarks they made criticizing President George Bush and the Iraq War. Later, Republicans complained loudly near the end of the campaign when Rock the Vote raised the possibility of a military draft in light of current U.S. military deployments.[20] RTV spokesperson Jay Strell defended the organization's action by citing a poll in which 46 percent of eighteen- to twenty-four-year-olds indicated that the draft would be an important issue in their decision to vote (R. Rose 2004). Rock the Vote also countered that it had worked with both major parties and their supporters, citing election-night TV-viewing parties that it hosted for College Republicans, performances by Bush-supporting headliners Toby Keith and Kid Rock at RTV concerts, and Choose or Lose television programs featuring Newt Gingrich and Republican National Committee chair Ed Gillespie. Finally, Rock the Voters pointed to the youth vote for Perot in 1992, Jesse Ventura in the 1998 Minnesota gubernatorial election, and John McCain in the 2000 Republican presidential primaries as evidence that they would lose credibility among young people if their organization was perceived to be partisan.[21] Regarding this matter, Moseley (1999) cites a sample of 1,500 completed voter registration forms from a Rock the Vote event indicating that over 50 percent registered "independent."

Recall that the *generational theory of participation* posits that persons of similar age may learn similar political lessons, and thus they may hold similar political views. When Rock the Vote political director Hans Riemer suggests that contemporary eighteen- to twenty-four-year-olds are linked by several core issues—jobs, environment, and tolerance—he is making a "political generation" argument. But what if young voters generally reflect the electorate at large? If so, the notion of a youth voting bloc is an illusion. As Andolina and Jenkins (2004) point out, young Americans are split along both ideological and partisan lines; if a consistent pattern exists, it is that moderates and independents outnumber liberals and conservatives as well as Democrats and Republicans on a host of measures.[22] A long-running national survey of college freshmen has consistently conveyed a "leftward" tilt (a very slight 24.2 percent liberal to 22.7 percent conservative in 2003) while simultaneously indicating that about 50 percent of incoming students are in the "middle of the road" (Higher Education Research Institute 2004). Lopez (2002) found that African Americans (41 percent) are the most likely eighteen- to twenty-five-year-olds to identify as Democrats; meanwhile, CD-buying white males who make up the consumer base of the recording industry marginally favor Republicans—32 percent, compared to 30 percent independent and 27 percent Democrat.

A majority 54 percent versus 44 percent of under-thirty voters went for John Kerry over incumbent George W. Bush in the 2004 presidential election. Given that this was the only age group to prefer the Democratic candidate, the Democratic Party might assume that it will fare well in future elections. Potentially complicating matters, however, are two groups of young people not appearing on conventional "radar screens." A Harvard Institute of Politics (2004) study found that college students "in the middle" divide almost evenly between *religious* and *secular* centrists. Neither are said to be predictably conservative or liberal; for example, the former support universal health care and affirmative action but oppose gay marriage. The U.S. "culture war" may or may not be as intense as media reports suggest. But the 23 percent of eighteen- to twenty-nine-year-old respondents to an MTV Choose or Lose (2004) poll who think of themselves as "evangelical" or "born again" Christians corresponds to the percentage of all voters identifying themselves as one or the other in 2004. One would not know that these persons exist from either MTV programming or Rock the Vote appeals.

## CONCLUSION

Youth music and politics have long been associated, although much of the emphasis has changed from message to marketing. In contrast to the confrontational and oppositional character of the late-1960s counterculture, pop stars and rock and rollers are socially acceptable today. The late Beatle George Harrison's 1971 *Concert for Bangladesh* gave birth to the "concert for a cause" that developed into the "political-artistic-philanthropic circus." Musicians then became associated with presidential candidates: Simon & Garfunkel and James Taylor on behalf of George McGovern in 1972, and the Allman Brothers Band for Jimmy Carter in 1976. As the 1970s drew to a close, rock and rollers, including Jackson Browne; Crosby, Stills, and Nash; Bonnie Raitt; and Bruce Springsteen, staged a series of concerts known by the shorthand tag "No Nukes" in response to the partial meltdown of a nuclear reactor in Pennsylvania. The phenomenon that Garofolo (1992, 16) calls the "full blown integration of popular music with the 'star making machinery'" arrived with 1985's Live Aid event to raise money for starving Ethiopians. The issue of hunger was relatively safe; "humanitarian aid" could appeal to most everyone, including principal underwriters Pepsi, Eastman-Kodak, AT&T, and Chevrolet, who had their corporate logos prominently displayed during the telecast of the event that was staged simultaneously in London and Philadelphia. The amount of money raised far exceeded expectations; moreover, new mass-communications technologies offered pop stars, record companies, and merchandisers access to a global audience of prospective new consumers. With this event, pop music transcended its conventional generational limits, entering fully into the realm of mainstream entertainment. If a "pop-politics" alliance had been acceptable for some time, it was now respectable. And, in a post–Live Aid world, the questions for similar efforts would be are the artists popular enough? and is the cause "too" controversial or partisan? Indeed, 2005's mammoth Live 8 concert for African debt relief was formulated so loosely that artists and politicos could share one another's stage.

Contemporary politics is conditioned by the work of "spin doctors" and "image makers." In this sense, Rock the Vote emerged as part of the "packaging" that has transformed politics into high-tech communications, and citizens into consumers (Bennett 1992; Franklin 1994). RTV's pithy sound bites exploit youthful antiauthority and rebellious posturing, its 2000 rallying cry "Piss off a Politician: Vote" paradoxically suggesting that casting a ballot is somehow "antiestablishment." Rock the Vote's website appeals for donations and directs you to "buy stuff." Wrapped in an alternative/hip hop/punk aesthetic, both the "fashion of politics" and the "politics of fashion" are on display here. One can purchase either a "Censorship is Un-American" or a "Give a Sh*t" T-shirt (the ironic juxtaposition of the two items is apparently lost on RTV's merchandising staff); a "Rock the Vote" thong (which would seem to have limited advertising reach); and logo ball caps, beanies, and other apparel.

While Rock the Vote does make generic appeals to ubiquitous politicians to "do the right thing" on a few select issues, as McKissack (1999, 12) writes,

"Just register to vote is all they ask." Thus, RTV expresses the "motor voter" law's intent: it principally addresses registration, not turnout; it is primarily about opportunity rather than motivation. The group's focus on voter registration allows corporations to benefit from their connection to pop musicians without being specifically associated with statements the latter might make. Meanwhile, it permits musicians to exploit their identification with an ostensibly political organization while avoiding the wrath of fans who might "boycott" their next recording in response to overt political leanings. The promotion of Rock the Vote as nonpartisan may suit the corporate sector, the music business, and the political mainstream, but does it serve its purported purpose of empowering the young?

For the most part, Rock the Vote offers what Henn, Weinstein, and Wring (2002) call a "politics of passive consumption rather than active participation." Governed by the need to offer a coherent voice and to stay "on message," office seekers can appear cautious in outlook and tone, neither of which is likely to make them especially attractive to younger voters. Further, many of today's marketing- and media-savvy youth are turned off by the collusion of politics and big business, and they easily detect the hollow prudence of keeping things apolitical, not that RTV events are unpopular with the young who enjoy free concerts. Rather, they take pleasure in what Rock the Vote offers while realizing, as Jackson Browne (1986) puts it, that "they sell us the President the same way they sell us our clothes and our cars." Curmudgeonly Curtis Gans of the Committee for Study of the American Electorate says, "People don't vote because of hip hop artists or rock stars" (Moody 2004). Well, mass marketing does not always work. In this sense, RTV is a symptom. Low voter turnout says more about politics as a media commodity than it does about mass political indifference. Given its consumer-oriented roots, Rock the Vote is unlikely to have a serious impact on youth voting, or more generally, on their political engagement. But perhaps there is no flaw in its design. Doing so might scare the establishment, upset the "status quo" (not the British rock band), and, pardon the pun, "rock the boat!"

## NOTES

1. For a contrary view suggesting that the "vanishing voter" in the United States is a myth, see McDonald and Popkin (2001). Employing a *voting eligible population* denominator that excludes the ineligible such as noncitizens and felons (both of which have increased in number) rather than the Census Bureau's *voting age population*, the authors maintain that there has been little decline in turnout during the previous three decades.

2. William Strauss and Neil Howe's (1991) "generational diagonal" concept—the life-cycle course, childhood through old age, lived by discrete birth-year groups—ambitiously attempts to reconcile "life-cycle" and "generational" theories.

3. The sharpest declines occurred between 1964 and 1974 (National Election Studies 2004).

4. Nonvoting throughout the political democracies has grown most markedly among the young. In South Africa, where the majority of the population has only recently gained the right to vote after decades of struggle, low youth participation prompted National Youth Commission chairperson Mahengi Bengi to comment, "Declining youth activism is part of a global trend. It shows that we are becoming a normal democracy" (Eveleth 1999).

5. *Generation X*: persons born between 1965 and 1977. The label is from the title of a 1991 Douglas Coupland novel lamenting the absence of significant sociopolitical events to mark his age group. *Generation Y*: those born since 1978 (of which there are about seventy million, making them the largest birth cohort in U.S. history). The *Gen Y* (as well as the lesser used *GenNext*) label refers to the fact that the cohort follows immediately upon the heels of Generation X.

6. Rock the Vote's founders were primarily motivated by two circumstances: (1) the labeling of records for "explicit language" and (2) the obscenity trial of rap group 2 Live Crew. Regarding the former, an organization called the Parents Music Resource Center (PMRC) had fought to make labeling an issue. The PMRC attracted attention, in part, because it included congressional spouses (including Tipper Gore, wife of then–Tennessee senator and future U.S. vice president Al Gore). Capitol Hill hearings on the matter featured testimony from the likes of Twisted Sister lead singer Dee Snider and the late Frank Zappa. In an effort to stave off federal regulatory action, the Recording Industry Association of America (RIAA) began attaching "Parental Advisory" warnings to product packaging. As for the latter situation, Broward County, Florida, banned the sale of the group's album "Nasty as They Wanna Be." The album was declared obscene by a federal judge whose decision was later reversed. 2 Live Crew were arrested during a live performance of songs from the album; they were subsequently acquitted. Then–Virgin Records America chairman Jeff Ayeroff was the principal mover and shaker in the launching of Rock the Vote. RTV made an initial splash with several "public service announcements" (PSAs) by Iggy Pop and Red Hot Chili Peppers proclaiming that "Censorship is Un-American."

7. Nonvoting Rock the Vote celebrities have included rocker Lenny Kravitz, folk/pop singer Jewel, and heartthrob actor Ben Affleck.

8. In addition to Clinton's skillful use of the popular media, Ross Perot announced his 1992 presidential candidacy on *Larry King Live* and campaigned largely by purchasing thirty-minute blocks of television airtime, former California governor Jerry Brown ran a 1-800 campaign, and Pat Buchanan went from playing a political pundit on TV to playing a political candidate on the small screen.

9. Producer Alison Stewart, recalling candidates' initial hesitancy to be interviewed by MTV, says that "they all thought we were going to ask them about the last five records they bought" (Solomon 1996, 20). Meanwhile, the network's political reporter

Tabitha Soren, who became something of a celebrity figure, recollects being interviewed by journalists as often as she interviewed candidates in 1992 (Sandler 2000).

10. Clinton's "payback" to the music industry for its efforts in helping elect him president was his administration's vigorous attempts to enforce U.S. copyright abroad and clamp down on pirated imports (Cloonan and Street 1998).

11. The achievement award was established to honor Rock the Vote's late executive director Patrick Lippert, who died of complications from AIDS in 1993. R.E.M. were the first recipients; others include Public Enemy's Chuck D, Hootie and the Blowfish, Sheryl Crow, Neil Young, Bono, Sting, Carlos Santana, Alanis Morissette, and Peter Gabriel. Representative Dan Glickman (D-KA) memorialized Lippert on the House floor; his remarks appear in the Congressional Record for July 13, 1993. http://thomas.loc.gov.

12. Attrition due to death, departure, and nonvoting removes voters from the rolls even as the voting-age population increases. Names disappear during nonpresidential election years when voter interest wanes. Finally, some "new" registrations are really address changes for people who were already on the rolls somewhere else. Ganz (1996) cites a 1988 Organizing Institute of San Francisco study comparing registration "transactions" with net increases in registration rolls. The study concluded that it took more than two registration transactions to net a single addition to the rolls.

13. According to a former Rock the Vote president (Strama 1998), the vast majority of voting "prompts" were (1) "It is my right as an American," (2) "because I love my country," and (3) "because people have fought and died for the right." Few persons cited issue- or candidate-based reasons.

14. Two studies investigating a potential correlation between receiving voter information through postal mail and actually casting a ballot produced quite different results. Pierce, Steel, and Lovrich's (2003) study of eighteen- to twenty-five-year-olds determined that receipt of a brochure and manual—accompanied by a request to visit a website—made no difference in the likelihood of respondent voting. In contrast, Iyengar and Jackman (2003) reported that among eligible voters aged eighteen to twenty-nine, those who were mailed a CD-ROM election handbook turned out at a much higher rate than did non-CD-ROM recipients.

15. To be fair, in 2005, Rock the Vote's website included a pro–Social Security video, and the organization teamed up with the AARP in support of strengthening the current system rather than moving toward privatization.

16. For an in-depth study that concludes that 501c3s typically interpret the law too broadly and are less politically involved than they legally could be, see Berry and Arons (2003).

17. In 1996, Rock the Vote did distribute over one million copies of a health care pamphlet and aired several videos that it produced with a $2.8 million grant from the Robert Wood Johnson Foundation. The project's impact on young people's knowledge and understanding of the health care system is not known, as no evaluation was done.

18. Time Warner's capitulation over criticism of rapper Ice-T's speed-metal band Body Count and its song "Cop Killer" was the defining moment in the music industry's retreat. RTV's foray into "grassroots politics"—for which the Pew Charitable Trusts

contributed \$2.5 million—proved a bust when organization staff and local activists each expected too much of the other. Rock the Voters saw their role in terms of attracting media attention for efforts addressing "teen curfews" or "three strikes and your out" laws. Locals apparently believed that connections to Rock the Vote would mean financial, technical, and celebrity resources that were not forthcoming.

19. Up-and-comers Black-Eyed Peas, Vanessa Carlton, Good Charlotte, Hoobastank, Maroon 5, and Josh Stone were all part of RTV's 2004 tour.

20. Rock the Vote's postings to its website and e-mails to a list of several hundred thousand addresses that it maintains prompted an angry letter from Republican National Committee chair Ed Gillespie who followed a reference to the organization's nonprofit, tax-exempt status with a "cease and desist" comment at www.rnc.org. In addition, the Republican leadership in the House of Representatives quickly brought a bill calling for renewal of the selective-service system to the floor, where it was soundly defeated 402–2 in a bipartisan display of opposition. Proposed by Democrat Charles Rangel (D-NY) prior to the start of the Iraq War in 2003, the bill had never received a committee hearing. Both President George Bush and challenger John Kerry indicated during the campaign that they opposed reinstating the draft.

21. Former Rock the Vote director Matt Moseley (1999) calls attention to lessons of the "Ventura effect" for youth turnout: (1) easier access to the voting booth—16 percent of Minnesota's voters in 1998 registered on election day, and (2) expanding the two-party system—Jesse Ventura was an independent candidate for governor of Minnesota.

22. According to Gallup, 32 percent of eighteen- to twenty-nine-year-olds identify as conservatives on both social and economic issues; 27 percent are liberal on the former, and 24 percent are liberal on the latter (Carroll 2003). Gallup also has eighteen- to twenty-nine-year-old Republican partisans running ahead of Democratic ones by 30 percent versus 24 percent. The Center for Information and Research on Civic Learning and Engagement found that 27 percent of African Americans aged eighteen to twenty-five are Republicans, and 21 percent are independents (Lopez 2002). White youth split quite evenly—32 percent Republican, 30 percent Democrat, and 28 percent independent.

# 9

# Mobilizing the Youth Vote in 2004 and Beyond

*Heather Smith and Ivan Frishberg*

November 2, 2004
"Good morning, this is your wake-up call. It's Election Day!"

$A$t 4:30 a.m. on November 2, 2004, each of the state Public Interest Research Group's (PIRG) New Voters Project state directors got a wake-up call. As it turns out, most of us never made it to bed from the night before and were busy making final preparations for election day when the call came. The leadership team had been working toward this day for almost a year, and the plan for the day started with that call. This first call set off a series of wake-up calls to hundreds of local organizers, and then to all of the volunteers, to make sure that the first shift of volunteers arrived at the polling stations for poll watching starting at 6:00 a.m.

Most of the campaign worked the same way as the wake-up calls—like a giant game of telephone. Campaign plans and goals were created centrally by our leadership team, which were passed on to the state directors, who then trained their canvass and campus directors, who then trained their canvassers and volunteers. Like in the game telephone, the end product in each city rarely looked like its original vision. Sometimes it worked, and we all learned from it. Sometimes it did not, and we were back on the phone restating the plan, a little clearer this time. This top-down approach worked. We had very ambitious goals for what was proposed as a historic plan to mobilize young voters, and to meet those goals required a witches brew of communication, trust, accountability, and plenty of hard work.

The State PIRGs' New Voters Project's overall goal was to increase turnout of eighteen- to twenty-four-year-old voters by five percentage points in the six states we targeted (Iowa, Colorado, New Mexico, Wisconsin, Oregon, and Nevada). Turnout among this age group had been declining sharply for over thirty years and in the last presidential election was at 36 percent of eligible voters, so stopping the decline would be an accomplishment, and increasing statewide turnout in six states by five percentage points seemed quite far fetched to most observers. But that was our goal.

To get to our goal, the New Voters Project team had registered 349,000 young people ages eighteen to twenty-four to vote and had contacted over 529,000 young registered citizens about going to the polls in the three weeks prior to election day.

And then there was election day itself.

Based on previous work, we calculated exactly how many young voters we would have to contact on election day and how many would have to go to the polls in order to hit our goals. We recruited the necessary thousands of volunteers to be on the phones, knocking on doors, and standing at the polls all day on election day. We had the logistics to think about; we found phones, copied maps for the canvassers, planned for who would go to which polling station, and arranged transportation. The amount of work that had to happen in one day was daunting, so we planned to start with wake-up calls to make sure everyone showed up.

By 6:00 a.m., the office was filled with volunteer poll watchers awaiting their instructions. These poll watchers would stand at the polling stations for every youth-dense precinct, armed with a list of all registered eighteen- to twenty-four-year-olds registered in that precinct, tracking who showed up to vote.

By 7:00 a.m., the poll watchers were at their polls, and the phone bankers began to arrive. The phone bankers' job was to work with the poll watchers. Every hour, the poll watchers would report on who had voted, and the phone bankers would call anyone that hadn't shown up at a poll yet. By 8:00 a.m., there were hundreds of phone bankers sitting on the floors, on top of tables, and in chairs across the states ready to use cell phones, land lines, and palm pilots to get their list of voters to the polls.

When the first reports from the poll watchers came in, the calling began.

By late afternoon, it slowed down. After a good morning rush of voters— including lines that had formed for poll openings in some locations—there was quite a lull. The callers had been dialing nonstop for seven plus hours, and even though we were sticking to our plan, there were not enough young people rushing the polls. By 3:00 p.m., we knew the evening hours were going to be critical; we would have to contact even more people than planned to make up for the slow afternoon. So we collected every last T-shirt, hat, wristband, flyer, sticker, button, and pen, and special teams of volunteers hit the streets.

We raced out of our offices in every direction and gave away materials to the commuters in rush hour, students on campus, or anyone else that would take and wear the items, and we asked everyone to come back to our offices and volunteer for the final push. The volunteer teams expanded exponentially, we set a goal for contacts, and we got back on the phones.

The state directors knew that our goals were daunting, but we were filled with optimism and determination. We checked in as a team one last time and pledged to serve hot chocolate in the freezing rain until the middle of the night if that's what it took to keep the last voter in line.

Less than two hours to go, and the phone calls from the poll watchers started to come at a panicked pace. "We need backup at Precinct Thirty-two; there are lines around the corner," David in Denver screamed. We immediately dispatched volunteers to help and bring hot chocolate.

Then Kate calls from Colorado Springs: "The gym has a line that snakes back and forth and out the door. This is amazing, but the wait is hours long." She called back thirty minutes later to announce that the student president was serving Kool-Aid and a band was setting up.

Then Corey in northern Colorado called. You can guess what he said. "Bring them hot chocolate; don't let a single person leave," we yelled back.

These same calls were coming in to our state offices around the country. "Bring them hot chocolate! Don't let them leave!" could be heard over and over again. The energy was amazing, the sound of thousands of young people calling their peers with urgency in their voices, the tension of being so close to hitting a seemingly unreachable goal, the constant ringing of the phone that resulted in cheers or cries for help, the sense that a community had been built and a movement was under way.

This is what it feels like when the impossible happens. We beat our goals. We crushed our goals. And what had seemed ridiculous for so long for so many volunteers and organizers became a beautiful truth swirling all around us.

## HOW IT ALL BEGAN

Seven years earlier, Robin Hubbard, an organizer for the Center for Campus Free Speech was using her network of student governments for a little side project. Those of us who had been involved with the low-energy 1996 elections, where young voter turnout dropped precipitously from the high of 1992, had come across some census data that showed college students voting at as high a rate as most other sectors of the electorate (in the mid-70 percent range). This was enough of a surprise, given the bad rap that young people had. If we, as the advocates for youth and voting were surprised, a lot of other people would be too.

Nonprofit organizations, foundations, and activists had always supported student voting projects under the assumption that the voting rate was low, but if you put some work into it, they would actually turn out and vote. That was the theory, but by the mid-1990s, most of these folks had pretty much given up under the assumption that it was not working and young people just did not vote.

Maybe for no other reason than generational pride, we came up with the idea of surveying college students on election night and trying to replicate what the Census Bureau had found. If the results held true, we thought that perhaps people would care more about what students thought. The Congress had just proposed almost $30 billion in cuts to student aid, and while students were organizing, Capitol Hill did not seem to be listening.

Robin found dozens of student governments in Mississippi, Kentucky, and Louisiana (states with odd-year gubernatorial elections) who had access to the student directories. Once the polls had closed, they called through a random selection of the students by picking every $n$th name in the directory and asked them if they had voted. Our suspicions were true: turnout among students rivaled that of older voters. We sent out a news release and renewed our conviction that students really do vote and should be paid attention to. (It was still true that young people were lagging the overall population in voter turnout, but that low turnout was primarily among the two-thirds of young people who were not in college. This group of potential voters remained the most significant challenge in increasing young voter turnout.)

Alas, the political world paid no attention to our great discovery, but the kernel of a strategy had been born. We were frustrated that the people with money and the people who made policy were not paying attention to young people and were writing off this generation. That frustration was a start, but it took a long time to develop into a real strategy.

Back during the snoozer of the 1996 elections, we had reassembled the Youth Vote Coalition from 1994 and decided that we had a message both for young people and for the decision makers: there's power in numbers; if we all got together, we would have power as a voting bloc. For decision makers, the pitch was that you should pay attention to this group because they are big. The reality was that in 1996, however, the numbers were not especially large, and no one really believed that young people had power.

By the 2000 election, Robin's study had helped to amend our strategy. We believed that young people would pay attention to politics when politics started paying attention to them. Many other measures showed young people to be engaged and interested in the political and service world, but few believed that voting was something for them. The term that was coined during that election among youth-vote organizers was "the cycle of mutual neglect." A youth advocacy group, Third Millennium, had been organized primarily around privatizing Social Security and reducing the deficit to save our generation from long-term financial crisis. They sought to make the point that long-term policies were not being paid attention to because young people were being neglected. They called their project "Neglection 2000."

It was a great campaign. Third Millennium analyzed where the presidential campaigns placed their ads (ten spots on *Friends* and some three hundred spots on *Good Morning America*), and they surveyed young and old alike to compare how much they were seeing and receiving information from the campaigns. The results were as clear as anyone would expect. We could use solid data to make our argument.

At the outset of 2000, our goal was to pressure, cajole, or shame politicians into paying attention to young people. Even with significant funding from the Pew Charitable Trusts, we realized that we did not have enough resources to go out and reach enough young people that their voice would matter or that they would have power in numbers. But we thought we could use our organizing to leverage the resources and attention of the campaigns, and they would go out and do the convincing.

Well, it did not really work again. The numbers were up slightly from 1996 but still showed no real impact. There really was not any evidence from the campaigns that they were paying attention to young voters. The exception was Senator John McCain, who talked about young voters all the way up until his concession speech. We learned later that the principal appeal to his talking about young voters in the primary was to older voters who were troubled about the cultural state of America and liked the idea of returning America to something that young people would be proud to serve, just as Senator McCain had done so valiantly.

While we had been trotting out new theories every two years and gradually building up the infrastructure and experience of the youth voting community, the academically inclined folks at the Pew Charitable Trusts were looking for more. As a part of our funding from the Trusts in 2000, the Youth Vote Coalition had worked with professors Don Green and Alan Gerber from Yale University.

We did not think much about the consequences of this work at the time, but the idea was to actually study the types of voter contact we were doing and quantify their impact. We were essentially running prescription drug trials for politics, where some people got a knock on the door or a phone call and some people in the control group did not. After the election, you go to the county records and find out at what rate people in the treatment and control groups voted, and there you have the answer about the impact of your door knocking or phone calling. (At the end of the chapter, we have a summary of more of their results).

The results were not really surprising, but they were very empowering—certainly more empowering than the nominal increase in youth turnout that the Census Bureau turned up for 2000. The Green and Gerber studies showed that talking to one hundred people resulted in eight new voters. So, rather than fifty people out of one hundred voting in a regular election, fifty-eight would vote after one talked to them all. This meant that organizers for youth-vote campaigns and political campaigns could actually start to predict with some reliability what the results of their work would be. It sounds like common sense, but it was brand new stuff, and we wanted more of it. More testing was done in the 2002 elections.

In addition to funding the continued youth organizing and research, the Pew Charitable Trusts had also funded CIRCLE, the Center for Information and Research on Civic Learning and Education. CIRCLE's mission was to do more of this research and to promote it with an academic credibility that we did not have as activists and advocates for youth.

The strategy was born for 2004: close the cycle of neglect, and engage political resources in young voter mobilization by proving the impact of best practices and appealing to political self-interest.

Our goal in 2004 was to use all of the research that was out there on how to mobilize young voters, and do it just as a professional and well-funded campaign would so that the political campaigns themselves would start to invest serious money into young voter outreach. This was not just the political effort we mounted in 2000. This time we were backed up with nearly $10 million of hardnosed person-to-person contact, proven by the professors and run by the state PIRGs—a nonpartisan public interest group with a strong track record for delivering high-quality grassroots organizing. All of this organizing was to be focused on just a handful of states to really demonstrate the impact that youth could have if they were paid attention.

If this did not get their attention, we were all going to quit—again.

## THE STATE PIRGS NEW VOTERS PROJECT

The state Public Interest Research Groups have long worked to make government accountable to ordinary citizens. Centuries of experience show that democratic government—government of the people, by the people, and for the people—is inevitably better than rule by elites, no matter how "enlightened" they may be. Civic participation is critical to this vision, as the strength of a democracy can be measured in large part by the participation of its citizens. Unfortunately, since young people were given the right to vote with the adoption of the Twenty-sixth Amendment in 1971, youth voting rates have been in steady decline.

The "cycle of mutual neglect" between young voters and politicians is a relationship in which youth are seldom the focus of campaign messages and rarely the recipients of person-to-person mobilization efforts. And when politicians don't pay attention to young voters, young voters become even less inclined to pay attention to them. It is little surprise, then, that barely one-third of eligible young people between the ages of eighteen and twenty-four voted in the 2000 election (36 percent), one of the closest in United States history.

In 2004, using the research and experience of the youth voting movement and funding from the Pew Charitable Trusts, the state PIRGs in partnership with the George Washington University Graduate School of Political Management launched the largest nonpartisan, grassroots youth voter-mobilization effort in the history of our nation, the New Voters Project.

The state PIRGs' New Voters Project ambitiously set out to increase youth participation and show politicians, political consultants, and opinion leaders that eighteen- to twenty-four-year-old voters could be an important constituency, deserving and demanding of their attention.

In 2004, the youth vote turned out in force. According to the 2004 U.S. Census Bureau report and analysis by the University of Maryland's CIRCLE, turnout among eighteen- to twenty-four-year-olds surged eleven percentage points to 46.7 percent, with more than 11.5 million votes cast—as high as the turnout in 1992, and the largest sheer number of votes cast by eighteen- to twenty-four-year-olds since they gained the right to vote in 1971.

We initially focused their work in six "core" states—Colorado, Iowa, Nevada, New Mexico, Oregon, and Wisconsin. Then, in June 2004, as we saw the impact of the work growing, we added organizers in fifteen "expansion" states, many of which had well-established student PIRG chapters. By leveraging connections with national partners, we registered thousands of additional young people to vote and garnered even more attention for young voters.

The eighteen- to twenty-four-year-old population in the six core states was approximately two million people. Of those two million young people, the goal was to register 265,000 and then conduct an intensive peer-to-peer grassroots get-out-the-vote (GOTV) campaign to get as many registered eighteen- to twenty-four-year-old voters to the polls as possible. We shattered the goal. The state PIRGs' New Voters Project

- Registered 349,000 eighteen- to twenty-four-year-olds in the six core states (more than one out of six people in our target audience) and 524,000 eighteen- to thirty-year-olds nationally.

- Made more than 530,000 GOTV personalized voter contacts in the weeks leading up to the election, including 48,000 GOTV contacts on election day itself.
- Worked at more than 150 colleges in twenty-one states.
- Recruited and trained more than 10,000 volunteers nationwide.

Of the approximately $4 billion spent in the 2004 election cycle, it is estimated that $50 million was targeted toward young voters—a mere fraction of the total dollars spent, but the most ever targeted toward young people. With an estimated eleven-point increase in turnout, it's clear that resources spent on the youth vote saw a significant return on investment. As Jane Eisner said in the *Washington Post*, "The youth vote is finding its voice again" (2004).

## STATE SELECTION

The state PIRGs selected six core states for the New Voters Project—Colorado, Iowa, Nevada, New Mexico, Oregon, and Wisconsin—after careful evaluation and analysis. Based on expected resources, geographic reach, and a population size on which we felt we could have a substantial impact; we initially targeted a population of approximately two million young people. By law, a nonpartisan registration effort must be active in a minimum of five states, so we needed a combination of at least five states where the population totaled two million. We also considered the following five criteria:

1. density and distribution of the youth population,
2. likely media attention toward the election in a given state,
3. voter registration and elections rules (that could make it easier or harder for young people to register and vote),
4. availability and quality of voter lists,
5. organizational capacity.

After considerable research, we enlisted our advisory committee to finalize the list of six states.

## PARTNERSHIPS

The New Voters Project built a wide-ranging nonpartisan network of more than one thousand partners nationwide to maximize our reach and effectiveness. We won the endorsement of eight governors, eleven secretaries of state, and fifty university and college presidents. Each of these relationships brought credibility and attention to the cause of youth voting.

We also worked with nonpartisan partners across the country. Rock the Vote (RTV) was the first organization to recognize that the state PIRGs' New Voters Project was a perfect partner. Rock the Vote matched its highly visible media presence and large membership with our field expertise on the ground. When the Rock the Vote bus visited a campus where the New Voters Project was active, we coordinated our efforts so that while the RTV bus drove around campus, we staffed voter registration stations, passed out information about student voting rights, and signed up students to volunteer with us on campus. In 2004, Rock the Vote also launched its online voter registration tool, which allowed young people to download a completed voter registration form that could be printed out and sent in to their local registrar. This tool was made even more powerful by the fact that anyone who filled out the registration form through www.rockthevote.com, or one of their online partners, was included as a target in the New Voters Project's core state GOTV operation.

We also partnered with Campus Compact, a national coalition of more than 950 college and university presidents committed to the civic purposes of higher education. Working together, the state PIRGs' New Voters Project was able to strengthen our relationships with college presidents, university student associations, and state student associations. In February and March of 2004, Campus Compact and the New Voters Project rallied 125 college and university presidents and administrators to sign a pledge card in which they promised to take an active role in developing institutional strategies to engage young people in the political process.

A selection of our other national partners includes Cast the Vote, Citizen Change, Declare Yourself, Every Child Matters, Frontier Airlines, Harvard University Institute of Politics, Headcount, Hip-Hop Summit Action Network, MTV, NAACP National Voter Fund, Patagonia, Project Vote, The Campaign for Young Voters, Tower Records, Voter Virgin, Voteworks, Businesses Promote the Vote, Women's Voices, Women Vote, Working Assets, World Wrestling Entertainment, Youth Venture, Youth Vote Coalition, and 18–35.org.

## REGISTRATION

Since only 50.7 percent of young people were registered in 2000, and information in voter files for those who are registered is weaker than for older voters, the state PIRGs' New Voters Project started with a major registration drive to significantly increase the pool of eligible voters and to build a reliable voter database. We employed several registration strategies in order to maximize outreach to all different groups of young people. In total, we registered more than 524,000 eighteen- to thirty-year-olds.

## On Campus

We knew it was most productive to register young people at the location where they would actually be voting—at their campus address instead of in their hometown, for example. We employed two strategies on campus. First, we worked with college presidents, administrators, and student government associations to institutionalize voter registration, making it a part of freshman orientation, move-in days, or other processes that most students participate in. Second, we ran grassroots, peer-to-peer voter registration drives, tabling in high-traffic areas like student centers and dining halls. The state PIRGs' New Voters Project had more than sixty campus organizers working with ten thousand volunteers on 150 college and university campuses to register nearly 197,000 young people on campuses in our six core states (89 percent of those in the final weeks before voter registration deadlines). In our expansion states, we registered an additional 90,000 eighteen- to thirty-year-olds.

## Off-Campus Youth

We prioritized outreach to young people who would have been less likely to register without the state PIRGs' New Voters Project. Nonstudents, for example, typically vote at rates about nineteen percentage points lower than students. Our fourteen canvass offices hired and trained canvassers to scour busy pedestrian areas, coffee shops, concerts, festivals, sporting events, malls, and other high-traffic locations where young people congregate. Canvassers put in nearly seventy thousand hours registering voters. By voter registration deadlines, we had registered 130,908 eighteen- to twenty-four-year-old off-campus youth in our six core states, as well as an additional 103,000 voters aged twenty-five and older.

## In High Schools

We reached out to high schools in our six core states to set up programs to register graduating seniors. State PIRGs' New Voters Project staff in Colorado secured commitments from several school systems to register at least 90 percent of their graduating seniors. And Wisconsin staff alone registered almost nine thousand students at sixty-eight high schools. All told, our high school outreach program registered almost fifteen thousand students.

## STORIES FROM THE FIELD: REGISTRATION

### Portland, Oregon: Midnight Madness!

The State PIRGs' New Voters Project worked with Oregon secretary of state Bill Bradbury on one final push to encourage young people in Portland to vote—Midnight Madness! Instead of sticking to the stated registration deadline of 5 p.m. on Tuesday, October 12 (when city and county offices officially close), Secretary Bradbury agreed to extend the deadline until midnight. We set up and staffed Midnight Madness registration tables across the city of Portland. There were stations on campuses, at pubs, and in community centers; we even had an outdoor drive-through drop-off station at Portland Community College.

### Las Vegas, Nevada: Voter Registration Goes to the Movies!

The New Voters Project joined forces with Cast the Vote and MTV's Choose or Lose to launch a three-week-long in-theatre voter registration drive at four megaplex movie houses in Las Vegas, Nevada. At each location, organizers and volunteers stationed registration tables in high-traffic areas and encouraged young people to register as they entered. "Register and Vote" public service announcements ran in the theaters for the duration of the drive. In just three weeks, we registered more than two thousand moviegoing youth.

## DATABASE

Contacting registered voters is critical to increasing voter turnout. But young people, more than any other demographic, are difficult to find and contact. Because young people move often and in recent years have tended not to have land-line telephones, young people are less likely to appear on commonly used lists, political or otherwise. And because young people historically register and vote at lower rates, government and vendor-supplied voter-file lists tend to be less useful than they are for files of older age groups.

We decided to start with the most reliable information we could find—the information from our own voter registration drives—and built the best database of young voters available. We set up state-of-the-art systems for tracking the contact information of people we registered to vote. We created our own method to collect cell-phone numbers and e-mail addresses—information that is not always collected on state registration forms but that is essential to contact young voters. We then supplemented the information we had collected from our registration drives with state and county voter lists and with data on young voters from coalition partners. By election day, we had built a database of 1.4 million records, including tens of thousands of cell-phone numbers and 150,000 e-mail addresses.

## GET OUT THE VOTE

The grassroots campaign experience of the State PIRGs and studies by Yale professors Don Green and Alan Gerber (2004) suggest that a large-scale effort of peer-to-peer voter contact can make a significant difference in the turnout rate of young voters. In studies summarized in their book, Green and Gerber found that door-to-door GOTV canvassing can increase voter turnout by eight percentage points, and high-quality GOTV phone banks can increase voter turnout by five percentage points among voters who are contacted.

In the weeks leading up to election day, we launched a large-scale effort to mobilize new voters we registered—as well as the broader population of registered youth—to turn out and cast their ballots. Our GOTV effort included a range of approaches like student-run campaigns on campuses, door-to-door canvassing, phone banks, and neighborhood-level volunteer-based efforts.

Other organizations reached out to young voters through sophisticated e-mail and media strategies. Taking full advantage of the state PIRGs' three decades of experience in coordinating person-to-person student and citizen mobilization efforts, the New Voters Project was the only nonpartisan youth mobilization operation to utilize this type of grassroots approach on a scale this large. The entire operation was centered on personalized interactions in which staff and volunteers talked to registered young voters about voting and provided them with information on where to vote and how to vote early or by absentee ballot.

In the final weeks leading up to election day, the New Voters Project made more than half a million personalized voter contacts, including forty-eight thousand contacts on election day itself.

*On campus.* We ran a comprehensive campus GOTV effort that combined dorm storming and phone banking with tabling and special events. Every activity was geared toward generating buzz around the elections and turning students out on election day. We made 159,421 voter contacts on campus.

*Off campus.* Our fourteen New Voters Project field offices operated a door-to-door field operation, reminding young voters to get to the polls on election day, offering absentee voting, and encouraging people to vote early whenever it was a convenient option. We made 112,140 face-to-face contacts through the canvass operation.

*GOTV phone banks.* The State PIRGs' four professional telephone outreach offices called round the clock and made 145,695 personal contacts in the last three weeks before the election, with a remarkable 15,000 contacts made on election day alone.

*Neighborhood voter program.* In New Mexico and Nevada, sixteen organizers phone banked from the voter files and contacted community groups and high schools to recruit neighborhood precinct captains in nonstudent precincts. New Voters Project organizers worked with precinct captains to contact young registered voters in their neighborhoods by phone and by canvassing door to door. By election day, the neighborhood program made 28,928 face-to-face contacts.

In the immediate hours and days following the election, some journalists reported that early exit polling showed no increase in turnout among young voters.[1] But they got it wrong. In fact, according to the 2004 U.S. Census Bureau report, young voters drove the overall turnout increase in the 2004 election. Turnout among eighteen- to twenty-four-year-olds increased eleven percentage points, while voter turnout increased by only four percentage points among the general population. According to CIRCLE, the eighteen- to twenty-four-year-old age group had the largest increase in turnout among all age groups between the 2000 and 2004 elections.

The state PIRGs' New Voters Project has been looking at early data, where available, from the counties in which we worked. So far, this information continues to indicate a dramatic increase in turnout among young Americans. In four counties in Iowa where the state PIRGs' New Voters Project was active, we saw a 76 percent increase in turnout among the eighteen- to twenty-four-year-old population, while turnout among voters aged twenty-five to thirty-six increased by 22 percent (see table 9.1).

## STORIES FROM THE FIELD: GOTV

### Voting Early in the Hawkeye State

New Voters Project organizers successfully petitioned Iowa secretary of state Chet Culver to bring polling stations to college and university campuses across the Hawkeye State. At Iowa State University (ISU) in Ames, Iowa, we arranged two "early-voting days" on campus. When Ames county officials tried to shut down the polling station on the second day of early voting—while two hundred students were still in line—our organizers sprang into action. We alerted the secretary of state's office to the problem and advised students to stay in line. New Voters Project organizers kept the ISU polling location open

**Table 9.1.  The Youth Vote, 2000 and 2004**

| Iowa | 2000 Turnout (18–24-year-olds) | 2004 Turnout (18–24-year-olds) | % Increase 2000 to 2004 | 2000 Turnout (25–36-year-olds) | 2004 Turnout (25–36-year-olds) | % Increase 2000 to 2004 |
|---|---|---|---|---|---|---|
| Dubuque | 2,564 | 4,797 | 87.09% | 4,896 | 5,841 | 19.30% |
| Johnson | 10,344 | 16,239 | 56.99% | 6,099 | 7,103 | 16.46% |
| Linn | 6,504 | 14,203 | 118.37% | 13,811 | 17,769 | 28.66% |
| Polk | 12,440 | 20,857 | 67.66% | 28,849 | 34,992 | 21.29% |
| Total | 31,852 | 56,096 | 76.11% | 53,655 | 65,705 | 22.46% |

*data provided by the Cedar Rapids Gazette (1/12/05)

and successfully lobbied for an additional "early voting day" on November 1, the day before the election.

## NEXT STEPS: THE STRATEGY CONTINUES

The task before us now is to build on the success of 2004 by registering even more young people to vote, by continuing to persuade the political establishment that youth are a vital constituency deserving of their resources, by building institutions that can mobilize youth, and by promoting reforms of our electoral processes that remove the barriers to participation.

In order to sustain this newly invigorated generation of young people and further expand political participation, we need to make sure that candidates and opinion leaders continue to see the power of the youth constituency; we cannot let the success of 2004 be an anomaly.

The Graduate School of Political Management at the George Washington University, a 2003 sponsor of the New Voters Project along with the state PIRGs, launched a project in 2004 (Young Voter Strategies) to take the lessons learned from the elections and market them to political campaigns, consultants, parties, and nonprofit organizations. The goal is to create confidence in the fact that young people are engaged and will turn out if you ask them, and to give the politicians the now-proven tools to do it.[2]

In the year since the elections, there has been a significant change in the conventional wisdom on young voters. Of course, not everyone is convinced, but there is a sense that something is happening, and many of the political elites want to know how to capitalize on it. In a recent meeting, a top campaign manager told us that he "was sick of the old moniker that young people don't vote. We all know they will vote; we just don't know how to get to them." The plan is working; we are generating interest and investment among the campaign practitioners. Here are some basic tactics that work to get to young voters:

1. *Person-to-personcontact* has the strongest impact on the likelihood that a young person will register and vote. Experiments by professors Don Green and Alan Gerber showed a five-percentage-point increase in turnout from phone calls and an eight-percentage-point increase in turnout from a conversation at the door. Use these assumptions to incorporate youth into your field plans. If you ask them, they will vote.
2. Ask everyone you talk to if they will *volunteer*. Young people today bring tremendous energy, creativity, and leadership to causes they care about. Also, developing volunteer networks allows for inexpensive peer-to-peer contacts.
3. Do *voter registration*. Many young voters move around. Registration efforts can help with the collection of updated contact information, including cell phones and e-mails. And this conversation when registering young people can double as a voter identification contact.
4. Go to *college campuses*. It is rare to find one place where so many potential voters from any demographic congregate like young people do on college campuses. Speak to classes and student organizations, spend time at a table, and walk the dorms and dense student neighborhoods. Tip: don't just do a photo shoot and leave; engage students in genuine dialogue.
5. When trying to reach young people *off campus*, think about how they live. Site-based canvassing at bars, clubs, concerts, gas stations, laundromats, community centers, festivals, and churches allows for high contact rates amongst critical groups of young voters.
6. You don't need a new *issue platform*, but you do need to talk about how your policies will relate to younger people's lives. For example, if you talk about your position on the Iraq War, explain how it will affect their brothers and best friends (as opposed to their sons and daughters).

Of course, we have come too far to leave the fate of our strategy in the hands of the newly converted political establishment; so as we move forward, youth voting organizations will also continue their work to engage young voters in the elections in 2005 and 2006 and will build an infrastructure for work in 2008.

Young Voter Strategies, with support from the Pew Charitable Trusts, will fund a dozen organizations to do nonpartisan voter registration work with segments of the youth population, and to track registration efforts with the same academic vigor as we did our mobilization work a few years back.

Student PIRG chapters—independent, state-based student organizations— will be the backbone of the state PIRGs' New Voters Project, are already active in the elections in New Jersey and Virginia in 2005, and are planning follow-up work in the six "core" states from 2004 in addition to expanding to even more states for 2006.

In addition to running voter registration drives, training student leaders, and continuing to make peer-to-peer voter contact a priority, the state PIRGs' New Voters Project will be reconvening with their partners and working to strengthen relationships with college and university officials. One of the most cost-effective ways to register and mobilize young voters is to increase the frequency of "institutionalized" voting; we need colleges and universities to make it easy for students to register, and we need elections offices and secretaries of state to protect young people's right to vote. Their focus will be to

- secure polling stations on campus for early voting;
- secure polling stations on campus for election day;
- institute voter registration for all incoming freshmen by making it a part of the freshman orientation, move-in process, and student identification process;
- work with local election officials to remove barriers to participation; and
- educate young people about their voting rights.

The student PIRGs and other youth organizing groups will also keep young people civically engaged during off-year elections through issue-based campaigns around topics we care about, like higher education, hunger, and homelessness.

Changing a thirty-five-year habit of politics and youth ignoring each other is not an easy task, but we have come a long way in the past twelve years. And the landscape is ripe for continued forward momentum: the youth-vote organizing community is more experienced, better funded, and increasingly stronger; young people today for reasons outside our control are much more engaged in their communities and civically inclined; and political campaigns are moving toward more peer-to-peer work overall, which makes the young-voter grassroots outreach a more natural fit. We like to think that a trend of increased youth participation in politics has begun; only time will tell. But for the next twelve years, we will continue to revise and pursue our strategy, and we will keep bringing hot chocolate to the polls.

## NOTES

1. The final exit-poll numbers suggest that turnout did increase among young voters, by seven percentage points.

2. See www.youngvoterstrategies.org for more information on this effort.

# 10

## Young Voter Mobilization Projects in 2004

*Daniel M. Shea and John C. Green*

After the 1996 election, politicians, pundits, and political scientists began to worry about the low level of voter turnout among young voters eighteen to twenty-four years old. According to U.S. Census figures, in that year only about one-third of eighteen- to twenty-four-year-olds turned out to vote, down about 15 percent from the previous election. But because the outcome of the 1996 election was never really in doubt (Bill Clinton easily defeated Republican Bob Dole), the decline in youth turnout did not set off alarm bells. After all, did it really matter if young voters sat out an election, particularly a dull one?

The 2000 election challenged that sort of thinking. The first open-seat presidential contest since 1988, the 2000 race was a dead heat from the beginning. It was a hard-hitting, dramatic campaign, and the candidates had clear differences on critical public policies. But for some reasons, most Americans seemed indifferent to the contest. In the end, the 2000 race proved to be one of the closest elections in American history. Indeed, only a handful of votes in a handful of states would have put Al Gore in the White House instead of George W. Bush. It was as if someone had tossed a coin in the air and it had landed on its edge. The outcome was that close, ultimately resolved by the U.S. Supreme Court, and the results mattered, because George W. Bush substantially shifted the direction of public policy.

Surely young voters returned to the polls for this controversial election, right? Turnout among young voters in the 2000 election remained mired at 36 percent. Suddenly *everyone* understood the significance of young voter withdrawal. A generation of voters turned off from politics was a big deal. From a philosophical perspective, it represented a worrisome problem with American democracy. Many argued that the concerns of young

Americans would be underrepresented in the policy process, thus distorting the link between the governed and the governors (Patterson 2003). From a pragmatic perspective, all understood that young voters could have glided either candidate safely into office. Operatives in both major political parties understood that young voters could be crucial in future elections.

All across the country, people decided it was time to do something about this "turned-off generation." In 2004, a stunning set of programs and new initiatives were created to encourage young Americans to participate in the democratic process. In many instances, existing programs were beefed up, but in other cases, entirely new projects were initiated. Simply stated, at no time in American history had there been more time, energy, and resources committed to mobilizing a particular group of voters. This chapter describes many of these varied efforts. It is by no means an exhaustive catalog, but rather a list of many of the most interesting and best-known projects.

For ease of presentation, these programs are sorted into five rough categories. The first category consists of projects sponsored by various elements of the entertainment industry, ranging from Rock the Vote to Smackdown Your Vote (see chapter 8). The second category includes initiatives funded principally by foundations, such as the New Voters Project (see chapter 9). The third category is a catchall of projects involved with new technology or institutional connections, including "computers, colleges, cities, and churches" (see Eisner 2004). The fourth category contains efforts by liberal interest groups, such as the New Voter Alliance and America Coming Together. The final category covers programs associated with the major political parties (see chapter 3). There is some overlap in these categories—for example, entertainers were involved in some programs outside of the first group—but this categorization provides a rough guide to the type and range of young voter projects in 2004.

It is simply honest to admit that we do not know if these programs made a difference in youth turnout. However, in 2004, turnout among eighteen- to twenty-four-year-olds skyrocketed by eleven points above 2000 figures—more than double the rate of increase for any other age group. Perhaps this increase resulted from the close and controversial 2000 election that pulled young voters to the polls, or the perception that the 2004 election was up for grabs. Certainly, the Republican and Democratic presidential campaigns waged an extraordinary campaign to turn out favorable voters, which may have reached the youth as well. Or perhaps controversial issues debated during the 2004 campaign, including the war in Iraq, sparked interest among the youth. Nonetheless, we believe that these special youth programs did make a difference, and more importantly, that they can make a contribution in the future, a point we will briefly address in the conclusion. If nothing else, some of these programs may help maintain or expand the 2004 positive results among young voters.

## ENTERTAINMENT INDUSTRY INITIATIVES

### Rock the Vote: The Crossroads of Entertainment and Engagement

In 1990, members of the music recording industry founded a unique organization in response to a series of perceived threats against the First Amendment rights of speech and expression. Rock the Vote (RTV), a nonpartisan and nonprofit organization, combined entertainment and politics to target young people and get them excited about and involved in politics. "From actors to musicians, comedians to athletes, Rock the Vote harnesses cutting-edge trends and pop culture to make political participation cool" (Rock the Vote 2004a).

Throughout the past fourteen years, RTV has run public service announcements (PSAs) starring an array of celebrities, produced documentaries and youth-friendly literature, lobbied Congress, and developed scores of voter registration initiatives (Rock the Vote 2004b). Street teams hit malls and concerts across the country while a voter registration bus traveled the nation to various college campuses, passing out voting information and introducing people to the interactive RTV website (Singer 2004). The organization even sent out preelection "Get Out the Vote" phone calls from various celebrities in the music entertainment industry (Rock the Vote 2004b).

Receiving its funding through corporate sponsors, private donations, and foundation grants, RTV was fairly well financed (Singer 2004). Its 1992 effort was aided by Bill Clinton's appearances on *The Arsenio Hall Show* playing his saxophone and on MTV answering the infamous "boxers or briefs?" question (Hampson 2004). RTV quickly became one of the most well-known youth voting initiatives in the country. Yet despite high publicity and praise, certain strategies seemed rather ineffective. For example, the nonpartisan stance of RTV weakens its message for American youth, who "want to vote for or against something or someone." Also, an increase in voter registration does not necessarily translate into an increase in voting. "Many of those registered by RTV might have registered anyway; others never went to the polls" (Hampson 2004).

Since 2002, it expanded its Community Street Teams to thirty-five cities, supplied schools nationwide with voter registration kits, and has partnered with eighty-five radio stations to air PSAs by celebrities such as Chris Rock, Eve, and Kelly Osborne (Rock the Vote 2004b). In 2004, the organization teamed up with Motorola to run "Rock the Mobile Vote," a nine-month program that featured "Get Loud" messages, polling questions, and special ring tones and graphics for members' cell phones. It even partnered with Ben & Jerry's Ice Cream to create its own flavor: a strawberry cheesecake ice cream named Primary Berry Graham, from which RTV received a donation for every pint sold (Spethmann 2004). These examples represent the kind of unconventional tactics that played a major part in the 2004 campaign.

In 2004, RTV registered 350,000 youth and brought "over two million new young voters to the polls." This reversed a long-standing trend of apathy and increased the youth turnout by 20 percent over the preceding presidential election (Rock the Vote 2004b). After the election, the Rock the Vote website proclaimed "You Did It!" signifying that young people turned out in record numbers in the election. But it also reminded youth that their job is never done. RTV continually works to increase youth involvement in the political process. "Regardless of whether youth are signing petitions, running for office, contacting their elected officials, or taking up a sign in protest, they are all rocking the vote" (Rock the Vote 2004a).

### Redeem the Vote: Fishers of Young Voters

Combining music and faith, Redeem the Vote marked a nonpartisan, nonprofit Christian effort to encourage young evangelicals to become active participants in the 2004 election. The goal of Redeem the Vote was simple but powerful: "to reach America's young people of faith and engage them in the 2004 election" (Redeem the Vote 2004). The primary motivation in establishing such an effort was to increase young voters' awareness of the cultural issues that have become so important in recent elections.

The hope was that Redeem the Vote would serve as "the religious community's answer to MTV's secular 'Rock the Vote'" (DiCarlo 2004). The organization put together tour groups of different Christian rock bands to promote the effort. Specifically, Redeem the Vote spent a majority of their time targeting the key swing states of Wisconsin, Pennsylvania, Ohio, and Florida. Through their music and lyrics, the artists encouraged young people to vote and provided several opportunities for them to do so (DiCarlo 2004).

The effort garnered much attention and success. As of late October, nearly sixty thousand people were in attendance at each festival, and by election day, forty-two thousand people had signed up to register on the website (Redeem the Vote 2004). Founder Randy Brinson noted that the response from churches was amazing. "People are getting in touch with us and asking how they can get it for their church," Brinson said (DiCarlo 2004).

### Choose or Lose: 280 Million Wowed

MTV launched "Choose or Lose" in 1992 as a way to reach young voters through the popular cable television network (Spethmann 2004). Working in collaboration with Rock the Vote, MTV believed that because of its large youth audience, it was in a unique position to promote voting among its audience. The best-known aspect of the Choose or Lose campaign has been the Choose or Lose bus, which has traveled the country each election year since the program's inception. This effort allows the program to reach young voters on a personal and local level, while the MTV network can broadcast its journey to a national audience (Atwood 1996). In recent years, many other organizations have adopted similar kinds of traveling programs to register voters.

MTV set a specific goal for itself in Choose or Lose 2004. By kicking off "20 Million Loud," the organization attempted, through television programming and online sources, to mobilize twenty million eighteen- to thirty-year-olds to vote. Special programs like news pieces, behind-the-scenes specials of the candidate's campaigns, and broadcasts of the Republican and Democratic national conventions served to inform young people about issues and policies (Singer 2004). Following these segments, viewers were encouraged to participate in the "PRElection" on the Choose or Lose website, which gave visitors a chance to both register to vote in the actual election and cast a vote in MTV's preelection poll via the Internet or mobile phone. Along with voting for their favored presidential candidate, participants also answered questions such as what issues they felt were important, why they believed voting is significant, and whether they planned to vote. Although the poll was not scientific, the three-week polling period did offer an interesting insight into the opinions of young people and succeeded in registering almost 120,000 new voters (MTV. com Choose or Lose 2004).

Funded by the MTV network, the organization has the ample resources of the popular cable channel at its disposal (Singer 2004). Apparently, this access is paying off. Estimates show that over thirty million people viewed some type of Choose or Lose programming in the months preceding the 2004 election (Singer 2004). MTV's Choose or Lose website has changed its "20 Million Loud" banner to now read "21 Million Proud," proclaiming that "over 21 million 18 to 30 year-olds made their voices heard" (MTV.com Choose or Lose 2004).

## HeadCount: Political Eye for the Young Guys

On its website, HeadCount boasts that their organization "registered more people than any all-volunteer group in the country. Our public service announcements made it to network TV. And perhaps most important, we gave hundreds of young people their very first taste of activism." Compared with many of the other youth projects in 2004, HeadCount started late but made a noticeable impression. After only about a month of planning, Marc Brownstein, the bass player of the electronic rock band "The Disco Biscuits," and

Andy Bernstein, a sports reporter, launched HeadCount in February 2004 (HeadCount 2004).

The organization consisted mainly of volunteers from around the country, promoters, and band members, all of which were unpaid. The organization relied primarily on artists to disseminate its message in the hope of reaching their goal of registering one hundred thousand young people. When a HeadCount artist traveled to a city with a street team, volunteers would be waiting for them, registering new voters. The artist would then speak during the show about not only the importance of registering, but about actually becoming informed on the issues and casting a ballot on election day. Head-Count headliners included Dave Matthews Band, Phish, and Carlos Santana. Such artists also put voting messages on their websites, as well as links to the HeadCount homepage. In addition, HeadCount produced a number of public service announcements featuring these artists and aired them on TBS, TNT, and other cable networks (HeadCount 2004). Relying on the strengths of its volunteers and the generosity of its contributors, HeadCount developed quickly and plans to expand its programs in future years.

### Hip-Hop Summit Action Network: Get-Out-The-Vizzle

Since its debut about thirty-one years ago, hip-hop music has become a mainstay in contemporary culture. Its ability to permeate differences of class and race has fueled not only its longevity, but also its importance to American youth (Busk 2002). The Hip-Hop Summit Action Network (HSAN) was formed to use this powerful art form in a constructive way. The group was cofounded by Russell Simmons and Benjamin Chavis. Simmons, often called the "godfather of hip-hop," is also founder of Def Jam Records and a pop-culture tycoon (Jones 2003), while Chavis, who serves as the HSAN president and CEO, is "a veteran of the Civil Rights movement and former Executive Director and CEO of the NAACP" (Hip-Hop Summit Action Network.org 2004a). Each believed this combination of hip-hop and civic engagement put HSAN in a unique position to encourage youth political engagement.

The mission of the Hip-Hop Summit Action Network is to harness "the cultural relevance of Hip-Hop music to serve as a catalyst for education advocacy and other societal concerns fundamental to the well-being of at-risk youth throughout the United States" (Hip-Hop Summit Action Network.org 2004a). By utilizing entertainers, youth leaders, and civil rights activists, HSAN put specific emphasis on organizing young African Americans into a significant voting bloc. Buses of HSAN organizers visited swing states throughout the year and set up "summits" at hip-hop concerts, seeking to register young people, engage them in discussions regarding important issues, and transform voting into a fashionable activity (Segal 2004). A special Get-Out-The-Vote Bus Tour ran from September 10, 2004, to election day and took young people across the country to encourage their peers to get out the vote (Hip-Hop Summit Action Network.org 2004b).

To appeal to young voters and develop a database of those eligible, HSAN asks youth to fill out a "hip-hop vote card" or sign up for the "Hip-Hop Team Vote" on the HSAN website, requesting their name, e-mail address, home phone number, and AOL Instant Messenger screen name. HSAN then uses this information to send important voting reminders through text messages, AOL Instant Messages, and e-mail (Segal 2004). Their website had a list of incentives for signing up, such as a personalized e-mail newsletter, information on hip-hop artists' new releases, and discounts on new clothing and shoes (Hip-Hop Summit Action Network.org 2004c). Although this nonprofit group works on a relatively small budget with only about twenty-five employees, its efforts are aggressive, far reaching, and appropriate for a young audience enraptured by the music, icons, and culture of hip-hop (Hip-Hop Summit Action Network.org 2004c).

## Citizen Change: Puffy Gets Political

After his efforts in 2004, Sean "P. Diddy" Combs, rap-musician-turned-producer/clothing designer/entertainer, can add youth-vote advocate to his résumé. Combs founded the national nonpartisan/nonprofit organization "Citizen Change" to "educate, motivate, and empower the more than 42 million Americans aged 18 to 30 that are eligible to vote." To sell its message, the group's strategy was to utilize the same marketing tools used to promote a CD, clothing item, or other product in the entertainment industry (Citizen Change 2004). Ultimately, Citizen Change attempted to sell voting's urgency.

With their in-your-face slogan, "Vote or Die!," Combs and his Citizen Change partners wished to convey the vital importance of voting on election day (Citizen Change 2004). Combs amassed a plethora of celebrities, such as Jay-Z, Ellen DeGeneres, 50 Cent, and Leonardo DiCaprio, to ensure that the "Vote or Die!" message permeated every facet of pop culture. Fashion designers, including Tommy Hilfiger and Phat Farm, were even commissioned to design limited-edition "Vote or Die!" T-shirts, the proceeds of which fueled Citizen Change's registration efforts (Citizen Change 2004).

Citizen Change did its best to capitalize on star power and the power of conformity to convince youth that not only is voting "in," but that their futures were at stake in the 2004 election. Combs himself appeared at the Republican and Democratic national conventions to spread the message that the outcome of the 2004 race would have serious implications concerning issues important to young Americans (Young 2004). He summed up his goal as he launched the initiative: "For the first time in history, we're going to make voting fashionable" (Amter 2004).

## Punk Voter: From Alienation to Anger to Activism

A group of punk-music listeners put aside their traditional feelings of estrangement from the world to join the ranks of those trying to mobilize new youth voters for the 2004 election. Punk Voter, founded in 2001 by punk bassist and vocalist Mike Burkett, targeted young fans of punk rock music with get-out-the-vote messages and anthems (Ross 2004). Unlike other organizations, however, Punk Voter was openly anti-President George W. Bush. Although some may be taken aback by their aggressive Bush bashing and antiwar messages, such as those on the compilation CD produced by Burkett's record label called "Rock against Bush," the group is well organized and has a large following (Ross 2004).

Punk Voter's primary mode of disseminating information is through booths set up at every stop along the "Warped Tour," a summer-long event filled with loud music and extreme sports demonstrations (Ross 2004). They use groups like Sum 41 and Green Day to entice and educate punk fans about "what is really going on in Washington DC" (Punk Voter 2004). Punk artists, fans, and labels look to translate the enthusiasm that drives the punk movement into the political arena. Claiming that "punks have always preached social change," their goal is to activate fans into bringing about that change through voter education, registration, and mobilization (Punk Voter 2004).

Their website included strong images of George W. Bush with a "VETO" stamp on his forehead and the word "deMOCKracy" written over it, graphic political cartoons, and messages encouraging the punk community to unite into a "political force to be reckoned with" (Punk Voter 2004). Although their efforts are focused on punk music fans, their messages are powerful, and their support, through individuals, corporations, and bands, is evident. Punks have channeled their rebellious ways into an effective form of political activism.

## Conservative Punk: Not Your Average Punks

While Punk Voter took pride in being "anti-Bush" in 2004, Conservative Punk was founded as a response to the traditional liberal nature of the punk genre, while, like Punk Voter, still targeting punk music's youth audience.

In developing his website, the founder of ConservativePunk.com, Nick Rizzuto, sought to motivate youth to register to vote and inspire young people to think independently about the choice they would be making on election day. Rizzuto aimed to discredit the stereotype that aligns "punk" voters with liberalism by informing younger people of more conservative ideals through punk music. Claiming that the numerous outlets emerging over the past few decades were too clouded in left-wing propaganda, Conservative Punk sought to create a forum that advocated an open atmosphere, more welcoming to conservatives. It tried achieving that by ridding the outlet of the "liberal sentiment" that, according to them, had too often been shoved down conservatives' throats (Conservative Punk 2004a). Rizzuto leaned toward Bush, but he claims that the organization was founded with the intention of being aligned with the idea of independence, not any particular political party. The name "Conservative Punk," then, apparently refers to the voting drive's conservative nature when compared to the other "punk" voting efforts (Lynskey 2004).

The privately funded website planned to remain active after 2004, serving as an established political forum, a place to download music from conservative punk groups, and a source for columns written by several different conservative columnists as different components of its site. Conservative Punk continues to offer a link to the universal voter registration form on the Federal Elections Commission website, as it strives to maintain its support for civic engagement, while attempting to create an ideological balance in the future of punk music and the punk movement (Conservative Punk 2004b).

### Your Country, Your Vote: Taking the Pickup Truck to the Polls

The popularity of country music has skyrocketed within recent decades. In 2004, country music stars took advantage of their rising success and launched a music-oriented get-out-the-vote effort entitled "Your Country, Your Vote." The goal for this initiative was to "reach the largest cross-section" of voting-age adults. The idea was born out of a discussion between musicians who acknowledged the growing apathy in young voters in the United States. Writer and director Ronald F. Maxwell stated, "What many people forget is that voting is a right, guaranteed by the Constitution, with the purpose of having leaders chosen by the people and for the people of our nation" (Northrop 2004).

Participants included country music stars such as Ricky Skaggs, Josh Turner, Marty Raybon, Lee Ann Womack, Blake Shelton, Darryl Worley, and Billy Dean, who previously appeared on a CD of songs that were inspired by the Civil War, called *America Will Always Stand*. Deciding to take the project a step further, these artists used the CD to motivate voters (Your Country, Your Vote 2004). The campaign kicked off in Nashville and included radio and television spots and announcements at country music concerts (Northrop 2004).

In addition, the website provided a plethora of information about election events. The site also included links to up-to-date information concerning the candidates and their platforms, as well as a link providing instructions on how to register to vote (Your Country, Your Vote 2004). The project was revolutionary for the country music community and garnered considerable support.

### Declare Yourself: Producing a New Series of Voters

Formed by famed television producer Norman Lear, who produced television shows such as *All in the Family* and *The Jeffersons*, "Declare Yourself" is a national nonprofit, nonpartisan organization created to energize and empower a new movement of young voters to participate in the 2004 presidential election" (Declare Yourself 2004). The campaign itself was one year long but was the result of a three-year project called the "Declaration of Independence Road Trip," a nationwide tour aimed at showing the "contemporary relevance of the nation's birth certificate" (Declare Yourself 2004).

Lear said that the project was rooted in his dismay over recent statistics on young voters, finding that in 1996 only 32 percent of eligible eighteen- to twenty-four-year-olds voted. To address this problem, Declare Yourself sought to "combine education, entertainment, and the Internet" to draw attention to the importance of voting (Gerhart 2003). The organization has reached young voters through nationwide rallies, public speeches, music tours, and visits to college students and high school seniors. The website provided useful information on voter registration and candidate platforms and issues (Declare Yourself 2004). Lear was able to garner much celebrity and media support for his initiative. Celebrities such as Drew Barrymore and companies like Home Depot are just a few Declare Yourself activists. Post-election results, surveys, and news have kept the website active as a force for youth political participation.

### Smackdown Your Vote!: Body-Slamming Apathy

With the presidential election shaping up to be an electoral cage fight, a group of professional wrestlers saw 2004 as the perfect opportunity to become politically involved. World Wrestling Entertainment Inc. took some time out of the ring to jump into the political arena in 2004 when it initiated Smackdown Your Vote!, an "apartisan" campaign focused at young voter involvement (WWE Vote 2004a). Like Choose or Lose, Smackdown Your Vote! is funded by its parent organization, World Wrestling Entertainment (Singer 2004). Partnering with other young voter projects, such as Rock the Vote and Citizen Change, the group's ultimate goals included organizing mass voter registration drives and asking candidates to address more issues relevant to Americans under thirty (WWE Vote 2004b).

Focusing primarily on four presidential candidates (Republican president George W. Bush, Senator John Kerry [D-MA], independent Ralph Nader, and Libertarian Michael Badnarik), Smackdown Your Vote! was especially active in encouraging youth to know the candidates' stances on issues important to them. One of the group's key initiatives was a policy pamphlet known as the national Voter Issues Paper, or "the 18–30 VIP," deemed most relevant to the eighteen- to thirty-year-old age bracket. The campaign focused on obtaining responses from presidential candidates concerning their thoughts on the issues presented in this paper. To show their progress, the website featured ideas, quotes, and reports from both state and national candidates concerning "the 18–30 VIP." In addition to those candidate responses, the site also provided a host of information for young voters. It featured candidate platforms and updates, news concerning both the Democrat and Republican national conventions, voting statistics, and post-election results and news. Aside from the Internet, the Smackdown Your Vote! campaign visited college and university campuses and assisted them with their voter registration efforts (WWE Vote 2004c). On election day, Smackdown's efforts bore fruit, laying a "smackdown" on youth voting apathy (WWE Vote 2004b).

## PHILANTHROPIC INITIATIVES

### New Voters Project: A New Strategy for an Old Plan

Political scientists often wonder how to turn American youth into a significant voting population, yet the perfect strategy to accomplish this goal remains elusive. Enter the New Voters Project, which has proven to be "the largest grassroots youth voter mobilization campaign in history" (New Voters Project 2004a). This enormous get-out-the-vote campaign targeted eighteen- to twenty-four-year-olds in Colorado, Iowa, Oregon, Wisconsin, New Mexico, and Nevada, due to the large young adult populations of these states (New Voters Project 2004a). The project was organized through the collaborative efforts of the Pew Charitable Trusts, the George Washington University School of Political Management, and the state Public Interest Research Groups (PIRGs), which seek to activate young voters through intense mobilization projects (New Voters Project 2004a).

Prior to the election, officials asked young people for their "pledge" to vote. In a drive in Wisconsin, nearly 22,500 eighteen- to twenty-four-year-olds pledged to vote on election day (Epstein 2004). Professor Kathleen Dolan of University of Wisconsin–Milwaukee said that the pledge drives were a good idea: "Mobilization is all about asking people to participate. At some level, it can demystify the process when someone who looks just like you demographically asks you to be a part of the process" (Epstein 2004). Though the original goal of the organization was to register 265,000 youth, New Voters Project surpassed that goal with an impressive 348,187 registrations as of election day (New Voters Project 2004b).

One initiative of the New Voters Project was to allow youth to submit questions that they would like to ask the 2004 presidential candidates Republican president George W. Bush, Democratic nominee John Kerry, and independent candidate Ralph Nader—twelve of which would be submitted to the candidates, whose responses were published on the New Voters Project website. The group successfully received more than five thousand questions for the initiative (Bethea 2004). New in both time frame and innovations, the New Voters Project's unique means of mobilizing youth voters and providing them with access to the candidates helped bring young Americans to the polls in 2004.

### Cast the Vote: Sending Youth from the Box Office to the Ballot Box

Pledging "to enliven participation in voting among America's young people" (Cast the Vote 2004b), Cast the Vote was a nonpartisan effort to target and mobilize eighteen- to twenty-four-year-olds by attempting to build a connection between youth and political engagement in and around movie theaters. Anne Judge, an experienced professional from the nonprofit sector, and Bill Miller, an expert in cinematic promotions, founded the organization in 2003 (Cast the Vote 2004a). The effort is now a project of the nonprofit Tides Center, and as such, is funded by foundation money, as well as corporate donations (Cast the Vote 2004a).

Cast the Vote sought to remove itself from the traditional protocol of GOTV campaigns, such as traveling door to door, and narrowed its focus to cinemas as it sought to target those attending movie theaters—something that has become a rite of passage for young adults—in its quest for youth mobilization. By lining up support from the largest movie theater chains in the country, Cast the Vote was able to prepare public service announcements to be shown immediately preceding the featured film (Ives 2004). In addition to their PSA campaign, beginning in September, the organization placed voter registration tables in the lobbies of movie theaters. They started with a pilot project in multiplexes around Las Vegas in order to make a more direct attempt at mobilizing young theater-going voters (Singer 2004).

As it grew, Cast the Vote made efforts to ally itself with other youth mobilization projects, like Rock the Vote and the New Voters Project, in order to make the execution of its own projects more simple and effective. The result was an effort that expanded across the country. As of October 5, 2004, the campaign had registered approximately one thousand voters (Singer 2004). This statistic, though, does not represent the growth the campaign experienced throughout the month of October.

### Youth Vote Coalition: Coalition of the Voting

In the early 1990s, efforts to inform young Americans about the importance of voting gained newfound importance as media outlets, private organizations, and partisan groups developed numerous youth voter mobilization programs and activities. The 1992 success in voter turnout among youth spawned even more enthusiasm. Thus, in 1994, an umbrella organization known as Youth Vote Coalition was formed to unify these groups and streamline their tactics. Permanently established in 2001, Youth Vote Coalition formed its national headquarters in Washington, D.C. Though Youth Vote Coalition began with just seventeen member organizations, it encompassed over one hundred groups by the 2004 election. Such a broad alliance was central to Youth Vote Coalition's success because it recognized that increasing civic and political participation can only be achieved though the combined efforts of like-minded organizations (Youth Vote Coalition 2004).

The Youth Vote Coalition's role in this endeavor was multifaceted. Not only did it serve as a hub for all those individual organizations working to increase youth turnout, but the group also conducted extensive research on the most effective way to reach young voters. Both nonpartisan groups, like Rock the Vote and Smackdown Your Vote, and candidates were free to utilize their findings. Youth Vote Coalition also conducted door-to-door campaigns across the nation to ask young Americans to get involved in the election (Macel 2002). After years of service, the Youth Vote Coalition ended its operations as of March 31, 2005.

## COMPUTERS, COLLEGES, CITIES, AND CHURCHES

### Justvotenow.org: Driving Voters Down the Information Superhighway

One of the more noticeable differences between the 2004 campaign and past elections was the use of the Internet, and more specifically, the use of e-mail. This new reliance on cyberspace was first exemplified in the Howard Dean campaign in the 2004 Democratic primaries, but it grew throughout the spring and summer months and played a prominent role in both the Kerry and Bush campaigns during the general election.

Justvotenow.org was certainly responsible for some of the prominence e-mail enjoyed in the 2004 election. In late October, the organization launched a viral get-out-the-vote (GOTV) effort, using software from the progressive iCanvas.org, to reach a goal of 250,000 new voters. Through its website, people pledged to vote, and after doing so, they were asked to provide the names and e-mail addresses of five additional people that might also pledge their vote, with these five then providing five more names each, and so on. The goal, explains Sunil Paul, the founder of both justvotenow.org and its sister site iCanvas.org, was to link the speed of email to the average person's address book (Provo 2004).

While a GOTV operation typically relies upon face-to-face contact, justvotenow.org's attempts to conduct online GOTV operations in 2004 were largely successful (Provo 2004). Over 300,000 voters were registered using the new technology justvotenow.org offered (Just Vote Now 2004). This program not only assisted in increasing turnout, but it also enabled citizens to run their own small voting drives (Just Vote Now 2004). By linking these smaller-scale drives together into one megadrive, justvotenow.org effectively linked technology and civic engagement.

### Working Assets/BearShare Voter Registration: Sharing Files and Voter Registration

There were many technological firsts in the 2004 election, but one of the more interesting was the combination of "the world's leading file-sharing client" and Working Assets' "Your Vote Matters" nonpartisan voter registration website. The pairing of BearShare and Your Vote Matters yielded a nonpartisan, nonprofit voter registration program that was able to attract larger numbers than other drives as a result of its quick and unparalleled access to millions of Americans. Each BearShare user was provided a link to Working Assets' Your Vote Matters registration site on a Web page only accessible to Bear-Share users (Free Peers Inc. 2004). "The Signup form asks users which state they reside in and then presents the appropriate form for each state. Working Assets worked closely with each state's head of elections to make the process as simple as possible," explained BearShare's John Busher (P2PNet 2004).

As of September 7, 2004, the program had allowed approximately 800,000 new voters to register in a simple online process (Free Peers Inc. 2004). While the project certainly could be deemed a success with the large number of voters registered, it should be pointed out that the get-out-the-vote aspect of the drive was missing. As a result, there most likely were some voters who either registered without actually intending to vote, or registered and simply failed to cast a vote for one reason or another. The partnership also appears to have only lasted until election day 2004, as the program's website, www.yourvotematters.org, has since been shut down.

## Swarthmore College Voter Registration: A "Tide"-al Wave of New Youth Voters

The rise in political activism among youth in 2004 was apparent on college campuses nationwide. Voter registration tables could be seen in campus centers and student unions across the country. One institution, Swarthmore College in Pennsylvania, founded a Voter Registration Coalition that united several groups' voter registration efforts into one large-scale registration drive that encapsulated not only the Swarthmore campus, but the suburban Philadelphia communities of Chester and Upper Darby as well (Heyman-Kantor 2004).

While most of the groups that joined the coalition were partisan, such as the Swarthmore College Democrats and the Swarthmore Progressive Action Committee, the coalition itself was nonpartisan, as the group claimed to "register everyone, Republicans and Democrats alike" (Heyman-Kantor 2004).

Christian DeSimone, a cofounder of the coalition, explained that while prior to 2004, four-fifths of Chester's eligible residents were registered, a much smaller fraction of voters actually turned out to vote. Thus, the group concentrated on raising turnout by reminding people to vote after they registered and by providing free transportation to and from polling places. In order to register those citizens who had not been reached, the coalition planned a community registration drive each weekend in September before Pennsylvania's early-October registration deadline (Heyman-Kantor 2004).

On campus, the coalition attempted to boost voter registration and turnout with a program called "Every Swattie Votes," consisting of a number of activities and services that made the process easier for students. Nonregistered students were registered, and those previously registered to vote in another state received assistance in changing their registration to Pennsylvania, due to its "swing state" status. Through the acquisition of students' names who were planning to study abroad or off campus during the fall semester, the campaign was able to send absentee ballot packets to all students regardless of whether they were registered at Swarthmore or in their home state. The coalition's on-campus program was especially successful during the school's orientation and first week of classes, registering over 150 first-year students (Heyman-Kantor 2004).

## Riverside, California, Youth Council—"Stand Up and Vote!": Count Riverside In

While some youth chose to participate on college campuses, other younger students chose to get involved in their community to boost turnout rates. The community of Riverside, California, is an example, where the rising youth interest in politics and civic engagement grew into a large-scale voter registration drive during the months leading up to the 2004 election.

A panel of twenty-four teenagers led the project, and the Riverside City Council provided ten thousand dollars to fund the effort. "Stand Up and Vote: Count Riverside In," the full name of the project, was founded as a response to the poor turnout rate of Riverside citizens in 2000 (only 32.9 percent of those eligible to vote in Riverside did so in that presidential election). Jesse Melgar, seventeen, the council chairman, criticized the apathy that was exhibited during that election by Riverside citizens, calling it a "slap in the face." He explained that while most Riverside citizens are given the right to vote but do not make use of it, it seems that the youth are the only ones engaging in the political process, "trying to make a difference" (Haberman 2004).

The Youth Council urged all high school students to acquire pledges to vote in the November 2004 election from ten different people by requesting permission to address government classes at various high schools. Members also spoke at service club meetings—asking for support, volunteers, donations, and pledges to vote—while also working with local companies to register and mobilize their employees. As a last step, phone and e-mail reminders were sent to citizens a few days prior to election day (Haberman 2004).

This individual drive sponsored by the Youth Council was part of a nationwide nonpartisan, nonprofit campaign called "Freedom's Answer," which intended to show students the benefits of political participation. The Riverside Youth Council, and other students participating in Freedom's Answer, refrained from asking citizens to vote for a certain party or candidate. Instead, they simply asked those who could to vote, so that those putting their lives at risk for freedom may be honored. Freedom's Answer was founded in order to provide high school students with a way to respond to the terrorist attacks of September 11, 2001 (Haberman 2004).

### Christian Youth Voter Project: The Voting Ministry

The Christian Youth Voter Project (CYVP) is a project of the Citizen Leader Coalition, an organization "dedicated to restoring America's constitutional government and founding principles" (Citizen Leader Coalition 2004). As the name indicates, the project was yet another effort during the 2004 campaign to register religious youth to vote in the presidential election. With an emphasis placed on direct contact with college campuses nationwide, the CYVP aimed to politically engage young conservative voters of faith.

First-time Christian voters (ages eighteen to twenty-one) in ten battleground states were targeted using demographic and geographic studies, as the CYVP sent direct mail to Christian colleges and universities, which encouraged youth to visit their website, and they allowed their articles to be repeatedly republished in as many of these schools' newspapers as possible. Using these methods, the CYVP was then able to educate, register, and mobilize conservative Christian youth across America. Though they claim they have no way of knowing the exact number of voters they have registered (Citizen Leader Coalition 2005a), the CYVP was certainly one of the more successful faith-based registration drives in the country.

The CYVP is still in existence, and it is currently in the process of mobilizing new, young conservative Christians for the midterm elections in 2006. Through a preliminary program called CVOTER.com—2006, the drive will again attempt to focus its efforts on a handful of competitive states. This time, though, the CYVP looks to broaden its methods of registration and mobilization by building a volunteer organization that will establish groups on Christian college campuses, by using churches and schools to distribute voter registration packets, and by providing students attending Christian colleges or those in the military with absentee ballots (Citizen Leader Coalition 2005b).

## PROGRESSIVE INTEREST GROUP PROJECTS

### Young Voter Alliance: Progressives Unite!—
### A New Model for New Voters

While many groups had their own individual voting drives during the 2004 campaign, there were some groups that pooled their efforts in order to create megadrives. One example was the Young Voter Alliance, an organization funded by private donations that was the largest partisan youth voting effort of the 2004 campaign. The alliance took the efforts of groups such as the Young Democrats of America (YDA)—the College Democrats of America's sister organization—the League of Pissed Off Voters, the League of Hip-Hop Voters, MoveOn Student Action, and the National Stonewall Democrats and organized them into a large youth-voting outreach organization. In pledging to target the youth vote so that the number of eighteen to thirty-five-year-old progressive voters increased in five swing states (Florida, New Mexico, Ohio, Pennsylvania, and Wisconsin), its short-term goal was similar to that of other youth voting drives: to mobilize America's youth so that the youth vote would become the swing vote needed to elect progressives to as many offices as possible in 2004. Making the youth vote a tangible voting bloc of the Democratic Party has become the long-term goal of the alliance (Fleming 2004).

The group's get-out-the-vote efforts in the 2004 election included "Trick or Vote," which involved dressing up in costumes and handing out special "Trick or Vote" goodie bags filled with voter-rights and political information, magazines, and CDs. The Young Voter Alliance has also developed the "New Voter

Model," a new way of communicating with younger voters using a combination of traditional methods, like door-to-door canvassing, and nontraditional methods, such as appearing at community centers, gyms, and nightclubs—common youth magnets (Fleming 2004). The national field directors, Malia Lazu and Colin O'Dea, explained that in many ways the youth vote's advantage has not been realized. "Young voters are untapped, untargeted and will be the X factor in this close election. It is essential that we go out and find young people and invite them into the political process," said Lazu and O'Dea (Fleming 2004).

Using its New Voter Model between July and October 2004, the group knocked on 208,311 doors while also contacting 43,828 additional youth in nontraditional political settings (Fleming 2004). As the end of October approached and registration deadlines began to draw near, the GOTV campaign increased in priority. The group began to reinitiate contact with many of the same youth in an effort to remind them to get to the polls on election day.

### Black Youth Vote!: Educating and Activating

The National Coalition on Black Civic Participation is an organization dedicated to increasing the participation of African Americans in every aspect of civil society by providing them with the necessary resources to become politically active. Founded in 1976, the coalition now has eighty-six member organizations working together to educate and activate the black community (National Coalition on Black Civic Participation 2004a). The newest program of the coalition is Black Youth Vote! (BYV!), a group created to target the eighteen- to thirty-five-year-old demographic. The new program seeks to increase voter participation by reaching all young African Americans, "including student, street, and incarcerated youth" (National Coalition on Black Civic Participation 2004b).

On its website, BYV! states that its goal is "to empower black youth by educating youth about the political process and training youth to identify issues and influence public policy through participation." The group's objectives include educating black youth on voting and public policy and creating a national media campaign that stresses the value of political participation (National Coalition of Black Civic Participation 2004b). Funded by individual donors, businesses, and foundations, BYV! relies heavily on outside support to finance their efforts (Singer 2004).

### Vote for Change: Electoral Targeting through Music

The politically charged environment in 2004 saw Hollywood celebrities and musicians become more vocal and politically active than in previous elections.

During the 2004 campaign, musicians supporting the Kerry campaign organized themselves into a "loose coalition" of artists performing in swing states believed to be the most crucial for the Democratic candidate. This series of performances, cosponsored by MoveOn PAC and America Coming Together (ACT), was named "Vote for Change," and it targeted younger Americans that might be influenced by the music of the artists on the tour (MoveOn PAC 2004a).

The tour itself consisted of thirty-seven concerts in thirty cities and ended with an "all-star finale," starring all of the tour's thirteen headliners, in Washington, D.C., on October 11, 2004. The finale was broadcast on pay-per-view television on the Sundance Channel, and the proceeds for all concerts benefited ACT, the tour's sponsor. Many Hollywood stars, famed bands and individual musicians, used the Vote for Change tour to show their support for John Kerry, such as Bruce Springsteen and the E Street Band, R.E.M., Pearl Jam, Death Cab for Cutie, Tim Robbins, John Fogerty, John Mellenkamp, Kenneth "Babyface" Edmonds, Dave Matthews Band, Ben Harper and the Innocent Criminals, James Taylor, the Dixie Chicks, and Bonnie Raitt (Orloff 2004). Throughout the concerts, between songs the musicians entertained audiences with commentary regarding the election, and sometimes the stars had a few surprising statistics to offer. For instance, in a Toledo, Ohio, show, Eddie Vedder, lead singer of Pearl Jam, offered an eye-opening statistic of his own. "Four percent of the whole U.S. population is in Ohio," said Vedder. "You account for twenty-five percent of the jobs that have been lost in the last four years. That's staggering. And this is a swing state?" (Orloff 2004).

The concerts were meant to increase enthusiasm for the Kerry campaign while benefiting even more intensive approaches to targeting voters by MoveOn PAC and ACT. During the night of the finale, members of MoveOn PAC organized "watch parties" as a way of raising their own enthusiasm and organizing in accordance with the Vote for Change tour (MoveOn PAC 2004b).

## Music for America: Sounding the Call for Change

Music for America is a partisan "527 committee" that combined politics and music to raise awareness among young voters. A 527 committee is a type of fundraising organization named after a clause in the Internal Revenue Code that can raise unlimited funds as long as it identifies "the source of the contributions" (Green 2004). Yet rather than act on behalf of a particular candidate, the group decided upon an issue-based brand of activism (Green 2004). The group was started in 2003 when its founding members, fresh out of college, decided to try and change the nation's political climate. Eager to increase civic engagement, Music for America's overarching mission is to get the eigh-teen- to thirty-year-old age group involved at all levels of politics (Music for America 2004).

In order to increase support, the organization needed more members and money. As a result, Music for America volunteers tried to register youth's e-mail addresses at their events—a practice that garnered e-mail registration from about 10 percent of the audience on "good nights" (Green 2004). As of the spring of 2005, approximately fifty thousand people—most of them between the ages of seventeen and twenty-four—had joined Music for America's mission to "reinvent progressive politics" (Music for America 2004).

With resources, the organization needed to spread their message to America's youth. To that end, Music for America visited many cities, spreading their message through concerts, comedy shows, tours, and festivals. The group's website provided visitors with the ability to access downloadable shows, e-mail members of Congress, and create a personal blog (Green 2004). Furthermore, the site dedicates a section to covering the issues it cares most about, such as the drug war and the economy. As stated at the bottom of each Web page, "Music for America is providing the cultural capital and political savvy" to allow America's youth to change the political process and will continue its efforts past the 2004 election (Music for America 2005). After November 2, 2004, Music for America took on the role of a "political watchdog," deter-mined to hold government accountable to its youth constituency.

### America Coming Together: Progressives Taking ACTion

Three days before the 2004 presidential election, Republican President George W. Bush and Democratic presidential nominee Senator John Kerry "unleashed the biggest and most aggressive voter-mobilization drives in the history of presidential politics" (Balz and Edsall 2004). A vast number of groups hit the streets on behalf of their favored contender, some working with, and others independent of, the candidates' campaigns. Among them was America Coming Together, a progressive 527 committee that turned out to be "the biggest" and perhaps "most important" such group of the election (Balz and Edsall 2004).

A 527 committee (named after a section of the IRS tax code), ACT col-lected large amounts of "soft money" from independent contributors such as billionaire George Soros, unions, and liberal interest groups. In fact, ACT raised much of its money jointly with the Media Fund, another progressive 527, through their collective fundraising group, the Victory Campaign 2004 (Nichols 2004). According to its website, ACT collected over $135 million "to begin the long-term process of identifying, registering, informing and organizing voters and grassroots activists to demand change" (America Coming Together 2005).

Though not formally connected to the Kerry campaign, the nonprofit ACT certainly worked hard to elect him. ACT's primary mobilization method was canvassing, where ACT members register people to vote, discover which issues are most important to them, and collect personal information such as phone numbers and driver's license numbers (Lieb 2004). Young voters were one of ACT's target groups. ACT undertook this massive effort to rectify what it saw as a very serious problem in our nation: prolonged Republican control of government. "Republicans have been investing heavily in political infrastructure for over 25 years. Vibrant state parties, candidate training programs, and community organizing are pillars of their plans for a 'permanent Republican majority'" (America Coming Together 2005). ACT was dedicated to combating "this threat [that] is more real than ever" (America Coming Together 2005).

Evidence of their success was already noticeable in July 2004. According to one of the organization's spokeswomen, ACT workers "have knocked on millions of doors and registered hundreds of thousands of new voters," about 65,000 of which were in the critical swing state of Ohio (Mooney 2004). Just six months after its January 2004 inception in Florida, "ACT's 110 paid canvassers [had] enrolled 33,580 new voters" in the state (Mooney 2004). As of October 2004, the group claimed to have registered 131,000 voters in the third of 2004's big swing-state triumvirate: Pennsylvania (Malone 2004). To say the least, ACT's efforts were met with success. By election day, "ACT volunteers reached over 4.2 million targeted voters" (America Coming Together 2005).

Though the 2004 election produced an unfavorable outcome, ACT planned to continue its efforts well into the future, quickly organizing its forces to focus on key races for the 2006 and 2008 elections (America Coming Together 2005). If ACT has anything to say about it, Americans will surely come together under the banner of civic engagement and exercise their right to vote.

## POLITICAL PARTY PROGRAMS

### Democratic National Committee: Youth Voting Is on the Way!

The Democratic National Committee's (DNC) efforts to engage youth in the political process mostly utilized the existing institutions of the party, such as the Democratic National Convention, and also the College Democrats of America (CDA) and the Young Democrats of America, the official youth outreach arms of the party organization. Through these means, the DNC bolstered enthusiasm among the youth for the 2004 election.

The 2004 Democratic National Convention was heavily geared toward youth. Its programs included acts like the Black Eyed Peas and Wyclef Jean, while an essay contest was established especially for youth. The youth had their own caucus during the week of the convention, which attracted big-name guests such as Teresa Heinz Kerry, Jerry Springer, and P. Diddy. Candidates were repeatedly introduced by their children, and older members of other delegations told some youth that the 2004 convention had one of the youngest delegations overall in recent memory. Rock the Vote held nightly parties during the week tailored to youth, and Sarah Bender, the youngest convention delegate, at seventeen, from Ohio, led the convention in the Pledge of Allegiance during Wednesday night's ceremonies. Those who tuned in to or attended the 2004 Democratic National Convention might remember the hope and optimism expressed ("Hope is on the way!"), and in many ways, this attitude reflected the status of a political party being injected with energy and exuberance after two unsuccessful elections (Cole 2004).

The convention also heavily catered to the elements of the official party organization responsible for reaching out to youth: the College Democrats and the Young Democrats. Numerous training sessions through the DNC's new Grassroots Action Institute and Network (GAIN) were held that taught youth delegates how to organize and run an effective grassroots campaign at home or on a college campus (Cole 2004). As a result of this training, over a thousand chapters of CDA and YDA were effectively campaigning for the Kerry-Edwards Democratic ticket in the fall.

### Republican National Committee: "Rigging" up a Plan to Snag Young Voters

The Republican National Committee (RNC) took an unusual approach with their youth voting outreach initiative in the 2004 election. With three million young voters as its ultimate goal, the RNC took to the streets of swing states with "Reggie the Registration Rig," an 18-wheel truck furnished with entertainment devices such as an Xbox and a soundstage. The Omaha, Nebraska, husband and wife that drove the semi, Deke and Christine, are Republicans. "Reggie" roams the country, making stops at events like swap meets and NASCAR races, encouraging young voters to register to vote (Fanelli 2004). As of October 11, 2004, the 18-wheeler had logged 19,109 miles while visiting twenty-two states (GOP Team Leader 2004).

The RNC also utilized their "Team Leader" program as a way of providing tools online to young activists wishing to get involved. The Team Leader website provides younger Republicans with GOP talking points while providing them with the ability to write their local officeholders, and it provides information about candidates running for office in the user's area and preliminary research on legislation in front of Congress or state legislatures. Perhaps most importantly, the site allowed users to form communities with which they can share information they find interesting with other users (GOP Team Leader 2005).

In addition to these two initiatives, the RNC sought to increase youth participation within its own party through the "Party for the President" program. This campaign encouraged youth to throw parties for President Bush, increasing enthusiasm for the president, while also increasing momentum for the campaign among youth.

### College Democrats of America: Covering All Its Bases

The College Democrats of America describes itself as "the official student outreach arm of the Democratic Party" (College Democrats of America 2005a). As such, the group's efforts to complete its main objectives, "to mobilize campuses across the country for Democratic candidates, train new generations of progressive activists, and shape the Democratic Party with voices from America's youth," are mostly funded by the Democratic National Committee, while also occasionally supported by private donations solicited by the organization's honorary cochairs and its alumni association (College Democrats of America 2005b).

The CDA's effort to attract more young voters to the Democratic Party is split into several subgroups, labeled "base-vote caucuses." Groups that have their own caucuses are, as the name indicates, important pieces of the Democratic base. The African American Caucus, the Disabilities Caucus, the GLBT Caucus, the Hispanic Caucus, and the Women's Caucus all have their own leaders, appointed by the executive board, who are responsible for attracting members of these communities found in the electorate to the Democratic Party. In addition, the CDA also staffs coordinators for those students in the Jewish community and those that study abroad. The goal is for these communities to attract those Americans that the Democratic Party can best appeal to and then translate those attracted into votes.

The CDA grew in the election year of 2004, increasing its presence on campuses nationwide from 500 chapters to 1,260. The CDA's membership has increased twentyfold, while the annual budget of the organization is ten times the size of the 2003 budget. The organization has launched an eChapters initiative that enables the national leadership to better organize nationally. This initiative divides the country up by states, and once the user selects the state he or she wants to view, campuses with CDA chapters in that state are listed with respective officer and contact information (Geldon 2005). The growth of the organization, not surprisingly, has led to the CDA's increased ability to draw youth toward the Democratic Party. In what could be a sign intimating this newfound strength, 54 percent of voters aged eighteen to twenty-nine voted for John Kerry, the Democratic candidate in the 2004 election, giving the Kerry campaign a 10 percent margin of victory—five times the size of the margin of victory Al Gore enjoyed in 2000 (Tanner 2004). With this kind of progress, the future looks bright for the CDA. With their use of technology and caucuses built around traditional Democratic communities, the CDA has dramatically increased their membership, as well as enthusiasm toward politics in American youth.

## College Republican National Committee: College GOP working to GOTV

The College Republican National Committee (CRNC) differs from its counterpart, the College Democrats of America, in not being financially dependent on the Republican National Committee, but instead is dependent on donations from the public. In October 2001, the CRNC declared themselves independent of the Republican Party organization and became a 527 committee instead (Center for Public Integrity 2003). This decision enabled the CRNC to create their own outreach programs while supporting the RNC, leading to initiatives like the Field Program and the Fieldman School that have helped the committee reach out to many conservative college students in order to register and mobilize these potential voters.

The CRNC, largely more stable than other voter mobilization efforts while also enjoying more of a connection to the major parties than other voter registration drives, has been able to develop a more complex strategy that first relies upon the organization and operations of the individual chapters in order to succeed on a second level, registering and mobilizing voters. The Field Program, "the cornerstone of the Republican National Committee" (College Republican National Committee 2005), had helped the CRNC establish approximately 1,150 chapters at colleges and universities across America. The program of 2005, run from late August through election day, planned to use approximately thirty-five field representatives, who travel to crucial states in order to effectively organize those state federations (College Republican National Committee 2005). The Field Program enables the CNRC to register and mobilize voters more effectively so that the new voters then, in turn, are able to register and mobilize other future conservative voters.

In order to fine-tune the program, the CRNC also established the Fieldman School. From the CRNC website, "The Fieldman School is a crash-course in grassroots youth politics that trains College Republicans in the four pillars of a mass-based youth effort: membership tables, the campus canvass, mock elections, and special projects" (College Republican National Committee 2004). The school teaches the members of the CRNC, especially in swing states, the most effective way to register and turn out conservative college students.

The group enjoyed widespread success with their voter mobilization efforts in 2004, reaching far beyond expectations. The committee was able to register 36,999 new Republican voters, while the group distributed over 23,000 absentee ballots. The CRNC had 16,735 volunteers help with their intense seventy-two-hour voter mobilization program, and in general, the committee accumulated 52,436 new College Republicans. Roughly 350 new chapters were started after the 2004 campaign was finished, while the group was able to send fifty-six full-time field representatives (while only expecting to send roughly thirty-five prior to the election) into key swing states in order to build solid networks between the chapters in those states to better coordinate campaign efforts (Keough 2005).

The CRNC is already planning to build off this success in its preparations for the 2006 midterm congressional elections. From the CRNC website, "Field [representatives] will also be responsible for building up state organizations in anticipation of targeted 2006 senate [*sic*] races" (Heyman-Kantor 2004). Through the coordination between its Field Program, grooming individuals in political organizing, and the Fieldman Program, teaching groups commonplace tactics and strategy in political campaigns, the CRNC has not only been able to bring young voters into the voting booth, but it has also helped to forge a connection between youth and the bigger political process.

## MODELS FOR THE FUTURE?

At this juncture, it is difficult to say with any certainty exactly what contribution these projects made to the increase in youth turnout in 2004. Some of the new programs appear to have been successful enough to have continued after the election, while others folded shortly after the ballots were cast. Some of these projects were the results of individual entrepreneurs and thus were subject to personal idiosyncrasies, while others were the project of long-standing institutions, and still others were alliances of groups. It will be fascinating to see if this level of youth projects reappears in 2008—another "open seat" presidential election, like 2000.

The success of any particular project aside, we can speculate about the place of these different types of projects in a future campaign. The entertainment industry is likely to continue to be a source of youth mobilization efforts, using the appeal of musicians, movie stars, and professional wrestlers (and their money) to reach young voters. These are potent resources and can provide a potent "top-down" approach to youth registration and GOTV efforts. However, they are likely to lack a grassroots connection to young voters, and such efforts exist at the pleasure of entertainers, who may shift their interests to other worthy causes at a moment's notice.

Philanthropic youth projects played a major role in the 2004 campaign, reflecting the widespread dismay with low youth turnout. These funds allowed for the pooling of talent, academic and practical, to develop and test new methods of reaching the youth vote. The results of these efforts may make a difference for years to come. By the same token, however, foundations may not stay focused on the day-to-day, year-to-year efforts to register and mobilize the regular waves of young citizens who come of age. In fact, the very success of many of these projects may lead the foundation community to shift its interests to other pressing problems.

The new use of Web-based technologies and the embedding of young voter programs in ongoing institutions may be a future growth area. The Internet just came of age politically in 2004, and its potential in this regard has hardly been exploited. Indeed, one valuable feature of the Internet is its ability to quickly and efficiently link together people and institutions all across the nation. This possibility may be especially important for existing institutions that wish to encourage youth participation in politics. Colleges, city governments, and churches are numerous in the United States, and if they adopted effective youth programs as a regular activity, it could make an enormous difference. Of course, these institutions have other missions, and they may not initiate such programs or maintain them over time.

One of the major innovations of the 2004 election was the rise of the 527 committees. This fundraising mechanism was most widely used by liberal interest groups, and some of these groups focused on youth mobilization. This device allowed progressive organizations to raise money in large amounts from unions and wealthy individuals and direct it toward grassroots programs. However, this virtue is also a potential vice: wealthy patrons, organizational or individual, may or may not fund these efforts in the future. Indeed, the future development of 527 committees is unclear. Another innovation of 2004 was the development of alliances of progressive interest groups for the purposes of sharing information and coordinating their grassroots activities. This innovation may well persist in the future.

Reinvigorated youth programs by the major party organizations—national, state, and local—harkens back to a form of politics once dominant in American politics, although parties often lack the resources and commitment to voter mobilization that the other kinds of projects exhibit. However, parties have two strengths. First, they are permanent institutions dedicated to electoral politics. Second, and more important, they regularly face strong incentives to mobilize voters of all kinds, including the youth. Put another way, political parties are the key voter mobilizing institutions in the United States. Simply put, voter participation has been the highest historically when such mobilizing institutions are vital and vibrant. And as we have seen, party organizations have the potential to recapture their past glory at the grass roots. In this regard, party programs may be the best long-term way to bring the youth into the political process.

# V

**CONCLUSION**

# 11

## Faces of the Future

### John Kenneth White

Nearly half a century ago, in 1966, the political scientist V. O. Key published a book entitled *The Responsible Electorate* (1966). Key began his groundbreaking work with this simple idea: "The perverse and unorthodox argument of this little book is that voters are not fools" (Key 1966).[1] This "perverse" notion led Key to classify voters into one of three categories: (1) standpatters (those who stay with their party of choice no matter what), (2) switchers (those who drift from one party to another depending on the issues and personalities of the moment), and (3) new voters (those entering the electorate for the first time). Young voters are the most regular source of new voters.

In many respects, these three types of voters are windows into the past, present, and future of American politics. Standpatters have their thinking shaped by a prior cataclysmic event. In Key's time, the standpatters were the offspring of the Great Depression—a disaster so large and encompassing that those who were touched by it gravitated to Franklin D. Roosevelt and the New Deal Democrats as welcome economic resuscitators. Today's standpatters are those influenced by a series of economic and cultural shocks that occurred during the 1970s. Back then, the confluence of high inflation and unemployment led many to agree with Ronald Reagan's conclusion in his 1981 inaugural address: "In the present crisis, government is not the solution to our problem; government is the problem" (Reagan 1981). Simply put, voter discontent with an inattentive and ineffective government and a perceived decline in the country's moral values became the basis for the Reagan Revolution.

These Reagan voters are today's new standpatters. In 2004, the Reagan generation, now aged thirty-five to forty-nine, voted decisively for George W. Bush. According to polls taken in the key states of Florida, Ohio, Iowa,

Nevada, and New Mexico, the Reagan standpatters gave Bush decisive majorities ranging from 54 percent to 59 percent, thereby clinching his reelection (Pontell and Coker 2004).[2] Even as Ronald Reagan became a historic icon with his passing in 2004, his standpatters continue to give the Republicans sustenance—thanks to their ongoing agreement with the party's conservative economic and cultural stands—and the Democrats fits.

The second group Key identified was the switchers. In 1952 and 1956, switchers determined the presidential outcome as they voted en masse for Dwight D. Eisenhower. Switchers were disenchanted with the Korean War and were attracted to the Republican candidate's charisma and lengthy military résumé (Key 1966). During the 1980s, switchers gravitated to Ronald Reagan, who, like Ike, had a winning persona. Later, they moved to Bill Clinton and Ross Perot, thanks to the country's lackluster economic performance and their conviction that George H. W. Bush did not comprehend the problem. But their dalliances with Eisenhower and Reagan represented no long-term commitment to the GOP, as their switches to Democrat Bill Clinton and independent Ross Perot demonstrated. Some switched back to George W. Bush in 2000 and 2004. To Key, switchers mattered because their behavior provided important clues to present-day winners.

But the most fascinating group is Key's new voters. In many ways, this group replenishes the old memories held by the standpatters with new ones that shape the politics of the future. Indeed, of the three categories, Key believed new voters were the most important:

> Though we commonly ascribe great significance to the switchers, they are in many elections, outnumbered by the "new voters." In some elections, indeed, the "new voters" contribute significantly to the outcome, if they do not determine it. Hence this group presents a continuing challenge to the contending parties, which must seek to recruit young voters . . . to maintain their position. (Key 1966)

Thus, the perpetual challenge that political parties face is this: which party will recruit the most new voters into its ranks, especially among the youth? At the onset of the twenty-first century, it is impossible to know *what* events will make today's youth the standpatters of the future and even *when* they will decide to enter the polling booth. What we do know is *who* these new voters are. The first wave is poised to enter politics, the eighteen- to twenty-four-year-olds. This group grew up during the administrations of George W. Bush and Bill Clinton and will carry into the politics the events of this era. The subsequent waves of new voters are found among today's children. In my case, I see the future when I look into the face of my eight-year-old daughter, Jeannette. As my daughter ages, she will experience the social trends of the early twenty-first century. She and her cohort will eventually reflect the effects of these trends at the polling booth.

One of the most important of these social trends is the dramatic changes in ethnicity and race. For example, in the Montgomery County, Maryland, public school system that Jeannette presently attends, only 45 percent of the students are white (Perlstein 2003). Watching high school graduates traverse various stages to receive their diplomas in 2004, and knowing that many got their start in such diverse places as Kenya, El Salvador, Vietnam, and Iran, school super-intendent Jerry D. Weast observed, "Sometimes you see an 'aha' in the crowd, the realization of what we've been saying all along: 'It's not coming. It's here'" (Perlstein 2004). Since 1991, Montgomery County schools have added 16,000 Hispanics, 12,000 blacks, and 7,000 Asians, while at the same time losing 3,000 white students (Perlstein 2004). In her local primary school, Jeannette is already a racial minority: African Americans constitute 32 percent of the students, Hispanics 30 percent, whites 27 percent, and Asians 10 percent.[3]

The impact of such ethnic and racial change can already be seen in today's eighteen- to twenty-four-year-olds. For example, the 2004 national exit polls revealed that they were more diverse in these terms than their elders (National Election Pool 2004). Overall, 77 percent of all 2004 voters nationally reported being white, but just 66 percent of young voters. Hispanics and Latinos made up just 8 percent of all voters and were almost twice as numerous among young voters. Even starker figures appeared in California. There, whites made up 65 percent of all 2004 voters, but just 44 percent of the eighteen- to twenty-four-year-olds. Despite increased turnout in 2004, young voters were still sub-stantially underrepresented in the electorate. As a consequence, the effects of ethnic and racial diversity were understated. But the impact of these trends is likely to accelerate as the subsequent waves of new voters enter the electorate. Put another way, the new voters of today and tomorrow are going to steadily transform American politics.

## "THE THIRD GREAT REVOLUTION"

Speaking at the 1998 commencement exercises at Portland State University, Bill Clinton cast his eye toward the impending new century and saw a nation transformed. The president told the graduates that the United States was experiencing a "third great revolution"—one as powerful as the American Revolution, which gave birth to the democratic ideas of the eighteenth and nineteenth centuries, and as imposing as the civil rights and women's rights revolutions that broadened the definition of personal liberties in the twentieth century. According to Clinton, this new revolution is produced by an army of immigrants: "Today, largely because of immigration, there is no majority race in Hawaii or Houston or New York City. Within five years there will be no majority race in our largest state, California. In a little more than fifty years, there will be no majority race in the United States" (Clinton 1998).

The facts bear out Clinton's argument. Consider: when Richard M. Nixon took the presidential oath in 1969, there were 9.6 million foreign born residing in the United States. Thirty-two years later, when George W. Bush raised his hand to repeat the same oath, that figure was 28.4 million (Williams, forthcoming). Today, there are more foreign born living in California—8.4 million—than people residing in the entire state of New Jersey, and more foreign born located in New York than in all of South Carolina (Buchanan 2002). The influx of so many immigrants is altering once-given stereotypes about certain ethnic communities. For example, in Boston—the ancestral home to the Kennedy family dynasty—nonwhite immigrants are populating once Irish-dominated neighborhoods. Indeed, for the first time since 1790, whites are Boston's newest minority group.[4]

These new immigrants are destined to write a lengthy chapter in tomorrow's twenty-first-century politics. Like their forebearers, ethnic identification with a fellow party candidate can spur many to the polls. Sam Yoon is one example. In 2005, Yoon, a Korean immigrant, ran for an at-large seat on the Boston city council. Yoon campaigned heavily in immigrant-dominated neighborhoods, including Fields Corner, an area heavily populated by immigrants from Vietnam, Cape Verde, and elsewhere, and his website was a multilingual panacea, with portions translated into Chinese, Korean, Spanish, Vietnamese, Haitian Creole, and Cape Verdean–Creole. Yoon's basic message was simple: "I'm one of you." Angel Bermudez, a senior director at the Boston Foundation, believed that Yoon's ethnic appeal was well founded: "The political capital of these communities of color as a whole and the respective immigrant communities is growing" (Wangsness 2005a). She was proved right when Yoon became the first Asian American to win a seat on the city council. Basking in victory, Yoon gave an election night "shout out" to various Asian American groups, saying, "This is for the Chinese Americans! This is for the Japanese-Americans!" (Wangsness 2005b). 2005 was the year that Boston's "new voters" wrote a new page into the city's history books.

Today, whites are the majority in just fifty-two of the nation's one hundred largest cities—down from seventy in 1990. Overall, the nation's largest cities lost more than two million whites between 1990 and 2000. But in the twenty fastest-growing cities, the number of blacks rose 23 percent, Asians 69 percent, and Hispanics 72 percent (Schmitt 2001). The rise of Hispanics is just as astonishing. From 1990 to 2000, the nation's largest cities gained 3.8 million

Hispanic residents, a 43 percent increase (Schmitt 2001). Here are some specific examples: New Jersey experienced a 51 percent rise in the number of its Hispanics; Loudon County, Virginia, one of many suburbs that ring Washington, D.C., had an astounding 368 percent increase; Chicago gained 208,000 Hispanics; in Milwaukee County, Wisconsin, the number of Hispanics rose by 84 percent (Armas 2001; Russakoff 2001).

The young voters of today and tomorrow embody these changes both directly, in their own ethnicity and race, and indirectly, in their experience of this new diversity. This fact adds a note of urgency to the political participation among young voters. Low levels of youth voting mean that these new perspectives are likely to be initially underrepresented in the electorate, and thus in party coalitions and the government. Under these conditions, American democracy may cope less effectively with the conflicts that might arise from the arrival of new racial identities, cultures, and languages.

## A BILINGUAL (AND BIFURCATED) NATION

Everywhere one looks, the evidence is overwhelming that the United States is rapidly becoming a multiracial, multicultural, and multilingual polity. In 2004, for example, California's Los Angeles County provided special ballots for its Latino, Chinese, Filipino, Japanese, Korean, and Vietnamese residents.[6] But this new cultural diversity hardly signifies the emergence of an ethnic "melting pot."[7] In the twenty-first century, many see two distinct Americas coming into focus: one, mostly white and English speaking, and another, mostly Hispanic and Spanish speaking. Nationwide, 47 million Americans converse in a language other than English, with 26 million speaking Spanish (Huntington 2004a).[8] Of these, 21.3 million say they know English less than "very well." In some states, the need to learn English is acute: in Massachusetts, for example, 460,000 people do not speak good English, and the waiting list for English-as-a-second-language courses is two to three years (Huntington 2004a).

Of these two Americas, it is the Hispanic and Spanish-speaking portion that is likely to dominate twenty-first-century politics. Signs of that emerging dominance are everywhere. In 2004, the Census Bureau reported that the Latino population stood at a record 41.3 million. With numbers like these, it is not surprising that in 1998 "Jose" replaced "Michael" as the most popular name for a baby boy (Huntington 2004b). Should present trends continue, it is estimated that Hispanics will approach 25 percent of the total population in 2050 (Etzioni 2001).

The political ramifications have been dramatic. Simply put, the twentieth-century white-dominated version of California that elected Ronald Reagan governor in 1966 and 1970, and president in 1980 and 1984, no longer exists—except, perhaps, on the commemorative state license plates honoring the late president. By 2000, Democrats assumed a dominant position in the Golden State. That year, Al Gore handily beat George W. Bush, 53 percent to 42 percent, accounting for Gore's "victory" in the national popular vote. Hispanics constituted 14 percent of California's electorate, and they gave 68 percent of their votes to Gore (Barone and Cohen 2003). Four years later, John Kerry bested Bush by a healthy margin of 54 percent to 45 percent. Once again, Kerry's decisive victory can be attributed to the 63 percent support he received from California's Hispanics, whose electoral presence increased to 21 percent of the votes cast (National Election Poll 2004). One year later, Antonio Villaraigosa became the first Latino mayor of Los Angeles to win the seat in 133 years (Finnegan and Barabak 2005).

The infusion of Hispanics into the U.S. population has produced a powerful political backlash. Conservative commentator and 2000 Reform Party presidential candidate Patrick J. Buchanan writes, "With their own radio and TV stations, newspapers, films, and magazines, the Mexican Americans are creating a Hispanic culture separate and apart from America's larger culture. They are becoming a nation within a nation" (Buchanan 2002). In 2004, the Department of Homeland Security estimated that there were 34 million immigrants residing in the United States, and of these, 8 million were illegal (Cohn 2004). Recent polls show that 77 percent of the public want to "restrict and control people coming into our country"; 53 percent say immigration hurts more than it helps; 83 percent think federal authorities should "crack down hard on all non-citizens entering the country by using such procedures as fingerprinting and random interviewing"; and 56 percent oppose "new laws making it easier for illegal immigrants to become legal workers."[9]

But while the backlash against the new immigrants (both illegal and legal) is considerable, it is slowly bending to present-day realities. George W. Bush has led the way. In 2001, Bush became the first president to utter a few Spanish words before a joint session of Congress. Pleading for support for his domestic agenda, Bush told lawmakers, "Juntos podemos" (Together we can) (Bush 2001). A few months later, he paid tribute to the Mexican holiday, Cinco de Mayo, by becoming the first president to broadcast his weekly radio address in both English and Spanish (Allen 2001). Later that same year, the White House website was modified to include Spanish translations of the administration's press briefings, biographies of the president and first lady, and Bush's radio addresses (Cohn 2004). Finally, accepting renomination at the Republican National Convention in 2004, Bush referred to his signature No Child Left Behind law this way: "No dejaremos a ningun nino atras!" (We will leave no child behind!) (Bush 2004). Bush has backed these symbolic gestures by proposing substantive policy changes designed to benefit Hispanics (and his political standing with them). For example, at the start of his second term, Bush proposed overhauling the nation's immigration laws (2005).

Whether Bush succeeds in keeping pace with the future—even with a Republican-controlled Congress—is unclear. What is certain is that the intersection of demography and politics is well understood in the Bush White House. And these facts are not lost on other aspiring politicians of many political persuasions either. The young voters of today and tomorrow are the critical factor in such strategic calculations because they will present a challenge to the old paradigm of ethnicity and race in American politics.

## A MULTIRACIAL FUTURE

In 1992, several hundred multiracialists came together in Bethesda, Maryland, for the "first national gathering of the multiracial community." The so-called Loving Conference—named in honor of the Supreme Court's 1967 decision in *Loving v. Virginia* that struck down state laws prohibiting interracial marriage—was not just a celebration of the right to marry and have children across racial lines. It marked—or so its organizers hoped—the public launching of a new and potent political movement (Cose 1997). Four years later, their hopes became reality when the first-ever "multiracial solidarity march" was held in Washington, D.C. (Williams, forthcoming). Today, the number of Americans who consider themselves belonging to more than one race or who have trouble labeling their own racial backgrounds has grown. Pattia Rodriquez is one example. A thirty-one-year-old, light-skinned sales director for a woman's magazine living in New York City, Rodriquez does not think of herself as either black or white:

> I acknowledge that I have both black and white ancestry in me, but I choose to label myself in nonracial terms: Latina. Hispanic. Puerto Rican. Nuyorican. I feel that being Latina implies mixed racial heritage, and I wish more people knew that. Why should I have to choose? White means mostly privilege and black means overcoming obstacles, a history of civil rights. As a Latina, I don't try to claim one of these (Navarro 2003).

The question of racial self-identification is hardly a new one. Alan Corcos, author of several books on race, writes, "Race is a slippery word because it is a biological term, but we use it every day as a social term. . . . Social, political, and religious views are added to what are seen as biological differences. . . . Race also has been equated with national origin . . . with religion . . . with language" (Etzioni 2001). For most of American history, the "slippery" definition of race was solved by applying the "one-drop" rule—meaning citizens who were white but could point to one-fourth of their relatives as being black (Davis 1991; Etzioni 2001).[10] Thus, from 1850 to 1890, the term "mulatto" appeared on all U.S. census forms. In 1890, the terms "Quadroon" and "Octoroon" made a one-time appearance (Williams, forthcoming). After the immigrant tide at the turn of the twentieth century, Jewish, Slavic, Irish, Polish, and other ethnic groups were listed as races on the 1910 census forms (Etzioni 2001).

But as the twenty-first century dawns, defining the term "race" has become much more complicated. Eduardo Diaz, a social service administrator, says of his Hispanic heritage, "There is no place called Hispanica. I think it's degrading to be called something that doesn't exist. Even Latino is a misnomer. We don't speak Latin" (Etzioni 2001). One Mexican American office worker says that whenever she is called a "Latina," it makes her think "about some kind of island" (Etzioni 2001). The complexity of racial self-identification prompted Ellis Cose, author of *Color Blind: Seeing Beyond Race in a Race-Obsessed World*, to observe, "Tomorrow's multiracial people could just as easily become the next decade's something else. A name, in the end, is just a name. The problem is that we want those names to mean so much—even if the only result is a perpetuation of an ever-more-refined kind of racial madness" (Cose 1997).

The question of racial identity becomes even more complicated given the 1.1 million black-white and Asian-white couples in addition to the biracial Hispanic marriages. Take the story of novelist Gish Jen, a Chinese American married to a man of Irish descent. At school, classmates taunted her son, calling him "Chinese," even as he futilely insisted he was not. Jen and her husband originally hoped their child would "grow up embracing his whole complex ethnic heritage." Today, they accept the fact that their son "is considered a kind of Asian person" (Cose 1997). Sherry Ly, a fifteen-year-old Chinese American, sympathizes: "It's crazy growing up as an Asian-American. I can't say I'm Asian. I don't really know. I couldn't deal with being 100 percent Chinese, but I don't really fit in with American society" (Gore and Gore 2002). The complexity of racial self-identification is clearly evident in a 2001 poll: 9 percent use different terminology to describe their race in different social situations, 28 percent say they are of mixed race, and 48 percent always self-identify with one race.[11]

This trend toward a more blended society has the potential to transcend the "us vs. them" racial politics of the past. But that is some time in the future. Meanwhile, those immigrants and children of immigrants who enter politics are likely to stress their racial heritage (even if it is a blurred one) and appeal to new voters much the same way their twentieth-century immigrant predecessors did. This process is already under way in the next generation of political leaders.

## TWO FUTURE FACES

Just before 5 p.m. on a sunny August summer day in 2004, a bride entered one-hundred-year-old St. Ann's Episcopal Church, a seaside structure located in Kennebunkport, Maine, and married the person she met in a trial advocacy class at her law school. The couple's story was like so many others. They sat next to each other in class passing notes, and in one of them the groom asked his future bride if she would like to play a round of golf (Silverman and Elkins 2003). Things moved forward, so to speak, from that point. At the wedding, the bridesmaids wore floor-length orange dresses as they entered a stone-structured church located near the water's edge. Half an hour later, the party emerged to have their pictures taken before heading off to a reception under a tent pitched behind a local inn.

The principal difference between this wedding and many others was the presence of two presidents: George H. W. Bush and George W. Bush, affectionately known within the family as forty-one and forty-three, and the Coast Guard ships and Secret Service agents that kept watch over the proceedings. While reporters commented on the presence of the two presidents along with the governor of Florida, they hardly mentioned the race of the bride and groom, George P. Bush and Amanda Williamson (Allen 2004; Ellis and Bell 2004; Kornblut 2004).

George P. Bush's Hispanic roots are well known. In the Bush dynasty, George Prescott Bush—son of Florida governor Jeb Bush and his Mexican-born wife, Columba—symbolizes the twenty-first century's multiracial future. In 1988, the young George P. was referred to by his grandfather, George H. W. Bush, as one of the family's "little brown ones"—a description Democrats immediately derided as racially insensitive (Margolick 2001). As he matured, George P. became a family asset and was often seen campaigning for his father, Jeb, and his uncle, George W. In a 2000 television commercial for the Republican presidential nominee, the youthful George P. declared, "I am a young Latino in the U.S. and very proud of my bloodline" (Contreras 2000). Addressing the delegates at the Republican National Convention that year, George P. extolled George W. as "un hombre con grandes sentimientos . . . who really cares about those he was elected to serve, including those of us whose faces look different" (Bush 2000).

That same year, *People* magazine gave the young Bush the number-four slot on its list of the country's one hundred most eligible bachelors (Ferullo

2000). *USA Today* noted the excitement he generated on the campaign trail and dubbed him a Hispanic hybrid of John F. Kennedy and Ricky Martin (Contreras 2000). Frank Guerra, whose Austin-based marketing company has done work for Jeb and George W. Bush, says of George P., "He is intelligent, he's articulate, he's handsome, he has a very clean, clear communication style, and he has the kind of charisma you can't buy" (Farrington 2004). Angela Figueroa, managing editor of *People en Espanol*, the popular magazine's Spanish-language offshoot, agrees: "He just popped out of nowhere, and now it's like, 'Ooh, la-la! He's hunky.' There's definitely a buzz" (Sharp 2000).

But in news accounts of his wedding day, neither the mixed race of twenty-eight-year-old George P. Bush nor the fact that his bride, Amanda Williamson, was white, were mentioned. Instead, the articles that reporters filed that day dwelt on the couple's résumés. *The Austin American-Statesman*'s story was typical: "She works for the Jackson Walker law firm in Fort Worth. He works as an assistant to U.S. Judge Sidney Fitzwater in Dallas, but he plans to leave that post in the fall to work for the Dallas office of Akin, Gump, Strauss, Hauer, and Feld" (Anders 2004). After the ceremony, a proud Governor Jeb Bush told reporters, "I am very happy for my son. He is marrying a wonderful young woman. Life can't get any better." For his part, George P. told reporters that he wants to "start a family as soon as possible," adding, "I want a lot of kids" (Silverman and Elkins 2003).

One month later, the future manifested itself in Mexico, where the Bush newlyweds campaigned for the reelection of the groom's uncle, George W. Bush. As George P. told a reporter in Spanish, "It was a surprise for me [to learn] that there are over one million U.S. citizens living in Mexico, and that hundreds of thousands of them vote each election" (Salinas 2004). Their efforts undoubtedly helped Bush secure a narrow victory. On election day, George W. Bush received an astonishing 40 percent of the Latino vote—a feat that gave the president crucial margins in key states over his Democratic rival (National Election Pool 2004).

George P. Bush, Amanda Williamson, and their children are the future. *How* they will transform twenty-first-century politics is a matter of conjecture. One can speculate that the ethnic and racial paradigm, as it was once understood in the last century, will be redefined for the next one. *What* will motivate these future standpatters to vote, and *when* they will exercise the franchise are also speculative matters. In Boston, Hartford, and Los Angeles, the future seems to have arrived ahead of schedule. In other places, the future is yet to come. But one thing we know for certain is *who* these potential new voters are. Years ago, political commentators Richard M. Scammon and Ben J. Wattenberg (1970) wrote, "Demography is destiny." If that saying still holds true, we know that the altered ethnic and racial demography of this country provides important clues to the politics of the future. And the young voters of today and tomorrow will steadily transform American politics.

## NOTES

1. Key died in 1963, and the book was brought to publication by a collection of friends who understood the importance of his final work and wanted to see it published.

2. In Florida, Bush captured 56 percent of the "Reagan generation" vote; Ohio, 59 percent; Iowa, 56 percent; Nevada, 56 percent; and New Mexico, 54 percent.

3. Montgomery County, Maryland, Whetstone Elementary School, 2003–2004 data report. See www.mcps.k12.md.us/schools/whetstonees.

4. According to the 2000 Census, 297,850 Bostonians listed themselves as minority or multiracial; only 291,561 defined themselves as white (Grossfeld 2001).

5. The U.S. Justice Department mandates that counties offer second-language ballots when more than 5 percent of their voting-age citizens are part of a single-language minority that does not speak or understand English adequately to participate in elections. That includes having an English illiteracy rate higher than the national average within the minority group (McLaughlin 2004).

6. The "melting pot" was an image that was both conjured and dispelled by Nathan Glazer and Daniel Patrick Moynihan in their seminal 1963 book titled *Beyond the Melting Pot: The Negroes, Puerto Ricans, Jews, Italians, and Irish of New York City* (Glazer and Moynihan 1963).

7. See U.S. Department of Commerce, "Number of Foreign-Born Up 57 Percent Since 1990, According to Census 2000."

8. Princeton Survey Research Associates, poll, July 14–August 5, 2003. Text of question: "Now I am going to read you another series on some different topics. For each statement, please tell me if you completely agree with it, mostly agree with it, mostly disagree with it, or completely disagree with it. We should restrict and control people coming into our country to live more than we do now." Completely agree, 46 percent; mostly agree, 31 percent; mostly disagree, 13 percent; completely disagree, 6 percent; don't know, 4 percent. NBC *News/Wall Street* Journal, poll, December 9–12, 2005. Text of question: "Would you say that immigration hurts the United States more than it helps it?" Helps more than it hurts, 37 percent; hurts more than it helps, 53 percent; not sure, 10 percent. Opinion Dynamics, poll, April 6–7, 2004. Text of question: "Traditionally, the United States has had open borders and allowed most non-citizens to enter the country. Do you think the United States should continue this relatively open border policy, or should the United States crack down hard on all non-citizens entering the country by using such procedures as fingerprinting and random interviewing?" Continue to have open borders, 11 percent; crack down hard, 83 percent; not sure, 6 percent. NBC News/*Wall Street Journal*, poll, March 6–8, 2004. Text of question: "Would you favor or oppose new laws making it easier for illegal immigrants to become legal workers?" Favor, 40 percent; oppose, 56 percent; not sure, 4 percent.

9. A DNA study conducted by Howard University found 30 percent of black males tested had some white DNA. See Etzioni *The Monochrome Society,* pg. 18.

10. *Washington Post*/Henry J. Kaiser Family Foundation/Harvard University, poll, March 8–April 22, 2001. Text of question: "Do you identify your race differently in different situations, do you always identify yourself as mixed race, or do you always identify yourself as a particular race?" Identify your race differently in different situations, 9 percent; always identify yourself as mixed race, 28 percent; always identify yourself as a particular race, 48 percent; varies (volunteered), 7 percent; don't know, 5 percent; refused, 2 percent.

11. Associated Press, wire report, August 7, 2004.

# References

Abramowitz, Alan I., and Kyle L. Saunders. 1998. Party polarization and ideological realignment in the U.S. electorate, 1976–1994. In *The parties respond, changes in American parties and campaigns*, ed. Sandy L. Maisel, 3rd ed. Boulder, CO: Westview Press.

Abramowitz, Alan I., and Walter J. Stone. 1984. *Nomination politics: Party activists and presidential choice*. New York: Praeger.

Abramson, Paul R., and John H. Aldrich. 1982. The decline of electoral participation in America. *American Political Science Review* 76:502–21.

Agnello, Thomas. 1973. Aging and the sense of political powerlessness. *Public Opinion Quarterly* 37 (2): 251–59.

Ahrens, Frank. 2005. Radio: WHFS off the air. *Washington Post*, January 12.

Aldrich, John H. 1995. *Why Parties? The Origin and Transformation of Party Politics in America*. Chicago: University of Chicago Press.

Allen, Mike. 2001. Bush: Respect Mexican immigrants. *Washington Post*, May 6.

———. 2004. In Maine, one Bush wedding and a fish story. *Washington Post*, August 8.

America Coming Together (ACT). 2005. Building for the future. http://acthere.com/plan.

American National Election Studies (ANES). 2004. ANES guide to public opinion and electoral behavior. www.umich.edu/~nes/index.htm.

Amter, Charlie. 2004. Puffy gets political. *E! Online News*, July 21. www.eonline.com/News/Items/0,1,14556,00.html.

Anders, Helen. 2004. Cute Bush is altar-bound. *Austin American-Statesman*, August 16.

Anderson, Dave. 1997. Tiger Woods in a blaze, rewrites Masters' history. *New York Times*, April 14.

Anderson, Kristi. 1979. *The creation of a Democratic majority, 1928–1936*. Chicago: University of Chicago Press.

Anderson, Ronald B. 1995. Cognitive appraisal of performance capability in the prevention of drunk driving: A test of self-efficacy theory. *Journal of Public Relations Research*, 7 (3): 205–29.

——. 2000. Vicarious and persuasive influences on efficacy expectations and intentions to perform breast self-examination. *Public Relations Review* 26:97–114.

Andolina, Molly W., and Krista Jenkins. 2004. Don't write off the kids just yet. . . . Hopeful prospects for youth in the 2004 election. American Political Science Association.

Ansolabehere, Stephen, and Shanto Iyengar. 1997. *Going negative: How political advertisements shrink and polarize the electorate.* New York: Free Press.

Armas, Genaro C. 2001. Census highlights varied racial mix. *Boston Globe*, March 9.

Ascher, Carol. 1983. *The 1983 educational reform reports.* ERIC pub. no. ED252636.

Atwood, Brett. 1996. MTV renews "choose or lose" net rolls out rock the vote promo. *Billboard*, February 3.

Ayres, B. Drummond, Jr. 1997. Women in Washington state house lead U.S. tide. *New York Times*, April 14.

Balz, Dan, and Thomas B. Edsall. 2004. Unprecedented efforts to mobilize voters begin. *Washington Post*, November 1.

Bandura, Albert. 1977. *Social learning theory.* Englewood Cliffs, NJ: Prentice-Hall.

——. 1986. *Social foundations of thought and action: A social cognitive theory.* Englewood Cliffs, NJ: Prentice-Hall.

Barboza, David. 1997. Smaller investors keeping faith, despite stock market troubles. *New York Times*, April 14.

Barone, Michael, and Richard E. Cohen. 2003. *The almanac of American politics, 2004.* Washington, DC: National Journal.

Barzel, Yoram, and Eugene Silberberg. 1973. Is the act of voting rational? *Public Choice* 16:51–58.

Bauer, Gary. 1998. What aren't we teaching our children? *Citizen: A Web Site of Focus on the Family.* www.family.org/cforum/citizenmag/departments/a0001560.cfm.

Beem, Chris. 2005. From the horse's mouth: A dialogue between politicians and college students. CIRCLE: The Center for Information and Research on Civic Learning and Engagement, College Park, Maryland. www.civicyouth.org/PopUps/workingpapers/WP27Beem.pdf (accessed December 12, 2005).

Bennett, Lance. 1992. *The governing crisis: Media, money, and marketing in American Elections.* New York: St. Martin's Press.

——. 1998. The uncivic culture: Communications, identity, and the rise of lifestyle politics. *PS: Political Science and Politics* 31 (4): 741–61.

Bennett, Linda L. M., and Stephen Earl Bennett. 1990. *Living with Leviathan: Americans coming to terms with big government.* Lawrence: University of Kansas Press.

Bennett, Stephen E. 1997. Why young Americans hate politics, and what we should do about it. *PS: Political Science & Politics* 30 (1): 47–53.

——. 1998. Young Americans' indifference to media coverage of public affairs. *PS: Political Science and Politics* 31 (3): 535–41.

Bennett, Stephen E., and Stephen C. Craig, with Eric W. Rademacher. 1997. Generations and change: Some initial observations. In *After the boom: The politics of generation X*, ed. Stephen C. Craig and Stephen Earl Bennett. Lanham, MD: Rowman & Littlefield.

Bennett, William, ed. 1993. *Book of virtues: a treasury of great moral stories*. New York: Simon and Schuster.

Berry, Jeffrey, with David F. Arons. 2003. *A voice for non-profits*. Washington, DC: Brookings Institution Press.

Bethea, April. 2004. Election 2004: Young voters put issues up for debate. *The Atlanta Journal-Constitution*, October 12.

Bibby, John F. 1998. Party organizations 1946–1995. In *Partisan approaches to postwar American politics*, ed. Byron E. Shafer. New York: Chatham House.

———. 2002. State party organizations: Strengthened and adapting to candidate-centered politics and nationalization. In *The parties respond: Changes in American parties and campaigns*, ed. Sandy L. Maisel, 4th ed. Boulder, CO: Westview Press.

Bok, Derek C. 2002. The Trouble with Government. Cambridge, MA: Howard University Press.

Bork, Robert H. 1996. *Slouching towards Gomorrah*. New York: ReganBooks.

Boyte, Harry C. 2003. Civic education and the new American patriotism post 9/11. *Cambridge Journal of Education* 33 (1): 85–100.

Brady, Henry E., Kay Lehman Schlozman, Sidney Verba, and Laurel Elms. 2002. Who bowls? The (un)changing stratification of participation. In *Understanding public opinion*, ed. Barbara Narrande and Clyde Wilcox, 2nd ed. Washington, DC: CQ Press.

Braungart, Richard G., and Margaret M. Braungart. 1989. Political generations. *Research in Political Sociology* 4:281–319.

———. 1991. The effects of the 1960s political generation on former left- and right-wing youth activist leaders. *Social Problems* 38 (3): 297–315.

Brehm, John, and Wendy Rahn. 1997. Individual-level evidence for the causes and consequences of social capital. *American Journal of Political Science* 41 (3): 999–1023.

Broder, John M. 2005. Latino defeats incumbent in L.A. mayor's race. *New York Times*, May 18.

Browne, Jackson. 1986. "Lives in the balance." *Lives in the balance*. Elektra Records.

Buchanan, Patrick J. 2002. *The death of the West: How dying populations and immigrant invasions imperil our country and civilization*. New York: St. Martin's Press, 2002, 2.

Buckley, William F. 1996. Get out the hip-hop vote. *National Review*, October 14, 94.

Burnham, Walter Dean. 1970. *Critical elections and the mainsprings of American politics*. New York: W. W. Norton.

Burgess, Diana, Beth Haney, Mark Snyder, John L. Sullivan, and John E. Transue. 2000. Rocking the vote: Using personalized messages to motivate voting among young adults. *Public Opinion Quarterly* 64 (1): 29–52.

Burr, Ramiro. 2004. Sales of Latin music hold steady in 2003. *Houston Chronicle*, January 2.

Bush, George W. 2000. Address to the Republican National Convention. Philadelphia, Pennsylvania, August 2.

———. 2001. Address to Congress. Washington, DC, February 27.

———. 2004. Acceptance speech, Republican National Convention. New York City, September 2.

———. 2005. State of the Union Address. Washington, DC, February 2.

Busk, Celeste. 2002. Exhibit chronicles history of hip-hop, Chicago-style. *Chicago Sun-Times*, January 18.

Cacioppo, John T., Richard E. Petty, and Katherine J. Morris. 1983. Effects of need for cognition on message evaluation, recall, and persuasion. *Journal of Personality and Social Psychology* 4:62–93.

Callahan, Tom. 2003. *In search of tiger: A journey through gold with Tiger Woods*. New York: Crown Publishers.

Campaign Study Group. 2000. Y vote 2000: Politics of a new generation. www. yvoteonline.org (accessed August 8, 2004).

Campbell, Angus, Phillip E. Converse, Warren E. Miller, and Donald Stokes. 1960. *The American voter*. New York: Wiley.

Campbell, David. 2000. Social capital and service learning. *PS: Political Science and Politics* 33 (3): 641–45.

Campbell, Ronald, and Erica Perez. 2004. Minorities dominate "real" Orange County. *Orange County Register*, October 1.

Campo-Flores, Arian, and Howard Fineman. 2005. A Latin power surge. *Newsweek*, May 30.

Cannon, Lou. 2003. *Governor Reagan: His rise to power*. New York: Public Affairs.

Carnegie Corporation of New York and CIRCLE: The Center for Information and Research on Civic Learning and Engagement. 2003. *The civic mission of schools*. New York: Authors.

Carroll, Joseph. 2003. Gallup poll assesses views of young Americans. Gallup poll, November 5. www.gallup.com (accessed October 29, 2004).

Cast the Vote. 2004a. Cast the Vote, MTV's "Choose or Lose," and New Voters Project to launch in-theatre ad campaign with voter registration in movie theatre lobbies. September 10. www.castthevote.org/includes/091004_press_release.pdf.

———. 2004b. Our mission. www.castthevote.org/mission.html.

Center for Information and Research on Civic Learning and Engagement (CIRCLE). 2002a. Youth civic engagement: Basic facts and trends. University of Maryland, January 9, 3.

———. 2002b. Youth voter turnout has declined, by any measure. University of Maryland.

———. 2002c. Short-term impacts, long-term opportunities: The political and civic engagement of young adults in America. Analysis and report by Lake Snell Perry & Associates/The Tarrance Group Inc., March.

———. 2004a. Around the CIRCLE—research roundup. www.civicyouth.org/ PopUps/v1.i.3.pdf.

———. 2004b. Youth turnout up sharply in 2004. November 3.

———. 2005. Youth voting in the 2004 election. Center for Information and Research on Civic Learning and Engagement fact sheet.

Center for Public Integrity. 2003. Silent partners. www.public-i.org/527/report. aspx?aid=10.

Cho, Hyunyi, and Kim Witte. 2004. A review of fear appeal effects. In *Perspectives on persuasion, social influence, and compliance gaining*, ed. John S. Seiter and Robert H. Gass. New York: Pearson.

Choose or Lose. 2004. 18–29 year olds and the presidential election. CBS News, September 14. www.cbsnews.com (accessed October 2, 2004).

CIRCLE and the Pew Center for the People and the Press. 2002. Youth civic engagement after 9/11/01. January 9, 18–19.

Citizen Change. 2004. About us: Citizen Change's mission. www.citizenchange.com.

Citizen Leader Coalition. 2004. What is Citizen Leader Coalition? www.citizenleader .com/aboutclc.html.

———. 2005a. Phone interview to research assistant, by Craig Berger. May 24.

———. 2005b. Citizen Leader Coalition. www.citizenleader.com/cvoter/index.html.

Clark, Eric. 1988. *The want makers: The world of advertising; how they make you buy*. New York: Viking.

Clinton, Bill. 1998. Remarks by the president at Portland State University commencement. Portland, Oregon, June 13.

Cloonan, Martin, and John Street. 1998. Rock the vote: Popular culture and politics. *Politics* 18 (1): 33–38.

Cogan, John J. 1997. Crisis in Citizenship Education in the United States. *International Journal of Social Education*. 11: 21–36.

Cohn, D'Vera. 2004. Area immigration booming. *Washington Post*, November 23.

———. 2005. Hispanic growth surge fueled by births in U.S. *Washington Post*, June 9.

Cohn, D'Vera, and Carol Morello. 2001. Northern Virginia's growth outpaces state's. *Washington Post*, March 9.

Cole, Jacquelyn. 2004. DNC focuses on young voters. *Scripps Howard Foundation Wire*, July 29.

College Democrats of America. 2005a. Media FAQs. www.collegedems.com/news/ media.

———. 2005b. What is CDA? www.collegedems.com/about/whatiscda/index.php.

College Republican National Committee. 2004. Training program. www.crnc.org/ page.asp?LinkID=116.

———. 2005. Field program. www.crnc.org/fieldprogram.htm.

Comber, Melissa. 2005. The effects of civic education on civic skills. Washington, DC: The Center for Information and Research on Civic Learning and Engagement.

Committee on Political Parties, American Political Science Association. 1950. Toward a more responsible two-party system. *American Political Science Review*, Supplement.

Conover, Pamela Johnson, and Donald Searing. 2000. A political socialization perspective. In *Rediscovering the democratic purposes of education*, ed. Lorraine M. McDonnell, P. Michael Timpane, and Roger Benjamin. Lawrence: University Press of Kansas.

Conrad, Dan. 1991. School-community participation for social studies. In *Handbook of research on social studies teaching and learning*, ed. James P. Shaver, 548–48. New York: Macmillan.

Conservative Punk. 2004a. About. www.conservativepunk.com/about.asp.

———. 2004b. Conservative punk. www.conservativepunk.com/index.asp.

Contreras, Russell. 2000. Voters' vida loca. *Houston Press*. June 29.

Conway, Margaret. 2000. *Political participation in the United States*. 3rd ed. Washington, DC: Congressional Quarterly Press.

Cose, Ellis. 1997. *Color-blind: Seeing beyond race in a race-obsessed world*. New York: HarperCollins.

Cotter, Cornelius P., James L. Gibson, John F. Bibby, and Robert J. Huckshorn. 1984. *Party organizations in American politics*. New York: Eagleton Institute of Politics, Rutgers University.

Coupland, Douglas. 1991. *Generation X: Tales for an accelerated culture*. New York: St. Martin's Griffin.

Craig, Stephen C., and Stephen Earl Bennett, eds. 1997. *After the boom: The politics of Generation X*. Lanham, MD: Rowman & Littlefield.

Crawford, Amanda J., Elvia Diz, and Yvonne Wingett. 2004. Initiative raises questions. *The Arizona Republic*, November 4.

Crotty, William, and Gary Jacobson. 1980. *American parties in decline*. Boston: Little, Brown.

Currinder, Marian. 2005. Campaign finance: Funding the presidential and congressional elections. In *The elections of 2004*, ed. Michael Nelson, 108–32. Washington, DC: Congressional Quarterly.

Dahl, Robert. 1961. *Who governs?* New Haven, CT: Yale University Press.

Davis, F. James. 1991. *Who is black? One nation's definition*. University Park: Pennsylvania State University Press.

Declare Yourself. 2003. 2004 youth survey. November. www.declareyourself.com (accessed October 2, 2004).

———. 2004. About us. www.declareyourself.com/aboutus/htm.

Delli Carpini, Michael X., and Scott Keeter. 1996. *What Americans know about politics and why it matters*. New Haven, CT: Yale University Press.

Dewey, John. 1916. *Democracy and education*. New York: Free Press.

DiCarlo, Rachel. 2004. Rocking the Christian vote: Redeem the Vote encourages young evangelicals to register to cast their ballots. *Daily Standard*, October 21.

Dickens, Charles. 1842. *American notes*. London and Hall, 149. Cited in Howard Reiter, *Parties and elections in corporate America*, 2nd ed. (New York: St. Martin's Press, 1993), 6.

Dionne, Eugene J. 1991. *Why Americans hate politics*. New York: Simon & Schuster.

Dobson, James. 2005. That's entertainment. *Dr. Dobson's Newsletter*, Focus on the Family website, June. www.family.org/docstudy/newsletters/a0037038.cfm.

Donovan, Carrie. 2005. The civic effects of small school reform: A discussion. Meeting notes of the Center for Information and Research on Civic Learning and Engagement, July 6. www.civicyouth.org.

Doppelt, Jack, and Ellen Shearer. 2001. America's no shows—nonvoters: Who they are, why they don't vote, and what it could take to bring them back to the polls. The Pew Charitable Trusts, September. www.pewtrusts.com (accessed August 8, 2004).

Dowd, Timothy J. 2000. Rocking the vote: The music industry and the mobilization of young voters. *Soundscapes: Journal on Media Culture* 3 (August). www.icce.rug.nl (accessed October 19, 2004).

Downs, Anthony. 1957. *An economic theory of democracy.* New York: Harper & Row.

Dreier, Peter. 2003. Villaraigosa's challenge: Governing Los Angeles in the Bush and Schwarzenegger era. www.commondreams.org/views05/0528-23.htm.

Dye, Thomas, and Harman Zeigler. 1996. *The irony of democracy.* 10th ed. Belmont, CA: Wadsworth.

Eagles, Munroe, and Russell Davidson. 2001. Civic education, political socialization, and political mobilization. *Journal of Geography* 100:233–42.

Education Commission of the States. 2004. State citizenship education policies. April 2004. www.ecs.org.

Eisner, Jane. 2004. *Taking back the vote: Getting American youth involved in our democracy.* Boston: Beacon.

Ellis, Justin, and Tom Bell. 2004. Town bustles with Bush family. *Portland Press Herald,* August 7.

Epstein, Reid J. 2004. Will you vote on November 2nd? Really? Promise?: Youth project seeks pledges, follow up phone calls. *Milwaukee Journal Sentinel* (Wisconsin), October 4.

Etzioni, Amitai. 2001. *The monochrome society.* Princeton, NJ: Princeton University Press.

Eveleth, Ann. 1999. How do we get the youth voting? *Daily Mail & Guardian,* June 18. www.mg.co.za (accessed August 31, 2004).

Fanelli, Brian. 2004. Redeeming the youth vote. *Wiretap,* July 21.

Farhi, Paul. 2005. Shock jock's audience is beating him to the door. *Washington Post,* October 20.

Farrington, Brendan. 2004. Governor's son—and political hunk—to wed in Maine. Associated Press, August 5.

Ferullo, Mike. 2000. At GOP convention, Bush nephew appeals to young voters, Hispanics. CNN, August 4.

Finnegan, Michael. 2005. Villaraigosa will finally get his national presence. *Los Angeles Times,* May 18.

Finnegan, Michael, and Mark Z. Barabak. 2005. Villariagosa landslide: Voter discontent helps propel challenger to a historic victory. *Los Angeles Times,* May 18.

Fiorina, Morris P., Samuel J. Abrams, and Jeremy C. Pope. 2005. *Culture war? The myth of a polarized America.* 2nd ed. New York: Longman.

Fitzpatrick, John. 1939. *The writings of George Washington from the original manuscript sources.* Vol. 30. Washington, DC: Government Printing Office.

Flanagan, Constance. 2003. Developmental roots of political engagement. *PS: Political Science and Politics* 36 (2): 257–61.

Fleming, Jane. 2004. Young Democrats of America and progressive groups turn out the youth vote with the Young Voter Alliance; Alliance GOTV plan and "Trick or Vote" project will turn out record numbers of young voters to elect Democrats up and down the ticket on Nov. 2nd. *PR Newswire US,* October 19.

Franklin, Bob. 1994. *Packaging politics.* London: Edward Arnold.

Free Peers Inc. 2004. BearShare file-sharing service registers voters through the YourVoteMatters.org online voter registration service. September 7. www.bearshare.com/press/voter.htm.

Frendreis, John P., James L. Gibson, and Laura L. Vertz. 1990. The electoral relevance of local party organizations. *American Political Science Review* 84:225–35.

Frendreis, John P., and Alan R. Gitelson. 1993. Local political parties in an age of change. *American Review of Politics* 14:533–47.

———. 1999. Local parties in the 1990s: Spokes in a candidate-centered wheel. In *The state of the parties: The changing role of contemporary parties*, ed. John C. Green and Daniel M. Shea, 3rd ed. Lanham, MD: Rowman & Littlefield.

Frendreis, John, Alan R. Gitelson, Gregory Flemming, and Anne Layzell. 1996. Local political parties and legislative races in 1992 and 1994. In *The state of the parties: The changing role of contemporary parties*, ed. John C. Green and Daniel M. Shea, 2nd ed. Lanham, MD: Rowman & Littlefield, 149–62.

Friedland, Lewis, and Shauna Morimoto. 2005. The changing lifeworld of young people: Risk, resume-padding, and civic engagement. Working Paper 40, Center for Information and Research on Civic Learning and Engagement. www.civicyouth .org.

Frishberg, Ivan, and Michael X. Delli Carpini. 2005. A new generation gets increased attention. *Wingspread Journal*, 13–17.

Fuchs, Marek. 2005. Corzine selects Menendez to replace him in Senate. *New York Times*, December 9.

Galston, William. 2000. Civic education and political participation. The Democracy Collaborative. www.democracycollaborative.org (accessed August 8, 2004).

———. 2001. Political knowledge, political engagement, and civic education. *Annual Review of Political Science* 4 (June): 217–34.

———. 2003. Civic education and political participation. *Phi Delta Kappan* 85 (1): 29–33.

Ganz, Marshall. 1996. Motor voter or motivated voter. *The American Prospect* 28 (September–October): 41–48.

Garofolo, Reebee. 1992. Understanding mega-events: If we are the world, then how do we change it? *Rocking the boat: Mass music & mass movements*, ed. Reebee Garofolo. Boston: South End, 15–36.

Geldon, Dan. 2005. My profound thanks. Weblog comment at College Democrats of America, May 20. www.collegedems.com/blog.

Gerhart, Ann. 2003. Norman Lear, hoping youth will tune in to vote. *Washington Post*, November 14.

Gibson, Cynthia. 2001. *From inspiration to participation*. New York: Carnegie Corporation of New York.

Ginsberg, Benjamin, and Martin Shefter. 1990. *Politics by other means*. New York: W. W. Norton.

Giroux, Henry. 1998. *Channel surfing: Racism, the media, and the destruction of today's youth*. New York: St. Martin's Griffin.

Glass, Stephen. 1997. Rock the morons. *The New Republic*, February 10, 16–17.

Glazer, Nathan, and Patrick Moynihan. 1963. *Beyond the melting pot: The Negroes, Puerto Ricans, Jews, Italians, and Irish of New York City*. Cambridge, MA: MIT Press.

Glover, Mike. 2005. Hillary Clinton reinforces ties to moderate Democrats. Associated Press. Retrieved December 3, 2006, from LexisNexis.

Goldberg, Jonah. 2003. Vote rocking: Dems go for "the youth." *National Review Online*, November 5. www.nationalreview.com (accessed October 19, 2004).

Goodlad, John. 1996. Democracy, education, and community. In *Democracy, education, and the schools*, ed. Roger Soder, 87–124. San Francisco: Jossey-Bass.

Goodman, Ellan. 2003. "Why ask Y? Bogus 'PC or Mac' debate question trivializes Gen Y's growing political clout." Washington Post Writers Group, www.working forchange.com/article.cfm?ItemID=15997, accessed June 1.

GOP Team Leader. 2004. Reggie. www.gopteamleader.com/reggie.

———. 2005. About team leader. www.gopteamleader.com/about.asp.

Gore, Al, and Tipper Gore. 2002. *Joined at the heart: The transformation of the American family*. New York: Henry Holt & Company.

Graber, Doris. 1993. *Processing the news: How people tame the information tide*. Lanham, MD: University Press of America.

Green, Andrew. 2004. They've got rhythm; they've got politics. *Milwaukee Journal Sentinel* (Wisconsin), July 19.

Green, Donald P., and Alan S. Gerber. 2001. Getting out the youth vote: Results from randomized field experiments. Institution for Social and Policy Studies, Yale University, December 29. www.yale.edu/isps (accessed August 8, 2004).

———. 2004. *Get out the vote: How to increase voter turnout*. Washington, DC: Brookings Institution Press.

Green, Donald, and Ian Shapiro. 1994. *Pathologies of rational choice theory: A critique of applications in political science*. New Haven, CT: Yale University Press.

Green, Eric. 2002. Record number of Hispanics elected to U.S. House of Representatives. U.S. Department of State, International Information Programs, November 12.

Grossfeld, Stan. 2001. "It's a Good Life." *Boston Globe*, May 6.

Gutmann, Amy. 1987. *Democratic education*. Princeton, NJ: Princeton University Press.

———. 2000. Why should schools care about civic education? In *Rediscovering the democratic purposes of education*, eds. Lorraine McDonnell, P. Michael Timpane, and Roger Benjamin, ed. 73–90. Lawrence: University Press of Kansas.

Haberman, Doug. 2004. Teens plan voting drive; youth council aims to sign up as many unregistered citizens as possible by Oct. 17. *Riverside Press Enterprise*, September 18.

Hacker, Jacob S., and Paul Pierson. 2005. Abandoning the middle: The revealing case of the Bush tax cut of 2001. *Perspectives on Politics*. 3 (1): 33–53.

Hafer, C. L., K. Reynolds, and M. A. Obertynski. 1996. Message comprehensibility and persuasion: Effects of complex language in counter attitudinal appeals to laypeople. *Social Cognition* 14:317–37.

Hampson, Rick. 2004. Rocking a vote is one thing; casting it is quite another. *USA Today*, August 19.

Harvard Institute of Politics. 2004. The political personality of America's college students. Spring. www.iop.harvard.edu (accessed August 31, 2004).

Hays, Carol. 1998. Alienation, engagement and the college student. In *Engaging the public: How government and the media can reinvigorate American democracy*, ed. Thomas Johnson, Carol E. Hays, and Scott P. Hays. Lanham, MD: Rowman & Littlefield.

HeadCount. 2004. HeadCount. www.headcount.org/images/about.htm.

Henn, Matt, Mark Weinstein, and Dominic Wring. 2002. A generation apart: Youth and political participation in Britain. *British Journal of Politics and International Relations* 4 (2): 167–92.

Herivel, Tan, and Paul Wright. 2003. *Prison nation: The warehousing of America's poor*. London: Routledge.

Herrnson, Paul S. 2002. National party organizations at the dawn of the twenty-first century. In *The parties respond: Changes in American parties and campaigns*, ed. Sandy L. Maisel, 4th ed. Boulder, CO: Westview Press.

Heyman-Kantor, Reuben. 2004. Swarthmore College students, faculty unite to register voters. *Swarthmore Phoenix*, September 10.

Hicks, John D. 1949. *The American nation: A history of the United States from 1865 to present*. Boston: Houghton Mifflin, 62.

Higher Education Research Institute (HERI). 1999. Most of the nation's college freshmen embrace the Internet as an educational tool, UCLA study finds. HERI website, January 25. www.gseis.ucla.edu/heri/norms_pr_98.html.

———. 2004. Press release. University of California at Los Angeles, October 29. www.gseis.ucla.edu.

Hip-Hop Summit Action Network.org. 2004a. Our mission. http://hsan.org/content.

———. 2004b. Become a HHTV GOTV TOUR volunteer. http://hsan.org/content/main.aspx?contestId-15.

———. 2004c. Join hip-hop Team Vote today. http://hsan.org/content/main.aspx?pageid=30.

Hochschild, Jennifer L., and Nathan Scovronick. 2000. Democratic education and the American dream. In *Rediscovering the democratic purposes of education*, 209–42. Lawrence: University Press of Kansas.

Howe, Neil, and William Strauss. 2000. *Millennials rising: The next great generation*. New York: Vintage.

Huntington, Samuel P. 2004a. *Who are we? The challenges to America's national identity*. New York: Simon & Schuster.

———. 2004b. Jose, can you see? *Foreign Policy*. March–April.

Huthmacher, J. Joseph. 1969. *Massachusetts: People and politics, 1919–1933*. New York: Atheneum.

Inglehart, Ronald. 1990. *Culture shift in advanced industrial society*. Princeton, NJ: Princeton University Press.

Institute for Democracy and Electoral Assistance (IDEA). 2004. Voter turnout from 1945 to date. www.idea.int (accessed August 31, 2004).

Ives, Nat. 2004. The media business: Advertising; marketers discover election day, embracing get-out-the-vote efforts for young people as a way to reach potential consumers. *New York Times*, March 22.

Iyengar, Shanto. 1990. Shortcuts to political knowledge: The role of selective attention and accessibility. In *Information and democratic processes*, ed. John A. Ferejohn and James H. Kuklinski. Urbana: University of Illinois Press.

Iyengar, Shanto, and Simon Jackman. 2003. Technology and politics: Incentives for youth participation. International Conference on Civic Education Research, New Orleans, Louisiana, November 16–18. http://pcl.stanford.edu (accessed August 31, 2004).

Jacoby, Tamar. 2004. A line has been drawn in the Arizona sand. *Washington Post*, November 14.

Jamieson, Kathleen Hall. 1988. *Eloquence in an electronic age: The transformation of political speechmaking*. New York: Oxford University Press.

Jennings, M. Kent. 1981. *Generations and politics: A panel study of young adults and their parents*. Princeton: Princeton University Press.

Jennings, M. Kent, and Richard G. Niemi. 1974. *The political character of adolescence: The influence of family and schools*. Princeton: Princeton University Press.

Jones, Stephanie J. 2005. Sunday morning apartheid: A diversity study of the Sunday morning talk shows. Washington, DC: National Urban League Policy Institute.

Jones, Vanessa E. 2003. The brand name hip-hop heavy Russell Simmons has one eye on the bottom line and the other on higher callings. *Boston Globe*, December 7.

Just Vote Now. 2004. Just Vote Now. www.justvotenow.org/about.html.

Kaiser Family Foundation/MTV. 2000. Youth voting and the 2000 election. October 3. www.kff.org (accessed September 10, 2004).

Kamenetz, Amy. 2004. Rock the vote? Maybe not. *Salon.com*, April 23. www.salon.com (accessed October 26, 2004).

Kaplan, Robert. 1997. Was democracy just a moment. *Atlantic Monthly*, December.

Keeter, Scott, Cliff Zukin, Molly Andolina, and Krista Jenkins. 2002. The civic and political health of the nation: A generational portrait. The Center for Information and Research on Civic Learning and Engagement, September 19. www.civicyouth.org (accessed August 8, 2004).

Keough, Michael. 2005. College Republicans. Private e-mail message to research assistant Craig Berger, May 26. mkeough@crnc.org.

Kern, Montague. 1989. *30-second politics: Political advertising in the eighties*. New York: Praeger.

Key, Valdimer Orlando, Jr. 1966. *The responsible electorate: Rationality in presidential voting, 1936–1960*. Cambridge, MA: Belknap Press of Harvard University Press.

Kirkpatrick, Jeane. 1976. *The new presidential elite*. New York: Russell Sage and Twentieth Century Fund.

Kitwana, Bakari. 2003. *The hip hop generation: Young blacks and the crisis in African American culture*. New York: Basic Civitas Books.

Klecka, William R. 1971. Applying political generations to the study of political behavior: A cohort analysis. *Public Opinion Quarterly* 35 (3): 358–73.

Kohut, Andrew. 1998. *Deconstructing distrust: How Americans view government*. Washington, DC: Pew Research Center for the People and the Press.

Kornblut, Anne E. 2004. Little talk of dynasty as a Bush weds. *Boston Globe*, August 8.

Kurtz, Karl, Alan Rosenthal, and Cliff Zukin. 2003. Citizenship: A challenge for all generations. National Conference of State Legislatures. www.ncsl.org.

Ladd, Everett Carll, and Karlyn H. Bowman. 1998. *What's wrong: A survey of American satisfaction and complaint*. Washington, DC: American Enterprise Institute Press.

Lakoff, George. 1996. *Moral politics: What conservatives know that liberals don't*. Chicago: University of Chicago Press.

——. 2004. *Don't think of an elephant: Know your values and frame the debate*. New York: Chelsea Green.

Langton, Kenneth, and M. Kent Jennings. 1968. Political socialization and the high school civics curriculum. *American Political Science Review* 62:862–67.

Leming, James S. 1996. We the people: The citizen and the Constitution. Eric Digest EDO-SO-96-4.

Lengle, James I. 1981. *Representation and presidential primaries*. Westport, CT: Greenwood Press.

Levine, Peter. 2005. Youth voting in 2004: The myths and the facts. *Wingspread Journal* 3–6.

Levine, Peter, and Mark Hugo Lopez. 2002. Youth voter turnout has declined, by any measure. Center for Information and Research on Civic Learning and Engagement fact sheet. www.civicyouth.org.

Levinson, Meira. 2004. The civic achievement gap: Why poor and minority students are disproportionately disengaged in civic life—and what can be done about it. *Threshold*. Washington, DC: Cable in the Classroom.

Lieb, David A. 2004. AP enterprise: Political group paid felons for door-to-door voter registration drive. The Associated Press State & Local Wire, June 24.

Lijphart, Arend. 1997. Unequal participation: Democracy's unresolved dilemma. *American Political Science Review* 91 (1): 1–14.

Lind, Michael. 2003. Far from Heaven. *The Nation*, June 16.

Longo, Nicholas V. 2004. The new student politics: Listening to the political voice of students. *The Journal of Public Affairs* 7 (1): 61–85.

Lopez, Mark Hugo. 2002. Civic engagement among minority youth. Center for Information and Research on Civic Learning and Engagement, September. www.civicyouth.org (accessed August 8, 2004).

——. 2004. Volunteering among young people. Updated, 2004. CIRCLE working paper. www.civicyouth.org/popups/factsheets/FS Volunteering2.pdf. Accessed June 1, 2006.

Lopez, Mark Hugo, and E. Kirby. 2005. Electoral engagement among minority youth. Washington, DC: Center for Information and Research on Civic Learning and Engagement.

Lupia, Arthur, and Mathew McCubbins. 1998. *The democratic dilemma: Can citizens learn what they need to know?* Cambridge: Cambridge University Press.

Lynskey, Dorian. 2004. Meet the pro-Bush punks: The most anti-establishment of music genres is being used in support of the US Republican Party. *The Guardian* (London), July 7.

Macel, Emily. 2002. Coalition hopes to get youths to the polls. *Roll Call*, October 7.

Maibach, Edward, and June A. Flora. 1993. Symbolic modeling and cognitive rehearsal: Using video to promote AIDS prevention self efficacy. *Communication Research* 20 (4): 517–45.

Maio, Gregory R., David W. Bell, and Victoria M. Esses. 1996. Ambivalence and persuasion: The processing of messages about immigrant groups. *Journal of Experimental Social Psychology* 32:513–36.

Malbin, Michael J., ed. 2003. *Life after reform*. Lanham, MD: Rowman & Littlefield.

Malone, Julia. 2004. Intense interest, outside groups spur increased voter registration. *Cox News Service*, October 4.

Margolick, David. 2001. Brother dearest. *Vanity Fair*, July.

Martin, Joyce A., et al. 2005. Births: Final data for 2003. *National Vital Statistics Report* 54 (2). www.cdc.gov/nchs/data/nvsr/nvsr54/nvsr54_02.pdf.

Martinez, Michael, and David Hill. 1999. Did motor voter work? *American Politics Quarterly* 27 (3): 296–315.

McDevitt, Michael, Spiro Kiousis, Xu Wu, Mary Losch, and Travis Ripley. 2003. The civic bonding of school and family: How kids voting students enliven the domestic sphere. Working Paper 7, Center for Information and Research on Civic Learning and Engagement. www.civicyouth.org.

McDonald, Michael P., and Samuel L. Popkin. 2001. The myth of the vanishing voter. *American Political Science Review* 95 (4): 963–74.

McKibben, Bill. 2001. George Harrison and the concert for Bangladesh. *Salon*, December 1. http://dir.salon.com (accessed October 21, 2004).

McKissack, Fred. 1999. Lost in MTV land. *The Progressive*, June 12.

McLaughlin, Elliott C. 2004. Georgia's first Spanish ballots to debut in Hall County this November. *Associated Press*, April 13.

McMillan, Jill, and Katy Harringer. 2002. College students and deliberation. *Communication Education*, 51 (3): 237–53.

McWilliams, Wilson Carey. 1995. *The politics of disappointment*. Chatham: Chatham House Publishers.

Milbrath, Lester. 1965. *Political participation: How and why do people get involved in politics?* Chicago: Rand McNally.

Miller, Joanne M., and Jon A. Krosnick. 2004. Threat as a motivator of political activism: A field experiment. *Political Psychology* 25 (4): 507–23.

Miller, Warren E. 2002. Party identification and the electorate at the start of the twenty-first century. In *The parties respond: Changes in American parties and campaigns*, L. Sandy Maisel, 4th ed. Boulder, CO: Westview Press.

Miller, Warren E., and J. Merrill Shanks. 1996. *The new American voter*. Cambridge: Harvard University Press.

Moody, Nekesa Mumbi. 2004. Hip-hop to the ballot box. Associated Press, July 27. www.ap.org (accessed October 21, 2004).

Mooney, Brian C. 2004. Parties race to register new voters. *Boston Globe*, July 6.

Moseley, Matt. 1999. Young Americans volunteer but don't vote. *Campaigns & Elections*, April 4, 35.

MoveOn PAC. 2004a. Vote for Change tour. www.moveonpac.org/vfc.

——. 2004b. Voice for change. www.moveonpac.org/content/pdfs/VFC_MNR_ release.pdf (accessed October 6, 2004).

MTV.com Choose or Lose. 2004. John Kerry wins PRE-lection in a landside. www. mtv.com/chooseorlose/pre_lection, October 20.

Murphy, James. 2004. Against civic schooling. *Social Philosophy and Policy* 21 (1): 221–65.

Music for America. 2004. About. www.musicforamerica.org/about.

——. 2005. Politix. www.musicforamerica.org/politix.

National Association of Secretaries of State (NASS). 1999. New Millennium Survey: American attitudes on politics, citizenship, government & voting. www.stateofthe vote.org (accessed August 8, 2004).

National Center for Learning and Citizenship. 2003. *Citizenship education policy brief, state policies to support citizenship education.* November. www.ecs.org.

The National Coalition on Black Civic Participation. 2004a. About us. www.bigvote. org/index1.htm.

——. 2004b. Black youth vote! www.bigvote.org/byv.htm.

National Commission on Civic Renewal. 1998. *A nation of spectators.* College Park, MD: University of Maryland Institute of Philosophy and Public Policy.

National Election Pool. 2004. Exit poll. November 2.

National Election Studies. 2004. Trust the federal government, 1958–2002. *The NES Guide to Public Opinion and Electoral Behavior.* www.umich.edu/~nes/index.htm (accessed September 10, 2004).

National Institute on Drug Abuse. 2004. Teen drug use declines. National Institute on Drug Abuse Press Release, December 21. www.nida.nih.gov/Newsroom/04/ NR12-21.html.

National Public Radio. 1999. Think tanks. *All Things Considered*, August 31.

National Youth Development Center (NYDC). 2000. Barriers to core resources for positive youth development. www.nvdic.org (accessed September 10, 2004).

Navarro, Mireya. 2003. Going beyond black and white, Hispanics in census pick "Other." *New York Times*, November 9.

Nelson, Jack L. 1991. Communities, local to national, as influences on social studies education. In *Handbook of research on social studies teaching and learning*, ed. James P. Shaver, 332–44. New York: Macmillan.

New Voters Project. 2004a. Campaign plan. www.newvotersproject.org/campaign_ plan.

——. 2004b. About the new voters project. www.newvotersproject.org/about_the_ new_voters_project.

Nichols, John. 2004. The beat-Bush brigades. *The Nation*, April 26.

Nie, Norman, et al. 1996. *Education and democratic citizenship in America.* Chicago: University of Chicago Press.

Nie, Norman, and D. Sunshine Hillygus. 2001. Education and democratic citizenship. In Diane Ravitch and Joseph Viteritti, *Making good citizens: Education and civil society.* New Haven, CT: Yale University Press.

Niemi, Richard, and Jane Junn. 1998. *Civic education: What makes students learn.* New Haven, CT: Yale University Press.

Niemi, Richard G., and Julia Smith. 2001. Enrollments in high school government classes: Are we short-changing both citizenship and political science training? *PS: Political Science and Politics*, June, 281–87.

Northrop, Sheryl. 2004. Top country music stars campaign for your country, your vote. *Press Release News Wire*, August 17.

Nye, Joseph S., Jr., Philip D. Zelikow, and David C. King. 1997. *Why people don't trust government*. Cambridge, MA: Harvard University Press.

O'Brien, Nancy Frazier. 2004. At 29 percent of 109th Congress, Catholics remain largest faith group. *Catholic News Service*, November 11.

O'Neill, Tip, and Gary Hymel. 1994. *All politics is local*. New York: Times Books.

Orfield, Gary, and Chungmei Lee. 2005. *Why segregation matters: Poverty and educational inequality*. Cambridge, MA: Harvard Civil Rights Project.

Orloff, Brian. 2004. Voice for change. www.rollingstone.com/news/story/_/id/6537312.

P2Pnet. 2004. P2P client registers voters. http://p2pnet.net/index.php?page=reply&story=2373.

Pace University/Rock the Vote Survey Research Study. 2004. First time voters: You never forget your first presidential election. July 26. http://appserv.pace.edu (accessed August 8, 2004).

Page, Benjamin, and Robert Shapiro. 1992. *The rational public: Fifty years of trends in Americans' policy preferences*. Chicago: University of Chicago Press.

Panetta Institute. 2000. Poll results. January 11. www.panettainstitute.org (accessed July 28, 2004).

Pastor, Gregory S., Walter J. Stone, and Ronald B. Rapoport. 1996. Candidate-centered sources of party change: The case of Pat Robertson, 1988. University of Colorado.

Patrick, John J. 2000. Introduction to education for civic engagement in democracy. In *Education for civic engagement: Service learning and other promising practices*, ed. Sheilah Mann and John Patrick, 1–8. ERIC pub. no. ED447065.

———. 2002. Defining, delivering and defending a common education for citizenship in a democracy. Paper presented at the Summit on Civic Learning in Teacher Preparation, Boston, Massachusetts, May 15.

Patrick, John J., and John D. Hoge. 1991. Teaching government, civics, and law. In *Handbook of research on social studies teaching and learning*, ed. James P. Shaver, 427–36. New York: Macmillan.

Patterson, Thomas E. 2002. *The vanishing voter: Public involvement in an age of uncertainty*. New York: Knopf.

Peck, Don. 2002. The shrinking electorate. *Atlantic Monthly*, November, 48–49.

Perlstein, Linda. 2003. Montgomery schools at diversity landmark. *Washington Post*, October 14.

———. 2004. Class of diversity awarded diplomas. *Washington Post*, June 6.

Petty, Richard E., and John T. Cacioppo. 1979. Issue-involvement can increase or decrease persuasion by enhancing message-relevant cognitive responses. *Journal of Personality and Social Psychology* 37:1915–26.

——. 1986. *Communication and persuasion: Central and peripheral routes to attitude change.* New York: Springer-Verlag.

——. 1990. Involvement and persuasion: Tradition versus integration. *Psychological Bulletin* 107:367–74.

Petty, Richard E., Gary L. Wells, and Timothy C. Brock. 1976. Distractions can enhance or reduce yielding to propaganda: Thought disruption versus effort justification. *Journal of Personality and Social Psychology* 34:874–84.

Pew Research Center for the People and the Press. 2002. Americans struggle with religion's role at home and abroad.

Pierce, John C., Brent S. Steel, and Nicholas P. Lovrich. 2003. Analysis of impacts of the Project Vote Smart young voters program—2002. www.vote-smart.org (accessed August 31, 2004).

Pontell, Jonathan, and J. Brad Coker. 2004. The invisible generation elects a president. *Polling Report*, November 29.

Popkin, Samuel, and Michael Dimock. 1999. Political knowledge and citizen competence. In *Citizen competence and democratic institutions*, ed. Stephen Elkin and Karol Soltan. University Park: Pennsylvania State University Press.

Post-Modernity Project. 1996. *The state of disunion.* Charlottesville: University of Virginia.

Provo, Darcy. 2004. A quarter million newly registered voters encouraged to spread voting pledge to friends through JustVoteNow.org. *PR Newswire US*, October 21.

Punk Voter. 2004. About PunkVoter.com. www.punkvoter.com/about/about.php.

Putnam, Robert D. 1995. Bowling alone: America's declining social capital. *Journal of Democracy* 6 (1): 65–78.

——. 2000a. *Bowling alone: The collapse and revival of American community.* New York: Simon & Schuster.

——. 2000b. The prosperous community: Social capital and public life. In *Principles and practices of American politics*, ed. S. Kernell and S. S. Smith. Washington DC: CQ Press.

——. 2002. Bowling together. *American Prospect* 13 (3).

Putnam, Robert D., and Lewis M. Feldstein. 2003. *Better together: Restoring the American community.* New York: Simon & Schuster.

Rahn, Wendy. 1998. Generations and American national identity: A data essay. Prepared for presentation at the Communication in the Future of Democracy Workshop, Annenberg Center, Washington, DC, May 8–9.

——. 1999. Americans' engagement with and commitment to the political system: A generational portrait. Prepared for presentation at the COSSA congressional briefing, Washington, DC, July 16.

Reagan, Ronald. 1981. Inaugural address. Washington, DC, January 20.

Redbord, Ari. 1996. Rock the leftist vote. *Weekly Standard*, July 29, 18.

Redeem the Vote. 2004. Home. www.redeemthevote.com.

Robbins, Dean, and Rob Grabow. 2004. *What we think, young voters speak out.* Bothwell, WA: Book Publishers Network.

Rock the Vote. 2004a. About rock the vote. www.rockthevote.com/rtv_about.php.

——. 2004b. Rock the vote timeline. www.rockthevote.com/rtv_timeline.php.

———. 2004 & 2005. www.rockthevote.com.

Rose, Maria Matzer. 2004. Univision Net soars 62 percent on record viewership. *Hollywood Reporter.com*, February 20.

Rose, Ryan. 2004. Is "Rock the Vote" stoning Bush? *The Sacramento Union*, October 27. www.sacunion.com (accessed November 1, 2004).

Rosenstone, Steven J., and John M. Hansen. 1993. *Mobilization, participation, and democracy in America*. New York: Macmillan Publishing Company.

Ross, Curtis. 2004. Punks join crowd aiming to incite youth vote. *Tampa Tribune* (Florida), August 1.

Rothstein, Richard. 2004. *Class and schools: Using social, economic, and educational reform to close the black-white achievement gap*. Washington, DC: Economic Policy Institute.

Russakoff, Dale. 2001. Census finds diversity spreading to suburbs. *Washington Post*, March 9.

Sabato, Larry J. 1991. *Feeding frenzy: How attack journalism has transformed American politics*. New York: Free Press.

Salinas, Maria Elena. 2004. Bush: The Latino connection. *Herald News*, Passaic County, NJ, September 5.

Sandler, Lauren. 2000. Political (de)generation: MTV and America's youth vote. *Alternet*, October 27. www.alternet.org, September 16, 2004.

Sax, Linda J., Alexander W. Astin, Jennifer A. Lindholm, William S. Korn, Victor B. Saenz, and Katherine M. Mahoney. 2003. *The American freshman: National norms for fall 2003*. Los Angeles: Higher Education Research Institute, UCLA.

Scammon, Richard M., and Ben J. Wattenberg. 1970. *The real majority*. New York: Coward-McCann.

Schattschneider, E. E. 1942. *Party government*. New York: Farrar & Rinehart.

Schiller, Gail. 2004. Rock the vote irks Republicans. *Reuters*, November 2. www.reuters.co.uk (accessed November 3, 2004).

Schlozman, Kay Lehman, Sidney Verba, and Henry E. Brady. 1999. Civic participation and the equality problem. In *Civic engagement and American democracy*, Theda Skocpol and Morris P. Fiorina. Washington, DC: Brookings/Russell Sage.

Schmitt, Eric. 2001. Whites in minority in largest cities, the census shows. *New York Times*, April 30.

Schneck, Stephen. 1995. Political parties and democracy's citizens. In *The politics of ideas: Intellectual challenges to the party after 1992*, ed. John K. White and John C. Green. Lanham, MD: Rowman & Littlefield.

Segal, David. 2004. Vote, dude: Hip-hop singers and celebrities try to tap a potentially powerful force—black youth. *Washington Post*, October 30.

Selnow, Gary W. 1993. *High-tech campaigns: Computer technology in political communication*. Westport, CT: Praeger.

Shanks, Merrill, Douglas A. Strand, Henry E. Brady, and Edward G. Carmines. 2002. Public agendas and citizen engagement survey. Pew Charitable Trusts, September 23. www.pewtrusts.com (accessed July 28, 2004).

Sharp, Deborah. 2000. George P. Bush at center of campaign buzz. *USA Today*, June 18.

Shea, Daniel M., ed. 1999a. *Mass politics: The politics of popular culture*. New York: St. Martin's.

———. 1999b. The passing of realignment and the advent of the "base-less" party system. *American Politics Quarterly* 27 (1): 33–57.

———. 2003. Schattschneider's dismay: Strong parties and alienated voters. In *The state of the parties: The changing role of contemporary parties*, ed. John C. Green and Rick Farmer, 4th ed. Lanham, MD: Rowman & Littlefield, 287–99.

Shea, Daniel M., and John C. Green. 2004. *The fountain of youth: Political parties and the mobilization of young Americans*. Center for Political Participation, Allegheny College.

———. 2006. Local parties and mobilizing the vote: The case of young citizens. In *The state of the parties: The changing role of contemporary American parties*, ed. John C. Green and Daniel Coffey, 5th ed. Lanham, MD: Rowman & Littlefield.

Sigel, Roberta S., and Marilyn B. Hoskin. 1981. *The political involvement of adolescents*. New Brunswick: Rutgers University Press.

Silbey, Joel. 1991. *The American political nation, 1838–1993*. Stanford, CA: Stanford University Press, 1991.

Silverman, Stephen M., and Sarah Elkins. 2003. Bachelor Bush to change his ways soon. *People.com*, June 30.

Singer, Thea. 2004. Having their say: Mobilization efforts driving hard to bring youths to ballot in November. *Boston Herald*, October 5.

Skocpol, Theda. 1999. Advocates without members: The recent transformation of American civic life. In *Civic engagement in American democracy*, ed. Theda Skocpol and Morris P. Fiorina. New York: Sage.

Skocpol, Theda, and Morris P. Fiorina, eds. 1999. *Civic engagement in American democracy*. New York: Sage.

Sniderman, Paul M., Richard A. Brody, and Philip E. Tetlock. 1991. *Reasoning and choice: Explorations in political psychology*. Cambridge: Cambridge University Press.

Solomon, John. 1996. MTV news comes of age. *Columbia Journalism Review*, May–June, 20.

Soule, John W., and James W. Clarke. 1970. Amateurs and professionals: A study of delegates to the 1968 national convention. *American Political Science Review* 64 (3): 888–98.

Soule, Suzanne. 2001. Will they engage? Political knowledge, participation, and attitudes of generations X and Y. Center for Civic Education, Calabasas, California. www.civiced.org (accessed August 31, 2004).

Spethman, Betsy. 2004. Playing politics. *Promo*, July 1. http://promomagazine.com (accessed August 8, 2004).

Stagg, Allison. 2004. Service-learning in K–12 public education. Center for Information and Research on Civic Learning and Engagement fact sheet. www.civicyouth .org.

Stone, Walter J., L. R. Atkeson, and Ronald B. Rapoport. 1992. Turning on or turning off? Mobilization and demobilization effects of participation in presidential nomination campaigns. *American Journal of Political Science* 36 (3): 665–91.

Stone, Walter J., and Ronald B. Rapoport. 1998. A candidate-centered perspective on party responsiveness: Nomination activists and the process of party change. In Sandy L. Maisel, ed., *The parties respond: Changes in American parties and campaigns*, 3rd ed. Boulder, CO: Westview Press.

Stone, Walter J., Ronald B. Rapoport, and L. R. Atkeson. 1995. A simulation model of presidential nomination choices. *American Journal of Political Science* 39 (1): 135–61.

Strama, Mark. 1998. Overcoming cynicism: Youth participation and electoral politics. *National Civic Review* 87 (1): 71–78.

Strauss, William, and Neil Howe. 1991. *Generations: The history of America's future, 1584 to 2069*. New York: William Morrow.

Streisand, Betsy. 2003. Latino power: Big media tune in to the nation's largest minority. *U.S. News and World Report*, March 17.

Tanner, Seth. 2004. Young Voters Turn Out for Kerry. Weblog comment at College Democrats of America, November 10. www.collegedems.com/blog/archives/000266.

Polling Report. Election 2008. www.pollingreport.com/2008.htm (accessed December 3, 2005).

*Time*. 2004. Tiger tied. October 18, 97.

Tindell, John H., and Martin J. Medhurst. 1998. Rhetorical reduplication in MTV's Rock the Vote campaign. *Communication Studies* 49:18–28.

Tocqueville, Alexis de. 1835. *Democracy in America*. 2 vols. New York: Harper Perennial, 1969.

Torney-Purta, Judith. 2002. The school's role in developing civic engagement: A study of adolescents in twenty-eight countries. *Applied Development Science* 6 (4): 203–12.

Torney-Purta, Judith, Rainer Lehmann, H. Oswald, and W. Schultz. 2001. *Citizenship and education in twenty-eight countries: Civic knowledge and engagement at age fourteen*. Amsterdam: International Association for the Evaluation of Educational Achievement. www.wam.umd.edu/~iea.

U. S. Census Bureau. 2003. Generation X speaks out on civic engagement and the decennial census: An ethnographic approach. June 17.

———. 2005. Reported voting and registration by race, Hispanic origin, sex and age groups: November 1964 to 2004. *Current Population Survey*, May 26. www.census.gov (accessed August 6, 2005).

Vanishing Voter Project. 2000. Voter involvement and reactions to the campaign. October 29. www.vanishingvoter.org (September 16, 2004).

Verba, Sidney, and Norman Nie. 1972. *Participation in America: Political democracy and social equality*. New York: Harper & Row.

Verba, Sidney, Kay Lehman Schlozman, and Henry E. Brady. 1995. *Voice and equality*. Cambridge, MA: Harvard University Press.

Vogt, Heidi. 2003. TeleFutura, one year old, finds its legs. *Media Life Magazine*, January 3.

Vrome, Ariadne. 2004. Generation X retrieving net-based information: Political participation in practice. Australian Electronic Governance Conference, Melbourne, Australia, April 14–15. www.public-policy.unimebl.edu.au (accessed July 28, 2004).

Wangsness, Lisa. 2005a. Tapping new voters in city races. *Boston Globe*, July 12.

———. 2005b. Only modest changes expected in council focus. *Boston Globe*, November 9.

Wattenberg, Martin P. 1991. The rise of candidate-centered politics: Presidential elections of the 1980s. Cambridge, MA: Harvard University Press.

———. 1996. *The decline of American political parties, 1952–1996*. Cambridge, MA: Harvard University Press.

Weiss, Andrew R., Anthony Lutkus, Wendy Grigg, and Richard Niemi. 2001. The next generation of citizens: NAEP civics assessments: 1988 and 1998. *Education Statistics Quarterly* 3 (3): 21–24.

Westheimer, Joel, and Joseph Kahne. 2004. Educating the "good" citizen: Political choices and pedagogical goals. *PS: Political Science and Politics*, April, 241–47.

Whalen, Jack, and Richard Flacks. 1989. *Beyond the barricades: The sixties generation grows up*. Philadelphia: Temple University Press.

White, John Kenneth. 1990. *The new politics of old values*. Hanover, NH: University Press of New England.

White, John Kenneth, and Daniel M. Shea. 2004. *New party politics: From Jefferson and Hamilton to the Information Age*. Belmont, CA: Wadsworth.

Whitman, Christine T. 2005. *It's my party too*. New York: Penguin Press.

Williams, Kim M. Forthcoming. *Race counts: American multiracialism and civil rights politics*. Ann Arbor: University of Michigan Press.

Wilson, James Q. 1962. *The amateur Democrat*. Chicago: University of Chicago Press.

Wiltz, Teresa. 2005. Warming trend: El Zol Radio's Latino mix gains listeners. *Washington Post*, April 20.

Wiltz, Teresa, and Paul Farhi. 2005. WHFS changes its tune to Spanish. *Washington Post*, January 13.

*Wingspread Journal*. 2005. The Johnson Foundation.

Wirthlin, Richard B. 1980. *Reagan for president: Campaign action plan*. Unpublished campaign document, June 29.

Wolfe, Alan. 1998. *One nation, after all*. New York: Viking.

Wolfinger, Raymond E., and Jonathon Hoffman. 2001. Registering and voting with motor voter. *PS: Political Science and Politics* 34 (1): 85–92.

Wolfinger, Raymond E., and Steven J. Rosenstone. 1980. *Who votes?* New Haven, CT: Yale University Press.

Wood, Wendy, Carl A. Kallgren, and Rebecca M. Preisler. 1985. Access to attitude-relevant information in memory as a determinant of persuasion: The role of message attributes. *Journal of Experimental Social Psychology* 21:73–85.

WWE Vote. 2004a. What is Smackdown Your Vote! www.vote.wwe.com/news/whatisSYV.html.

———. 2004b. Smackdown Your Vote! feats record youth vote turnout in 2004. http://vote.wwe.com/news/SYV_Feats_Record.html.

———. 2004c. Smackdown Your Vote! http://vote.wwe.com.

Yankelovich, Daniel. 1994. How changes in the economy are reshaping American values. In *Values and Public Policy*, ed. Henry J. Aaron, Thomas E. Mann, and Timothy Taylor. Washington, DC: Brookings.

Young, Yolanda. 2004. P. Diddy backs up his call for change. *USA Today*, August 27.

Your Country, Your Vote. 2004. www.yourcountryyourvote.org/mission.html.

Youth Vote Coalition. 2004. Our history. www.youthvote.org/voter/history.cfm.

Zaller, John. 1992. *The nature and origins of mass opinion*. Cambridge: Cambridge University Press.

Zill, Nicholas. 2002. Civics lessons: Youth and the future of democracy. *Public Perspective*, January–February.

# Index